Taste of Home MOST REQUESTED RECIPES

TASTE OF HOME BOOKS • RDA ENTHUSIAST BRANDS, LLC • MILWAUKEE, WI

MADE IT, LOVED IT, SHARED IT!

Every year, the editors at *Taste of Home* receive hundreds of innovative recipes and mouthwatering inspiration from home cooks like you. That's what makes **Taste of Home Most Requested Recipes** your ultimate guide to the very best from our extensive collection—the most delicious, most talked about, most shared, top-rated stunners. These are the recipes that let you feel the joy of "I made that and everybody loved it!"

Discover 388 delectable homemade creations: craveworthy appetizers, fill-'em up casseroles and one-pot classics, breakfast and brunch specialties, hearty soups and sandwiches, colorful sides and salads, gorgeous desserts, and so much more.

Each dish was reviewed and approved by our experts in the *Taste of Home* Test Kitchen, and step-by-step instructions and vibrant full-color photos make it easy to cook with confidence.

221

145

TABLE OF CONTENTS

63

82

11

To find a recipe: tasteofhome.com
To submit a recipe: tasteofhome.com/submit
To find out about other *Taste of Home* products:
 shoptasteofhome.com

f LIKE US facebook.com/tasteofhome

TWEET US twitter.com/tasteofhome

Appetizers, Snacks & Beverages

Find the perfect nibble, bite and nosh among these killer appetizer recipes. A few are even ready in 30 minutes or less for those times you need apps in a hurry. Let's get this party started!

THE BEST HUMMUS

Hummus is my go-to appetizer when I need something quick, easy and impressive. Over the years I've picked up a number of tricks that make this the best hummus you'll ever have.
—*James Schend, Pleasant Prairie, WI*

- -

Prep: 25 min. • **Cook:** 20 min. + chilling
Makes: 1½ cups

- 1   can (15 oz.) garbanzo beans or chickpeas, rinsed and drained
- ½   tsp. baking soda
- ¼   cup fresh lemon juice
- 1   Tbsp. minced garlic
- ½   tsp. kosher salt
- ½   tsp. ground cumin
- ½   cup tahini
- 2   Tbsp. extra virgin olive oil
- ¼   cup cold water
  Optional: Olive oil, roasted garbanzo beans, toasted sesame seeds, ground sumac

1. Place garbanzo beans in a large saucepan; add water to cover by 1 in. Gently rub beans together to loosen outer skin. Pour off water and any skins that are floating. Repeat 2-3 times until no skins float to the surface; drain. Return to saucepan; add baking soda and enough water to cover by 1 in. Bring to a boil; reduce heat. Simmer, uncovered, until beans are very tender and just starting to fall apart, 20-25 minutes.
2. Meanwhile, in a blender, process lemon juice, garlic and salt until almost a paste. Let stand 10 minutes; strain, discarding solids. Stir in cumin. In a small bowl, stir together tahini and olive oil.
3. Add beans to blender; add cold water. Loosely cover and process until completely smooth. Add lemon mixture and process. With blender running, slowly add tahini mixture, scraping sides as needed. Adjust seasoning with additional salt and cumin if desired.
4. Transfer mixture to a serving bowl; cover and refrigerate at least 30 minutes. If desired, top hummus with additional olive oil and assorted toppings.
¼ CUP: 250 cal., 19g fat (3g sat. fat), 0 chol., 361mg sod., 15g carb. (2g sugars, 5g fiber), 7g pro.

MEXICAN LAYER DIP

This adaptable dip is like a magnet to hungry guests at our family gatherings and casual parties. It's tasty served hot or cold. Just one chip full and you're hooked!
—*Sheila Frasher, Crown City, OH*

Prep: 40 min. • **Makes:** 8 cups

- 1   lb. ground beef
- 1   medium onion, chopped, divided
- 1   can (15 oz.) tomato sauce
- 2   tsp. sugar
- 1   tsp. chili powder
- ⅛   tsp. salt
- ⅛   tsp. pepper
- 1   can (16 oz.) refried beans
- 2   medium tomatoes, seeded and chopped
- 1   small green pepper, finely chopped
- 2   cups sour cream
- 3   cups shredded Mexican cheese blend
     Optional: Chopped green onions and chopped tomatoes
     Corn chips

1. In a large skillet, cook beef and half of the onion over medium heat until meat is no longer pink; drain. Stir in the tomato sauce, sugar, chili powder, salt and pepper. Bring to a boil. Reduce heat; simmer, uncovered, until thickened, about 20 minutes.

2. Spread refried beans into a 13x9-in. dish; top with beef mixture, tomatoes, green pepper and remaining onion. Layer with the sour cream and cheese. If desired, top dip with chopped green onions and chopped tomatoes. Serve with chips.

1 SERVING: 117 cal., 8g fat (5g sat. fat), 29mg chol., 202mg sod., 5g carb. (2g sugars, 1g fiber), 6g pro.

CAYENNE PRETZELS

These seasoned pretzels were a huge hit at my daughter's graduation party. The longer they sit, the spicier they get!
—*Gayle Zebo, Warren, PA*

Prep: 10 min. • **Bake:** 1¼ hours
Makes: 3½ qt.

- 1   cup canola oil
- 1   envelope ranch salad dressing mix
- 1   tsp. garlic salt
- 1   tsp. cayenne pepper
- 1   lb. (12 cups) pretzel sticks

1. In a small bowl, combine the oil, dressing mix, garlic salt and cayenne. Divide pretzels between 2 ungreased 15x10x1-in. baking pans. Pour oil mixture over pretzels; stir to coat.
2. Bake at 200° for 1¼-1½ hours or until golden brown, stirring occasionally. Cool completely. Store in an airtight container.
¾ CUP: 236 cal., 15g fat (2g sat. fat), 0 chol., 690mg sod., 24g carb. (1g sugars, 1g fiber), 3g pro.

MANDY RIVERS
Lexington, SC

5i

HOMEMADE LIMONCELLO

This limoncello is better than any store-bought version. It's perfect as an after-dinner treat on its own, or whipped up in a cocktail.
—*Jenni Sharp, Milwaukee, WI*

Prep: 40 min. + standing • **Makes:** 1½ qt.

- 10 medium lemons
- 1 bottle (750 ml) vodka
- 3 cups water
- 1½ cups sugar

1. Using a vegetable peeler, peel rind from lemons (save lemons for another use). With a sharp knife, scrape pith from peels and discard. Place lemon peels and vodka in a large glass or plastic container. Cover and let stand at room temperature for at least 2 weeks, stirring once a week.
2. In a large saucepan, bring water and sugar to a boil. Reduce heat; simmer, uncovered, for 10 minutes. Cool completely.
3. Strain vodka mixture, discarding lemon peels. Return mixture to container; stir in sugar mixture. Pour into glass bottles; seal tightly. Let stand for 2 weeks. Serve chilled.
1½ OZ.: 87 cal., 0 fat (0 sat. fat), 0 chol., 0 sod., 9g carb. (9g sugars, 0 fiber), 0 pro.

5i

SLOW-COOKED SMOKIES

I include these little smokies smothered in barbecue sauce on all my appetizer buffets. They're popular with both children and adults.
—*Sundra Hauck, Bogalusa, LA*

Prep: 5 min. • **Cook:** 5 hours
Makes: 8 servings

- 1 pkg. (14 oz.) miniature smoked sausages
- 1 bottle (28 oz.) barbecue sauce
- 1¼ cups water
- 3 Tbsp. Worcestershire sauce
- 3 Tbsp. steak sauce
- ½ tsp. pepper

In a 3-qt. slow cooker, combine all ingredients. Cover and cook on low for 5-6 hours or until heated through. Serve with a slotted spoon.
1 SERVING: 331 cal., 14g fat (5g sat. fat), 32mg chol., 1694mg sod., 44g carb. (35g sugars, 1g fiber), 7g pro.

GRILLED CHIPOTLE SHRIMP

I originally created this for a Cinco de Mayo party, and it was a hit! It's so easy, yet has a serious wow factor. The creamy dipping sauce mellows out the shrimp's heat perfectly.
—*Mandy Rivers, Lexington, SC*

Prep: 25 min. + marinating • **Grill:** 10 min.
Makes: about 5 dozen (1¼ cups sauce)

- ¼ cup packed brown sugar
- 2 chipotle peppers in adobo sauce, chopped, plus ¼ cup adobo sauce
- 6 garlic cloves, minced
- 2 Tbsp. water
- 2 Tbsp. lime juice
- 1 Tbsp. olive oil
- ¼ tsp. salt
- 2 lbs. uncooked large shrimp, peeled and deveined

CILANTRO CREAM SAUCE
- 1 cup sour cream
- ⅓ cup minced fresh cilantro
- 2 garlic cloves, minced
- 1½ tsp. grated lime zest
- ¼ tsp. salt
- ¼ tsp. minced fresh mint

1. In a small saucepan, bring the brown sugar, chipotles, adobo sauce, garlic, water, lime juice, oil and salt to a boil. Reduce heat; cook and stir 2 minutes longer. Remove from the heat; cool completely.
2. Transfer mixture to a large bowl. Add the shrimp; turn to coat. Cover and refrigerate for up to 2 hours.
3. Meanwhile, combine the sauce ingredients; chill until serving.
4. Drain and discard marinade. Thread shrimp onto metal or soaked wooden skewers.
5. Grill shrimp on an oiled rack, covered, over medium heat or broil 4 in. from the heat until shrimp are pink, 6-8 minutes, turning once. Serve with sauce.
1 SHRIMP WITH 1 TSP. SAUCE: 27 cal., 1g fat (1g sat. fat), 21mg chol., 47mg sod., 1g carb. (1g sugars, 0 fiber), 3g pro.

ZUCCHINI PATTIES WITH DILL DIP

These crisp-tender patties are a nice alternative to crab cakes and taste very similar, thanks to the seafood seasoning. They always get gobbled up.
—*Kelly Maxwell, Plainfield, IL*

Prep: 25 min. • **Cook:** 10 min.
Makes: 2 dozen (¾ cup dip)

- ¾ cup sour cream
- 2 Tbsp. minced fresh dill
- 1 tsp. lemon juice
- ⅛ tsp. salt
- ⅛ tsp. pepper
- 2½ cups shredded zucchini
- 1 cup seasoned bread crumbs
- 1 tsp. seafood seasoning
- ¼ tsp. garlic powder
- 1 large egg, lightly beaten
- 2 Tbsp. butter, melted
- 1 large carrot, chopped
- ¼ cup finely chopped onion
- ¼ cup all-purpose flour
- ½ cup canola oil

1. For dip, in a small bowl, combine the first 5 ingredients. Cover and refrigerate until ready to serve.

2. Place zucchini in a colander to drain; squeeze to remove excess liquid. Pat dry; set aside.

3. In a large bowl, combine the bread crumbs, seafood seasoning and garlic powder. Stir in egg and butter until blended. Add the carrot, onion and zucchini.

4. Place flour in a shallow bowl. Shape zucchini mixture into 24 small patties; coat with flour.

5. Heat oil in a large skillet; fry patties, a few at a time, for 3-4 minutes on each side or until lightly browned. Drain on paper towels. Serve with dip.

1 PATTY WITH 1½ TSP. DIP: 93 cal., 8g fat (2g sat. fat), 12mg chol., 126mg sod., 5g carb. (1g sugars, 0 fiber), 2g pro.

DID YOU KNOW?

Whether you plan on purchasing zucchini from the farmers market or corner store, you'll get the best flavor from the freshest ingredients. Look for zucchini that's firm to the touch and has smooth, blemish-free skin. Beware of large, super-sized zucchini, as they can have bland flavor and woody texture.

🔒 BACON WATER CHESTNUT WRAPS

In our house, the Christmas season just wouldn't be the same without these classic bites. It's impossible to eat just one!
—*Laura Mahaffey, Annapolis, MD*

- -

Prep: 20 min. • **Bake:** 30 min.
Makes: about 2½ dozen

- 1 lb. bacon strips
- 2 cans (8 oz. each) whole water chestnuts, drained
- ½ cup packed brown sugar
- ½ cup mayonnaise
- ¼ cup chili sauce

1. Cut bacon strips in half. In a large skillet over medium heat, cook bacon until almost crisp; drain. Wrap each bacon piece around a water chestnut and secure with a toothpick. Place in an ungreased 13x9-in. baking dish.

2. In a small bowl, combine the brown sugar, mayonnaise and chili sauce; pour over water chestnuts. Bake, uncovered, at 350° until hot and bubbly, about 30 minutes.

1 APPETIZER: 75 cal., 5g fat (1g sat. fat), 6mg chol., 148mg sod., 6g carb. (4g sugars, 0 fiber), 2g pro.

AIR-FRYER TAQUITOS

I love serving these appetizers—they are perfect for any occasion. To spice them up, add sliced jalapenos.
—Mark Webber, Valdez, AK

- -

Prep: 20 min. • **Cook:** 15 min./batch
Makes: 10 servings

- 2 large eggs
- ½ cup dry bread crumbs
- 3 Tbsp. taco seasoning
- 1 lb. lean ground beef (90% lean)
- 10 corn tortillas (6 in.), warmed
  Cooking spray
  Optional: Salsa and guacamole

1. Preheat air fryer to 350°. In a large bowl, combine the eggs, bread crumbs and taco seasoning. Add ground beef; mix lightly but thoroughly.
2. Spoon ¼ cup beef mixture down the center of each tortilla. Roll up tightly and secure with toothpicks. In batches, arrange taquitos in a single layer on greased tray in air-fryer basket; spritz with cooking spray. Cook 6 minutes; turn and cook until meat is cooked through and taquitos are golden brown and crispy, 6-7 minutes longer. Discard the toothpicks before serving. If desired, serve with salsa and guacamole.
1 TAQUITO: 168 cal., 6g fat (2g sat. fat), 65mg chol., 336mg sod., 17g carb. (1g sugars, 2g fiber), 12g pro.

SLOW-COOKER CRAB DIP

With just 10 minutes of prep time, this creamy and delicious crab dip couldn't be easier. The recipe comes from my hometown cookbook. My co-workers rave about it every time I bring it to a potluck!
—Julie Novotney, Rockwell, IA

- -

Prep: 10 min. • **Cook:** 2 hours • **Makes:** 2 cups

- 1 pkg. (8 oz.) cream cheese, softened
- ½ cup grated Parmesan cheese
- ½ cup mayonnaise
- 4 green onions, finely chopped
- ½ tsp. garlic powder
- 1 can (6 oz.) crabmeat, drained, flaked and cartilage removed
- ½ cup sliced almonds, toasted
  Assorted crackers

1. In a 1½-qt. slow cooker, combine the first 5 ingredients. Stir in crab. Cook, covered, on low 2-3 hours, until heated through.
2. Just before serving, sprinkle with almonds. Serve with crackers.
2 TBSP.: 132 cal., 12g fat (4g sat. fat), 27mg chol., 185mg sod., 2g carb. (1g sugars, 0 fiber), 4g pro.

4. For Thai sauce, heat oil in a small saucepan over medium heat. Add ginger, garlic and chile pepper; cook and stir until fragrant, about 2 minutes. Stir in brown sugar and lime juice. Bring to a boil; cook until slightly thickened, about 5 minutes. Stir in cilantro and fish sauce.

5. For spicy barbecue sauce, heat prepared barbecue sauce in a small saucepan over medium heat. Stir in chipotle peppers, honey and vinegar. Bring to a boil; cook and stir until slightly thickened, about 5 minutes.

6. Toss wings with 1 of the sauces. If desired, sprinkle with green onion slices.

1 PIECE: 87 cal., 8g fat (2g sat. fat), 15mg chol., 218mg sod., 1g carb. (1g sugars, 0 fiber), 4g pro.

FRESH TOMATO BRUSCHETTA

The topping for this simple appetizer can be put together ahead of time and refrigerated. We also love the bruschetta on top of grilled chicken sandwiches, hamburgers and homemade pizza.
—*Samantha Cass, Swartz Creek, MI*

Takes: 25 min. • **Makes:** 3 dozen

- 4 plum tomatoes, seeded and chopped
- ½ cup shredded Parmesan cheese
- ¼ cup minced fresh basil
- 3 Tbsp. olive oil
- 2 Tbsp. minced fresh parsley
- 3 garlic cloves, minced
- 2 tsp. balsamic vinegar
- ⅛ tsp. salt
- ⅛ tsp. crushed red pepper flakes
- ⅛ tsp. pepper
- 1 French bread baguette (10½ oz.), cut into ½-in. slices
- ¼ cup butter, softened
- 8 oz. fresh mozzarella cheese, sliced

1. In a bowl, combine the first 10 ingredients.

2. Spread baguette slices with butter; top each with a cheese slice. Place on ungreased baking sheets. Broil 3-4 in. from the heat until cheese is melted, 3-5 minutes. With a slotted spoon, top each bread slice with about 1 Tbsp. tomato mixture.

1 APPETIZER: 81 cal., 5g fat (2g sat. fat), 9mg chol., 95mg sod., 7g carb. (0 sugars, 1g fiber), 2g pro. **DIABETIC EXCHANGES:** 1 fat, ½ starch.

BEST EVER FRIED CHICKEN WINGS

For game days, I whip up these saucy wings. When I run out, friends hover by the snack table until I bring out more. When they ask me how to fry chicken wings, they never believe it's so easy!
—*Nick Iverson, Denver, CO*

Prep: 10 min. + chilling • **Cook:** 20 min.
Makes: about 4 dozen

- 4 lbs. chicken wings
- 2 tsp. kosher salt
  Oil for deep-fat frying

BUFFALO WING SAUCE
- ¾ cup Louisiana-style hot sauce
- ¼ cup unsalted butter, cubed
- 2 Tbsp. molasses
- ¼ tsp. cayenne pepper

SPICY THAI SAUCE
- 1 Tbsp. canola oil
- 1 tsp. grated fresh gingerroot
- 1 garlic clove, minced
- 1 minced Thai chile pepper or ¼ tsp. crushed red pepper flakes

- ¼ cup packed dark brown sugar
- 2 Tbsp. lime juice
- 2 Tbsp. minced fresh cilantro
- 1 Tbsp. fish sauce

SPICY BARBECUE SAUCE
- ¾ cup barbecue sauce
- 2 chipotle peppers in adobo sauce, finely chopped
- 2 Tbsp. honey
- 1 Tbsp. cider vinegar
  Thinly sliced green onions, optional

1. Using a sharp knife, cut through the 2 wing joints; discard wing tips. Pat chicken dry with paper towels. Toss wings with kosher salt. Place on a wire rack in a 15x10x1-in. baking pan. Refrigerate at least 1 hour or overnight.

2. In an electric skillet or deep-fat fryer, heat oil to 375°. Fry wings in batches until skin is crisp and meat is tender, 8-10 minutes. Drain on paper towels.

3. For Buffalo wing sauce, bring the hot sauce just to a boil in a small saucepan. Remove from heat; whisk in butter 1 piece at a time. Stir in molasses and cayenne pepper.

AIR-FRYER PEPPER POPPERS

These creamy stuffed jalapenos have some bite. They may be the most popular treats I make! My husband is always hinting that I should make a batch.
—*Lisa Byington, Johnson City, NY*

Prep: 20 min. • **Cook:** 15 min./batch
Makes: about 2 dozen

- 1 pkg. (8 oz.) cream cheese, softened
- ¾ cup shredded cheddar cheese
- ¾ cup shredded Monterey Jack cheese
- 6 bacon strips, cooked and crumbled
- ¼ tsp. salt
- ¼ tsp. garlic powder
- ¼ tsp. chili powder
- ¼ tsp. smoked paprika
- 1 lb. fresh jalapenos, halved lengthwise and seeded
- ½ cup dry bread crumbs
  Optional: Sour cream, French onion dip and ranch salad dressing

1. Preheat air fryer to 325°. In a large bowl, combine the cheeses, bacon and seasonings; mix well. Spoon 1½-2 tablespoonfuls into each pepper half. Roll in bread crumbs.

2. Spritz air-fryer basket with cooking spray. Working in batches if needed, place poppers in a single layer in basket. Cook until the cheese is melted and peppers are heated through, 15-20 minutes. If desired, serve poppers with sour cream, dip or dressing.

1 STUFFED PEPPER HALF: 81 cal., 6g fat (4g sat. fat), 18mg chol., 145mg sod., 3g carb. (1g sugars, 1g fiber), 3g pro.

TEST KITCHEN TIP
Use a grapefruit spoon to core and seed a jalapeno pepper. The spoon's curved shape and serrated edges make it ideal for the veggie's shape. Remember to wear rubber or plastic gloves when cutting or seeding hot peppers to protect your hands, and avoid touching your face.

CHAMPAGNE SIPPER

This is a terrific cocktail for any holiday celebration. And because you make it by the pitcher, you can mingle with your guests instead of tending bar.
—*Moffat Frazier, New York, NY*

Takes: 10 min. • **Makes:** 12 servings

- 1½ cups sugar
- 1 cup lemon juice
- 3 cups cold water
- 1½ cups sweet white wine, chilled
- 1 bottle (750 ml) champagne, chilled
  Sliced fresh strawberries, optional

In a 3-qt. pitcher, dissolve sugar in lemon juice. Add cold water and wine. Stir in champagne. If desired, serve with strawberries.

¾ CUP: 168 cal., 0 fat (0 sat. fat), 0 chol., 2mg sod., 28g carb. (26g sugars, 0 fiber), 0 pro.

OBATZDA (GERMAN BEER CHEESE DIP)

Obatzda, otherwise known as German beer cheese dip, is so delicious and creamy. It's the perfect dip to make the night before a get-together.
—*Beate Trinkl, Einsbach, Germany*

Takes: 15 min. • **Makes:** 3½ cups

- 2 rounds (8 oz. each) Camembert cheese, rind on, sliced
- 1 pkg. (8 oz.) cream cheese, softened
- 1 medium onion, finely chopped
- 1 tsp. paprika
- ½ tsp. caraway seeds
- ¼ tsp. salt
- ⅛ tsp. pepper

In a small bowl, mash Camembert cheese with a fork to desired consistency. Beat in cream cheese, onion and seasonings. If desired, sprinkle with additional caraway seeds.

2 TBSP.: 79 cal., 7g fat (4g sat. fat), 20mg chol., 183mg sod., 1g carb. (1g sugars, 0 fiber), 4g pro.

CRANBERRY-ORANGE SANGRIA

Letting this sangria sit in the fridge overnight improves the fruitiness, making it the perfect ready-to-serve drink for a holiday party. It's also nice with a splash of brandy.
—*Maria Regakis, Saugus, MA*

Prep: 15 min. + chilling • **Makes:** 10 servings

- 1 medium orange, halved and thinly sliced
- 1 medium apple, quartered and thinly sliced
- ½ cup fresh or frozen cranberries
- 1 bottle (32 oz.) cranberry juice
- 1 bottle (750 ml) zinfandel or other fruity red wine
- 1 cup simple syrup
- ½ cup orange liqueur
  Ice cubes

GARNISHES

  Optional: Thinly sliced oranges, thinly sliced apples and fresh cranberries

In a large pitcher, combine first 7 ingredients; refrigerate overnight. Serve over ice; garnish with oranges, apples and cranberries if desired.

¾ CUP: 263 cal., 0 fat (0 sat. fat), 0 chol., 6mg sod., 47g carb. (44g sugars, 1g fiber), 1g pro.

SALMON DIP WITH CREAM CHEESE

Here's a delightful hors d'oeuvre that's excellent for any occasion. The combination of salmon, cream cheese and spices gives it terrific flavor.
—*Raymonde Hebert Bernier, Saint-Hyacinthe, QC*

Prep: 10 min. + chilling • **Makes:** 1½ cups

- 6 oz. cream cheese, softened
- 3 Tbsp. mayonnaise
- 1 Tbsp. lemon juice
- ½ tsp. salt
- ½ tsp. curry powder
- ¼ tsp. dried basil
- ⅛ tsp. pepper
- 1 can (7½ oz.) salmon, drained, bones and skin removed
- 2 green onions, thinly sliced
  Crackers and chopped vegetables

In a bowl, combine the cream cheese, mayonnaise and lemon juice. Add the salt, curry powder, basil and pepper; mix well. Gently stir in salmon and onions. Cover and refrigerate for at least 1 hour. Serve with crackers and vegetables.

2 TBSP.: 78 cal., 7g fat (2g sat. fat), 17mg chol., 234mg sod., 1g carb. (0 sugars, 0 fiber), 4g pro.

READER REVIEW

"Awesome! This recipe is very flexible and can be easily adjusted based on what you have on hand."
RHORTON22, TASTEOFHOME.COM

CURRIED BEEF BITES

These appetizers are so fast and easy to prepare. They're always the first to disappear at any party!
—Karen Kuebler, Dallas, TX

- -

Prep: 15 min. • **Bake:** 15 min.
Makes: 3 dozen

- 12 **slices white bread, crusts removed**
- 3 **Tbsp. butter, melted**
- ½ **lb. ground beef**
- 5 **celery ribs, chopped**
- ½ **cup seasoned bread crumbs**
- 2 **tsp. curry powder**
- ½ **tsp. garlic salt**
   Optional: Cucumber raita and chopped fresh cilantro

1. Preheat oven to 400°. Flatten the bread slices with a rolling pin; brush tops with butter. Set aside.

2. In a large skillet, cook beef and celery over medium heat until beef is no longer pink and celery is tender, 8-10 minutes, breaking the beef into crumbles; drain. Stir in the bread crumbs, curry powder and garlic salt.

3. Spoon beef mixture evenly among bread slices. Roll up bread slices and secure with toothpicks. Place on a greased baking sheet. Bake until golden brown, 12-15 minutes. When cool enough to handle, discard the toothpicks and cut each roll-up crosswise into 3 slices. If desired, serve warm with cucumber raita and chopped fresh cilantro.

1 ROLL-UP: 52 cal., 2g fat (1g sat. fat), 6mg chol., 114mg sod., 6g carb. (1g sugars, 0 fiber), 2g pro.

SAVORY CHEESE BALL

Blue cheese contributes a pleasant, tangy bite and olive a saltiness to this creamy cheese ball recipe. For the optimum taste, let the cheese ball stand at room temperature for 20 minutes before serving.
—Jan Stawara, Howell, MI

- -

Prep: 15 min. + chilling • **Makes:** 2 cups

- 1 **pkg. (8 oz.) cream cheese, softened**
- 1 **cup crumbled blue cheese**
- ¼ **cup butter, softened**
- 1 **can (4¼ oz.) chopped ripe olives**
- 1 **Tbsp. minced chives**
- ¾ **cup chopped walnuts**
   Assorted crackers

1. In a large bowl, beat the cream cheese, blue cheese and butter until smooth. Stir in olives and minced chives. Cover and refrigerate for at least 1 hour.

2. Shape cheese mixture into a ball; roll in walnuts. Wrap in plastic; refrigerate for at least 1 hour. Serve with crackers.

2 TBSP.: 145 cal., 14g fat (6g sat. fat), 27mg chol., 204mg sod., 2g carb. (1g sugars, 1g fiber), 3g pro.

AIR-FRYER CRISPY SRIRACHA SPRING ROLLS

While in the Bahamas, friends suggested a restaurant that serves amazing chicken spring rolls. When I got home, I whipped up my own version. Such a great appetizer to have waiting in the freezer!
—*Carla Mendres, Winnipeg, MB*

Prep: 50 min. • **Cook:** 10 min./batch
Makes: 2 dozen

- 3 cups coleslaw mix (about 7 oz.)
- 3 green onions, chopped
- 1 Tbsp. soy sauce
- 1 tsp. sesame oil
- 1 lb. boneless skinless chicken breasts
- 1 tsp. seasoned salt
- 2 pkg. (8 oz. each) cream cheese, softened
- 2 Tbsp. Sriracha chili sauce
- 24 spring roll wrappers
  Cooking spray
  Optional: Sweet chili sauce and additional green onions

1. Preheat air fryer to 360°. Toss coleslaw mix, green onions, soy sauce and sesame oil; let stand while cooking chicken. Place the chicken in a single layer on greased tray in air-fryer basket. Cook until a thermometer inserted in chicken reads 165°, 18-20 minutes. Remove chicken; cool slightly. Finely chop chicken; toss with seasoned salt.
2. Increase air-fryer temperature to 400°. In a large bowl, mix cream cheese and Sriracha chili sauce; stir in the chicken and coleslaw mixture. With 1 corner of a spring roll wrapper facing you, place about 2 Tbsp. of the filling just below center of wrapper. (Cover remaining wrappers with a damp paper towel until ready to use.) Fold bottom corner over filling; moisten remaining edges with water. Fold side corners toward center over filling; roll up tightly, pressing tip to seal. Repeat.
3. In batches, arrange spring rolls in a single layer on greased tray in air-fryer basket; spritz with cooking spray. Cook rolls until lightly browned, 5-6 minutes. Turn; spritz with cooking spray. Cook until golden brown and crisp, 5-6 minutes longer. If desired, serve spring rolls with sweet chili sauce and sprinkle with green onions.
1 SPRING ROLL: 127 cal., 7g fat (4g sat. fat), 30mg chol., 215mg sod., 10g carb. (1g sugars, 0 fiber), 6g pro.

AMBER MASSEY
Argyle, TX

BUFFALO CHICKEN MEATBALLS

I make these game-day appetizer meatballs with blue cheese or ranch salad dressing for dipping. If I make them for a meal, I may skip the dressing and serve the meatballs with blue cheese polenta on the side. Yum!
—*Amber Massey, Argyle, TX*

Prep: 15 min. • **Bake:** 20 min.
Makes: 2 dozen

- ¾ cup panko bread crumbs
- ⅓ cup plus ½ cup Louisiana-style hot sauce, divided
- ¼ cup chopped celery
- 1 large egg white
- 1 lb. lean ground chicken
  Reduced-fat blue cheese or ranch salad dressing, optional

1. Preheat oven to 400°. In a large bowl, combine bread crumbs, ⅓ cup hot sauce, celery and egg white. Add chicken; mix lightly but thoroughly.
2. Shape into twenty-four 1-in. balls. Place on a greased rack in a shallow baking pan. Bake 20-25 minutes or until cooked through.
3. Toss meatballs with the remaining hot sauce. If desired, drizzle with salad dressing just before serving.
1 MEATBALL: 35 cal., 1g fat (0 sat. fat), 14mg chol., 24mg sod., 2g carb. (0 sugars, 0 fiber), 4g pro.

READER REVIEW

"Loved these! I'm a huge fan of Buffalo wings, and this recipe is a perfect way to enjoy a healthier version of Buffalo chicken. I used Buffalo sauce instead of Louisiana-style sauce. Delicious!"

CHERSTAD, TASTEOFHOME.COM

PINEAPPLE SALSA

This mouthwatering salsa features fresh pineapple and cilantro. Besides serving it with chips, you can spoon it over grilled chicken or fish for a jazzed-up meal.
—*Suzi LaPar, Wahiawa, HI*

Takes: 20 min. • **Makes:** 3½ cups

- 2 cups diced fresh pineapple
- 2 medium tomatoes, seeded and chopped
- ¾ cup chopped sweet onion
- ¼ cup minced fresh cilantro
- 1 jalapeno pepper, seeded and chopped
- 1 Tbsp. olive oil
- 1 tsp. ground coriander
- ¾ tsp. ground cumin
- ½ tsp. salt
- ½ tsp. minced garlic
  Tortilla chips

In a large bowl, combine first 10 ingredients. Cover and refrigerate until serving. Serve with tortilla chips.

¼ CUP: 29 cal., 1g fat (0 sat. fat), 0 chol., 87mg sod., 5g carb. (4g sugars, 1g fiber), 0 pro.

SPICY CHICKEN WINGS WITH BLUE CHEESE DIP

These fall-off-the-bone-tender wings have just the right amount of heat, and cool blue cheese dressing creates the perfect flavor combination for dipping.
—*Kevalyn Henderson, Hayward, WI*

Prep: 25 min. + marinating • **Bake:** 2 hours
Makes: 2 dozen (1¾ cups dip)

- 1 cup reduced-sodium soy sauce
- ⅔ cup sugar
- 2 tsp. salt
- 2 tsp. grated orange zest
- 2 garlic cloves, minced
- ½ tsp. pepper
- 3 lbs. chicken wingettes and drumettes
- 3 tsp. chili powder
- ¾ tsp. cayenne pepper
- ¾ tsp. hot pepper sauce

BLUE CHEESE DIP
- 1 cup mayonnaise
- ½ cup blue cheese salad dressing
- ⅓ cup buttermilk
- 2 tsp. Italian salad dressing mix

1. In a small bowl, combine the soy sauce, sugar, salt, orange zest, garlic and pepper. Pour half of the marinade into a large shallow dish. Add the chicken; turn to coat. Cover and refrigerate for 1 hour. Cover and refrigerate remaining marinade.

2. Drain the chicken, discarding marinade. Transfer chicken to a greased 13x9-in. baking dish. Cover and bake at 325° for 1½ hours or until chicken juices run clear.

3. Using tongs, transfer chicken to a greased 15x10x1-in. baking pan. In a small bowl, combine the chili powder, cayenne, pepper sauce and reserved marinade. Drizzle over the chicken.

4. Bake, uncovered, for 30 minutes, turning once. In a small bowl, whisk dip ingredients. Serve with wings.

1 PIECE WITH 4 TSP. DIP: 237 cal., 19g fat (4g sat. fat), 47mg chol., 588mg sod., 4g carb. (3g sugars, 0 fiber), 11g pro.

CHICKEN CRESCENT WREATH

Here's an impressive-looking dish that's a snap to prepare. Even when my cooking time is limited, I can still serve this delicious crescent wreath. The red pepper and green broccoli add a festive touch.
—*Marlene Denissen, St. Croix Falls, WI*

Prep: 15 min. • **Bake:** 20 min.
Makes: 16 servings

- 2 tubes (8 oz. each) refrigerated crescent rolls
- 1 cup shredded Colby-Monterey Jack cheese
- ⅔ cup condensed cream of chicken soup, undiluted
- ½ cup chopped fresh broccoli
- ½ cup chopped sweet red pepper
- ¼ cup chopped water chestnuts
- 1 can (5 oz.) white chicken, drained, or ¾ cup cubed cooked chicken
- 2 Tbsp. chopped onion

1. Arrange crescent rolls on a 12-in. pizza pan, forming a ring with pointed ends facing the outer edge of pan and wide ends overlapping.
2. Combine the remaining ingredients; spoon over wide ends of rolls. Fold the points over filling and tuck under wide ends (filling will be visible).
3. Bake at 375° for 20-25 minutes or until golden brown.
FREEZE OPTION: Securely wrap cooled wreath in plastic and foil before freezing. To use, remove from freezer 30 minutes before reheating. Remove wreath from foil and plastic; reheat on a greased baking sheet in a preheated 325° oven until heated through.
1 PIECE: 151 cal., 8g fat (2g sat. fat), 11mg chol., 357mg sod., 14g carb. (3g sugars, 0 fiber), 6g pro.

CREAMY TACO DIP

You'll know this snack was a big hit when you come home with an empty pan!
—*Denise Smith, Lusk, WY*

Takes: 15 min. • **Makes:** 20 servings

- 1 pkg. (8 oz.) fat-free cream cheese, softened
- ⅓ cup fat-free sour cream
- ½ cup taco sauce
- 1 tsp. ground cumin
- 1 can (15 oz.) fat-free refried beans
- 1 cup shredded lettuce
- 1 cup shredded fat-free cheddar cheese
- 1 medium tomato, diced
- ¼ cup chopped ripe olives
- ¼ cup chopped green chiles
  Tortilla chips

1. In a large bowl, beat cream cheese and sour cream until smooth. Stir in taco sauce and cumin; set aside.
2. Spread the refried beans over the bottom on a serving platter or 13x9-in. dish. Spread cream cheese mixture over the beans, leaving about 1 in. uncovered around the edges. Top layer with lettuce, cheese, tomato, olives and chiles. Serve with tortilla chips.
¼ CUP: 57 cal., 0 fat (0 sat. fat), 3mg chol., 250mg sod., 8g carb. (1g sugars, 2g fiber), 6g pro.

HOT CRAB PINWHEELS

A friend gave me the recipe for these crab bites. They're delicious, but what amazed me most is that my husband, who hates seafood, couldn't stop eating them.

—Kitti Boesel, Woodbridge, VA

- -

Prep: 15 min. + chilling • **Bake:** 10 min.
Makes: 3 dozen

- 1 pkg. (8 oz.) reduced-fat cream cheese
- 1 can (6 oz.) crabmeat, drained, flaked and cartilage removed
- ¾ cup diced sweet red pepper
- ½ cup shredded reduced-fat cheddar cheese
- 2 green onions, thinly sliced
- 3 Tbsp. minced fresh parsley
- ¼ to ½ tsp. cayenne pepper
- 6 flour tortillas (6 in.)

1. Beat cream cheese until smooth; stir in the crab, red pepper, cheese, green onions, parsley and cayenne. Spread ⅓ cup filling over each tortilla; roll up tightly. Wrap in plastic, twisting ends to seal; refrigerate for at least 2 hours.

2. To serve, preheat oven to 350°. Unwrap rolls; trim ends and cut each into 6 slices. Place on baking sheets coated with cooking spray. Bake until bubbly, about 10 minutes. Serve pinwheels warm.

1 PINWHEEL: 44 cal., 2g fat (1g sat. fat), 10mg chol., 98mg sod., 3g carb. (0 sugars, 0 fiber), 2g pro.

TEST KITCHEN TIP
Be sure the canned crab is labeled "lump," which means it contains large pieces of crab. Or use 1 lb. of refrigerated lump crab if you prefer.

MARSHMALLOW FRUIT DIP

You can whip up this sweet and creamy dip in just 10 minutes. I like to serve it in a bowl surrounded by fresh-picked strawberries at brunches or luncheons in early summer.
—*Cindy Steffen, Cedarburg, WI*

Takes: 10 min. • **Makes:** 5 cups (40 servings)

- 1   pkg. (8 oz.) cream cheese, softened
- ¾   cup cherry yogurt
- 1   carton (8 oz.) frozen whipped topping, thawed
- 1   jar (7 oz.) marshmallow creme
  Assorted fresh fruit

In a large bowl, beat cream cheese and yogurt until blended. Fold in whipped topping and marshmallow creme. Serve with fruit.

2 TBSP.: 56 cal., 3g fat (2g sat. fat), 7mg chol., 24mg sod., 6g carb. (5g sugars, 0 fiber), 1g pro.

CONTEST-WINNING SUGAR & SPICE NUTS

My daughters, grandkids and just about everyone who visits me looks forward to this mix of crunchy nuts, spices and fruit during the holidays. And tucked in colorful tins, it makes a handy last-minute gift idea for busy hostesses or drop-in visitors.
—*Joan Klinefelter, Utica, IL*

Takes: 30 min. • **Makes:** 3½ cups

- ¼   cup packed brown sugar
- ½   tsp. ground cinnamon
- ¼   tsp. cayenne pepper
- 1   egg white
- 1   cup salted cashews
- 1   cup pecan halves
- 1   cup dry roasted peanuts
- ½   cup dried cranberries

1. In a small bowl, combine the brown sugar, cinnamon and cayenne; set aside. In a large bowl, whisk the egg white; add nuts and cranberries. Sprinkle with sugar mixture and toss to coat. Spread in a single layer on a greased baking sheet.

2. Bake at 300° for 18-20 minutes or until golden brown, stirring once. Cool. Store in an airtight container.

¼ CUP: 211 cal., 16g fat (2g sat. fat), 0 chol., 161mg sod., 13g carb. (8g sugars, 2g fiber), 5g pro.

STRAWBERRY SALSA

This deliciously different salsa is versatile, fresh-tasting and colorful. People are often surprised to see a salsa made with strawberries, but it's excellent over grilled chicken and pork and as a dip with corn chips.

—*Jean Giroux, Belchertown, MA*

- -

Prep: 15 min. + chilling • **Makes:** 4 cups

- 1 pint fresh strawberries, chopped
- 4 plum tomatoes, seeded and chopped
- 1 small red onion, finely chopped
- 1 to 2 medium jalapeno peppers, minced
- 2 Tbsp. lime juice
- 1 Tbsp. olive oil
- 2 garlic cloves, minced

1. In a large bowl, combine the strawberries, tomatoes, onion and jalapenos. Stir in the lime juice, oil and garlic. Cover and refrigerate for 2 hours.

2. Serve with cooked poultry or pork or as a dip for tortilla chips.

¼ CUP: 19 cal., 1g fat (0 sat. fat), 0 chol., 1mg sod., 3g carb. (2g sugars, 1g fiber), 0 pro. **DIABETIC EXCHANGES:** Free food.

2

3

QUICK PICANTE SAUCE

Hot pepper sauce and a jalapeno pepper give this snappy sauce just the right amount of zip. It makes a great dip for tortilla chips or a tangy sauce for tacos and fajitas. This is always a big hit at parties and office gatherings. I even make it for my mother when she needs to bring a dip to a party.
—*Barbara Sellers, Shreveport, LA*

Takes: 5 min. • **Makes:** 5 servings

- 1 can (14½ oz.) diced tomatoes, drained
- ½ cup coarsely chopped onion
- ½ cup minced fresh cilantro
- 1 jalapeno pepper, seeded and halved
- 3 Tbsp. lime juice
- 1 Tbsp. chili powder
- 1 garlic clove, halved
- ½ tsp. salt
- ¼ tsp. grated lime zest
- 5 drops hot pepper sauce
  Tortilla chips

In a blender, combine the first 10 ingredients; cover and process until smooth. Serve with tortilla chips.
¼ CUP: 32 cal., 0 fat (0 sat. fat), 0 chol., 415mg sod., 7g carb. (4g sugars, 2g fiber), 1g pro.

GINGERED MANGO SALSA

Zesty cilantro meets cool mint in this fruity salsa. We love it with grilled chicken. You can substitute papaya for the mango, if you like.
—*Barb Fore, McAllen, TX*

Prep: 15 min. + standing • **Makes:** 1¼ cups

- 1 cup chopped peeled mango
- ¼ cup chopped red onion
- ¼ cup minced fresh cilantro
- ¼ cup lime juice
- 2 Tbsp. minced fresh mint
- 1 Tbsp. minced fresh gingerroot
- ½ tsp. olive oil
- ¼ tsp. salt

In a bowl, combine all ingredients. Let stand for 30 minutes before serving.
¼ CUP: 39 cal., 1g fat (0 sat. fat), 0 chol., 120mg sod., 9g carb. (7g sugars, 1g fiber), 0 pro.

TEST KITCHEN TIP
To clean a mango, hold the whole fruit under cool running water. Rub gently with your hands as you rinse. You can also use a clean vegetable brush to gently scrub the surface. You won't be eating the skin; you just want to remove any dirt that might end up on your cutting surface and the fruit inside.

Breakfast & Brunch

Jump-start the day with these top-rated breakfast and brunch ideas. From stacks of pancakes to savory scramblers, this hearty roundup will make for your best mornings ever.

ITALIAN BRUNCH TORTE

We pair this impressive layered bake with a salad of mixed greens and tomato wedges. It's delicious served warm or cold, and it's one of our most-requested dishes for brunch.
—*Danny Diamond, Farmington Hills, MI*

Prep: 50 min. **Bake:** 1 hour + standing
Makes: 12 servings

- 2 tubes (8 oz. each) refrigerated crescent rolls, divided
- 1 tsp. olive oil
- 1 pkg. (6 oz.) fresh baby spinach
- 1 cup sliced fresh mushrooms
- 7 large eggs, divided use
- 1 cup grated Parmesan cheese
- 2 tsp. Italian seasoning
- ⅛ tsp. pepper
- ½ lb. thinly sliced deli ham
- ½ lb. thinly sliced hard salami
- ½ lb. sliced provolone cheese
- 2 jars (12 oz. each) roasted sweet red peppers, drained, sliced and patted dry

1. Preheat the oven to 350°. Place a greased 9-in. springform pan on a double thickness of heavy-duty foil (about 18 in. square). Securely wrap foil around the pan. Unroll 1 tube of crescent dough and separate into triangles. Press onto bottom of prepared pan to form a crust, sealing seams well. Bake 10-15 minutes or until set.

2. Meanwhile, in a large skillet, heat oil over medium-high heat. Add the spinach and mushrooms; cook and stir until mushrooms are tender. Drain on several layers of paper towels, blotting well. In a large bowl, whisk 6 eggs, Parmesan cheese, Italian seasoning and pepper.

3. Layer the baked crust with half of each of the following: ham, salami, provolone cheese, red peppers and spinach mixture. Pour half of the egg mixture over top. Repeat layers; top with remaining egg mixture.

4. On a work surface, unroll and separate remaining crescent dough into triangles. Press together to form a circle and seal seams; place over filling. Whisk remaining egg; brush over dough.

5. Bake, uncovered, 1-1¼ hours or until a thermometer reads 160°, covering loosely with foil if needed to prevent overbrowning. Carefully loosen sides from pan with a knife; remove rim from pan. Let stand 20 minutes.

1 PIECE: 403 cal., 24g fat (10g sat. fat), 167mg chol., 1360mg sod., 19g carb. (5g sugars, 0 fiber), 23g pro.

STUFFED HASH BROWNS

Ever since we met, my husband has made me hash browns with bacon, pepper jack and sour cream. We share it when we have guests, too.
—*Ann Ciszak Pazar, Anchorage, AK*

- -

Prep: 15 min. • **Cook:** 10 min./batch
Makes: 4 servings

- 1 pkg. (20 oz.) refrigerated shredded hash brown potatoes
- ¼ cup finely chopped onion
- ½ tsp. salt
- ¼ tsp. pepper
- 4 Tbsp. olive oil, divided
- ½ cup pepper jack cheese
- ½ cup crumbled cooked bacon
- ½ cup sour cream
- 2 green onions, thinly sliced

1. In a large bowl, toss potatoes with onion, salt and pepper. In a small cast-iron or other heavy skillet, heat 2 tsp. oil over medium heat. Add 1 cup potato mixture, pressing down to flatten with spatula. Cook, without stirring, until bottom is golden brown, 4-5 minutes. Drizzle with 1 tsp. oil; flip. Cook until bottom is golden brown, 4-5 minutes, sprinkling with 2 Tbsp. cheese and 2 Tbsp. bacon during the last minute of cooking.

2. Fold the hash browns in half; slide onto plate and keep warm. Repeat with remaining ingredients. Top with the sour cream and green onions.

1 SERVING: 410 cal., 27g fat (9g sat. fat), 26mg chol., 791mg sod., 30g carb. (3g sugars, 3g fiber), 13g pro.

MORNING ORANGE DRINK

I love to treat my overnight guests to this creamy orange frappe. Just blitz a few basic ingredients in your blender and enjoy.
—*Joyce Mummau, Mount Airy, MD*

- -

Takes: 10 min.
Makes: 6 servings (about 1 qt.)

- 1 can (6 oz.) frozen orange juice concentrate
- 1 cup cold water
- 1 cup whole milk
- ⅓ cup sugar
- 1 tsp. vanilla extract
- 10 ice cubes

Combine the first 5 ingredients in a blender; process at high speed. Add ice cubes, a few at a time, blending until smooth. Serve immediately.

¾ CUP: 115 cal., 1g fat (1g sat. fat), 6mg chol., 21mg sod., 24g carb. (23g sugars, 0 fiber), 2g pro.

READER REVIEW

"I have been making this for years. My family loves this in the summer at supper with a BLT or salad."

CHERYLMAC, TASTEOFHOME.COM

PRESSURE-COOKED BROCCOLI EGG CUPS

Serving brunch? This delicious egg bake is filled with crunchy bites of broccoli and served in ramekins. Your guests will love it!
—Edna Hoffman, Hebron, IN

Takes: 25 min. • **Makes:** 4 servings

7 large eggs
1½ cups half-and-half cream
3 Tbsp. shredded Swiss cheese
2 tsp. minced fresh parsley
1 tsp. minced fresh basil
¼ tsp. salt
⅛ tsp. cayenne pepper
1 to 1½ cups frozen broccoli florets, thawed and coarsely chopped

1. Whisk 3 eggs with next 6 ingredients; pour into 4 greased 1-pint canning jars. Divide the broccoli among jars; top each with 1 egg.
2. Place trivet insert and 1 cup water in a 6-qt. electric pressure cooker. Place jars on trivet. Center the lids on jars; screw on bands until fingertip tight. Lock lid; close pressure-release valve. Adjust to pressure-cook on high for 6 minutes. Quick-release pressure. Remove lid; using tongs, remove the jars. Let stand 3 minutes before serving.

1 SERVING: 274 cal., 19g fat (10g sat. fat), 375mg chol., 333mg sod., 5g carb. (4g sugars, 1g fiber), 16g pro.

SPICY BREAKFAST LASAGNA

It's fun to cook something new for family and friends—especially when it gets rave reviews. When I took this dish to our breakfast club at work, people said it woke up their taste buds!
—Guthrie Torp Jr., Highland Ranch, CO

Prep: 20 min. + chilling • **Bake:** 35 min.
Makes: 16 servings

3 cups 4% cottage cheese
½ cup minced chives
¼ cup sliced green onions
18 large eggs
⅓ cup 2% milk
½ tsp. salt
¼ tsp. pepper
1 Tbsp. butter
8 lasagna noodles, cooked and drained
4 cups frozen shredded hash browns, thawed
1 lb. bulk pork sausage, cooked and crumbled
8 oz. sliced Monterey Jack cheese with jalapeno peppers
8 oz. sliced Muenster cheese

1. Combine the cottage cheese, chives and onions; set aside. In another bowl, whisk eggs, milk, salt and pepper until blended. In a large skillet, heat butter over medium heat. Pour in egg mixture; cook and stir until the eggs are thickened and no liquid egg remains. Remove from heat; set aside.
2. Place 4 lasagna noodles in a greased 13x9-in. baking dish. Layer with 2 cups hash browns, scrambled eggs, sausage and half the cottage cheese mixture. Cover with Monterey Jack cheese. Top with the remaining lasagna noodles, hash browns and cottage cheese mixture. Cover lasagna with Muenster cheese. Refrigerate, covered, 8 hours or overnight.
3. Remove dish from refrigerator 30 minutes before baking. Preheat oven to 350°. Bake, uncovered, until a knife inserted in center comes out clean, 35-40 minutes. Let stand 5 minutes before cutting.

1 PIECE: 366 cal., 23g fat (11g sat. fat), 256mg chol., 640mg sod., 16g carb. (3g sugars, 1g fiber), 23g pro.

CHORIZO & GRITS BREAKFAST BOWLS

Growing up, I bonded with my dad over chorizo and eggs. My fresh approach combines them with grits and black beans. Add a spoonful of pico de gallo.
—*Jenn Tidwell, Fair Oaks, CA*

Takes: 30 min. • **Makes:** 6 servings

- 2 tsp. olive oil
- 1 pkg. (12 oz.) fully cooked chorizo chicken sausages or flavor of choice, sliced
- 1 large zucchini, chopped
- 3 cups water
- ¾ cup quick-cooking grits
- 1 can (15 oz.) black beans, rinsed and drained
- ½ cup shredded cheddar cheese
- 6 large eggs
  Optional: Pico de gallo and chopped fresh cilantro

1. In a large skillet, heat oil over medium heat. Add the sausage; cook and stir until lightly browned, 2-3 minutes. Add zucchini; cook and stir until tender, 4-5 minutes longer. Remove from pan; keep warm.

2. Meanwhile, in a large saucepan, bring water to a boil. Slowly stir in grits. Reduce heat to medium-low; cook, covered, until thickened, stirring occasionally, about 5 minutes. Stir in black beans and cheese until blended. Remove from heat.

3. Wipe skillet clean; coat with cooking spray and place over medium heat. In batches, break 1 egg at a time into pan. Immediately reduce heat to low; cook until whites are completely set and yolks begin to thicken but are not hard, about 5 minutes.

4. To serve, divide the grits mixture among 6 bowls. Top with chorizo mixture, eggs and, if desired, pico de gallo and cilantro.

1 SERVING: 344 cal., 14g fat (5g sat. fat), 239mg chol., 636mg sod., 30g carb. (4g sugars, 4g fiber), 24g pro. **DIABETIC EXCHANGES:** 3 medium-fat meat, 2 starch.

JENN TIDWELL
Fair Oaks, CA

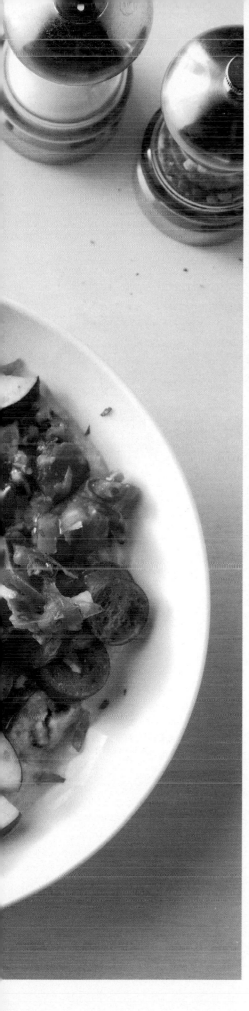

BUTTERMILK CHOCOLATE CHIP PANCAKES

At our house, Saturday morning always means pancakes for breakfast. I make the menu special by servings up stacks of these fluffy buttermilk treats studded with mini chips.
—*Julianne Johnson, Grove City, MN*

- -

Takes: 20 min. • **Makes:** 16 pancakes

- 2 cups all-purpose flour
- 2 tsp. sugar
- 2 tsp. baking powder
- 1 tsp. baking soda
- ¼ tsp. salt
- 2 large eggs, room temperature, lightly beaten
- 2 cups buttermilk
- ¼ cup vegetable oil
- ⅔ cup miniature semisweet chocolate chips

1. In a bowl, combine the first 5 ingredients. Combine the eggs, buttermilk and oil; stir into the dry ingredients just until moistened. Pour the batter by ¼ cupfuls onto a greased hot griddle.

2. Sprinkle each pancake with 2 tsp. mini chocolate chips. Turn when bubbles form on top of pancake; cook until second side is golden brown.

2 PANCAKES: 291 cal., 13g fat (4g sat. fat), 49mg chol., 487mg sod., 37g carb. (12g sugars, 2g fiber), 7g pro.

TEST KITCHEN TIP
When making pancake batter, be sure to not overmix. The more you stir, the more protein develops and the tougher and chewier your pancakes will be. After mixing the batter, let it sit for a while. This allows the proteins to relax, making for pillowy-soft flapjacks.

STRAWBERRY-BASIL REFRESHER

Fresh strawberries and basil are everywhere in the early summer, so get them together for a cooler that's pure sunshine. Garnish with basil leaves and sip it in the shade.
—*Carolyn Turner, Reno, NV*

Takes: 10 min. • **Makes:** 12 servings

- ⅔ cup lemon juice
- ½ cup sugar
- 1 cup sliced fresh strawberries
  Ice cubes
- 1 to 2 Tbsp. chopped fresh basil
- 1 bottle (1 liter) club soda, chilled

1. Place lemon juice, sugar, strawberries and 1 cup of ice cubes in a blender; cover and process until blended. Add basil; pulse 1 or 2 times to combine.

2. Divide the strawberry mixture among 12 cocktail glasses. Fill with ice; top with club soda.

1 SERVING: 40 cal., 0 fat (0 sat. fat), 0 chol., 18mg sod., 10g carb. (9g sugars, 0 fiber), 0 pro. **DIABETIC EXCHANGES:** ½ starch.

SPICED BLUEBERRY QUINOA

I started eating quinoa when I found out how much protein it has. This is an easy dish to experiment with; my first version of the recipe was made with shredded apples instead of blueberries. It's just as delicious either way!
—*Shannon Copley, Upper Arlington, OH*

Prep: 10 min. • **Cook:** 30 min.
Makes: 2 servings

- ½ cup quinoa, rinsed and well drained
- 2 cups unsweetened almond milk
- 2 Tbsp. honey
- ½ tsp. ground cinnamon
- ¼ tsp. salt
- 1 cup fresh or frozen blueberries, thawed
- ¼ tsp. vanilla extract
- 2 Tbsp. chopped almonds, toasted

1. In a small saucepan, cook and stir quinoa over medium heat until lightly toasted, 5-7 minutes. Stir in almond milk, honey, cinnamon and salt; bring to a boil. Reduce heat; simmer, uncovered, until quinoa is tender and liquid is almost absorbed, 20-25 minutes, stirring occasionally.

2. Remove from heat; stir in blueberries and vanilla. Sprinkle with almonds.

1 CUP: 352 cal., 10g fat (1g sat. fat), 0 chol., 479mg sod., 59g carb. (25g sugars, 7g fiber), 9g pro.

MAPLE FRENCH TOAST BAKE

This yummy French toast casserole is a breeze to whip up the night before a busy morning. My family loves the richness it gets from cream cheese and maple syrup.
—Cindy Steffen, Cedarburg, WI

Prep: 15 min. + chilling • Bake: 50 min.
Makes: 8 servings

- 12 slices bread, cubed
- 1 pkg. (8 oz.) cream cheese, cubed
- 8 large eggs
- 1 cup 2% milk
- ½ cup maple syrup
   Additional maple syrup

1. Arrange half of the bread cubes in a greased shallow 2-qt. baking dish. Top with cream cheese and remaining bread. In a large bowl, whisk the eggs, milk and syrup; pour over bread. Cover and refrigerate overnight. Remove from the refrigerator 30 minutes before baking.
2. Cover and bake at 350° for 30 minutes. Uncover; bake 20-25 minutes longer or until golden brown. Serve with additional syrup.
1 SERVING: 372 cal., 17g fat (8g sat. fat), 218mg chol., 464mg sod., 42g carb. (17g sugars, 1g fiber), 14g pro.

ENGLISH MUFFIN EGG SANDWICHES

You can't beat the delicious combination of mushrooms, onions, peppers and cream cheese. Don't like it too spicy? Leave out the red pepper flakes for less heat.
—Amy Lloyd, Madison, WI

Takes: 25 min. • Makes: 8 servings

- ½ lb. sliced fresh mushrooms
- 1 small sweet red pepper, chopped
- 1 small sweet onion, chopped
- ½ tsp. garlic salt
- ¼ tsp. pepper
- ¼ tsp. crushed red pepper flakes, optional
- 7 large eggs, lightly beaten
- 8 whole wheat English muffins, split and toasted
- 4 oz. reduced-fat cream cheese

1. Place a large nonstick skillet over medium-high heat. Add sliced mushrooms, red pepper, onion and seasonings; cook and stir until mushrooms are tender, 5-7 minutes. Remove from pan.
2. Wipe skillet clean and coat with cooking spray; place skillet over medium heat. Add eggs; cook and stir just until the eggs are thickened and no liquid egg remains. Add vegetables; heat through, stirring gently.
3. Spread muffin bottoms with cream cheese; top with egg mixture. Replace tops.
1 SANDWICH: 244 cal., 9g fat (4g sat. fat), 173mg chol., 425mg sod., 30g carb. (7g sugars, 5g fiber), 14g pro. DIABETIC EXCHANGES: 2 starch, 1 medium-fat meat, ½ fat.

ARTICHOKE & POTATO FRITTATA

This potato frittata is a delicious brunch dish, but it's hearty enough for a weeknight dinner, too. If you like Greek or Mediterranean cuisine, you'll want to add this to your keeper files.
—Sarah Newman, Harvest, AL

Prep: 35 min. • **Bake:** 25 min.
Makes: 4 servings

- 3 Tbsp. olive oil, divided
- ½ cup finely chopped red onion
- 1 garlic clove, minced
- 2 medium Yukon Gold potatoes (about 10 oz.), thinly sliced
- 8 large eggs
- ¼ cup 2% milk
- 2 medium tomatoes, chopped
- 1 can (14 oz.) water-packed artichoke hearts, drained and chopped
- ¼ cup crumbled goat cheese, divided
- 2 Tbsp. minced fresh basil or 2 tsp. dried basil, divided
- 1 tsp. salt
- ½ tsp. pepper

1. Preheat oven to 350°. In a 10-in. ovenproof skillet, heat 1 Tbsp. oil over medium heat. Add onion; cook and stir until tender, 3-4 minutes. Add garlic; cook 1 minute longer. Remove onion mixture from pan.
2. Add remaining oil to same pan; arrange the potatoes on bottom of pan. Cook over medium-low heat until tender, 15-20 minutes, stirring occasionally.
3. In a large bowl, whisk eggs and milk. Stir in tomatoes, artichokes, onion mixture, 2 Tbsp. goat cheese, 1 Tbsp. fresh basil, salt and pepper. Pour egg mixture over potatoes; sprinkle with remaining cheese. Bake until eggs are completely set, 25-30 minutes.
4. Let stand for 5 minutes. Sprinkle with remaining basil. Cut into wedges.
1 WEDGE: 420 cal., 22g fat (6g sat. fat), 382mg chol., 1039mg sod., 35g carb. (5g sugars, 3g fiber), 20g pro.

DID YOU KNOW?
A frittata is the Italian version of the French omelet. Since the meat, cheese and/or vegetables are mixed in with the egg mixture, frittatas are easier to make than an omelet, but take longer to cook. The round frittata is cut into wedges and can serve two or more people. An omelet usually serves one or two.

LYNN DANIEL
Dallas, TX

STRAWBERRY-HAZELNUT FRENCH TOAST

When my husband and I discovered this decadent French toast at a bed-and-breakfast in Arkansas, we bought the inn's cookbook so we could enjoy the same treat at home. We've changed the recipe a bit since then, but it still reminds us of that lovely B&B.
—Lynn Daniel, Dallas, TX

Prep: 15 min. + chilling • **Bake:** 35 min.
Makes: 10 servings

- ½ cup butter, cubed
- 1 cup packed brown sugar
- 2 Tbsp. light corn syrup
- 10 slices French bread baguette (1 in. thick)
- 5 large eggs
- 1½ cups half-and-half cream
- 2 Tbsp. hazelnut liqueur or hazelnut flavoring syrup
- 1 Tbsp. vanilla extract
   Sliced fresh strawberries and chopped hazelnuts

1. In a microwave, melt butter with brown sugar and corn syrup; stir until brown sugar is blended. Pour into a greased 13x9-in. baking dish; top with bread.
2. In a large bowl, whisk eggs, cream, liqueur and vanilla; pour over bread. Refrigerate, covered, overnight.
3. Preheat oven to 350°. Remove French toast from refrigerator while oven heats. Bake, uncovered, until the top is puffed, edges are golden and a knife inserted in the center comes out clean, 35-40 minutes. Let stand 5-10 minutes before serving. Serve with strawberries and hazelnuts.
1 SERVING: 304 cal., 15g fat (9g sat. fat), 135mg chol., 184mg sod., 34g carb. (29g sugars, 0 fiber), 5g pro.

OVERNIGHT BAKED OATMEAL

My husband and I spent a long weekend at a bed-and-breakfast not far from our home. The owners shared this delicious recipe with me, which I made my own after a couple of simple changes.

—Jennifer Cramer, Lebanon, PA

Prep: 10 min. + chilling • **Bake:** 45 min.
Makes: 8 servings

- 2 large eggs, room temperature, lightly beaten
- 3 cups 2% milk
- ¾ cup packed brown sugar
- ¼ cup canola oil
- 1½ tsp. ground cinnamon
- 1 tsp. salt
- 2 cups old-fashioned oats
- ¼ cup dried blueberries
- ¼ cup dried cherries
- ¼ cup sliced almonds

1. In a large bowl, whisk together the first 6 ingredients. Stir in oats, blueberries and cherries. Transfer to a greased 8-in. square baking dish. Refrigerate, covered, for 8 hours or overnight.

2. Preheat oven to 350°. Remove oatmeal from refrigerator while oven heats. Stir oatmeal; sprinkle with almonds. Bake, uncovered, until golden brown and a thermometer reads 160°, 40-50 minutes. Serve warm.

½ CUP: 331 cal., 13g fat (2g sat. fat), 54mg chol., 364mg sod., 46g carb. (30g sugars, 4g fiber), 8g pro.

GREAT GRANOLA

Oats, nuts and dried fruit make a crunchy homemade topping for yogurt or for eating by the handful. It also makes a delicious gift.

—Johnna Johnson, Scottsdale, AZ

Prep: 25 min. • **Bake:** 25 min. + cooling
Makes: 7 cups

- 2 cups old-fashioned oats
- ½ cup chopped almonds
- ½ cup salted pumpkin seeds or pepitas
- ½ cup chopped walnuts
- ¼ cup chopped pecans
- ¼ cup sesame seeds
- ¼ cup sunflower kernels
- ⅓ cup honey
- ¼ cup packed brown sugar
- ¼ cup maple syrup
- 2 Tbsp. toasted wheat germ
- 2 Tbsp. canola oil
- 1 tsp. ground cinnamon
- 1 tsp. vanilla extract
- 7 oz. mixed dried fruit (about 1⅓ cups)

1. In a large bowl, combine first 7 ingredients; set aside.

2. In a small saucepan, combine the honey, brown sugar, syrup, wheat germ, oil and cinnamon. Cook and stir over medium heat until smooth, 4-5 minutes. Remove from the heat; stir in vanilla. Pour over the oat mixture and toss to coat.

3. Transfer to a greased 15x10x1-in. baking pan. Bake at 350° until golden brown, stirring occasionally, 22-27 minutes. Cool completely on a wire rack. Stir in dried fruit. Store in an airtight container.

½ CUP: 290 cal., 14g fat (2g sat. fat), 0 chol., 49mg sod., 38g carb. (25g sugars, 4g fiber), 6g pro.

BREAKFAST QUICHE

With two kinds of cheeses, lots of crispy bacon and a dash of cayenne, this airy quiche makes a big impression with brunch guests. It's the recipe my friends always ask for.
—Mark Clark, Twin Mountain, NH

- -

Prep: 15 min. + cooling
Bake: 30 min. + standing
Makes: 6 servings

- 1¼ **cups all-purpose flour**
- ¼ **tsp. salt**
- ½ **cup cold butter**
- 3 **to 5 Tbsp. ice water**
FILLING
- 12 **bacon strips, cooked and crumbled**
- ½ **cup shredded pepper jack or Monterey Jack cheese**
- ½ **cup shredded sharp cheddar cheese**
- ⅓ **cup finely chopped onion**
- 4 **large eggs**
- 2 **cups heavy whipping cream**
- ¾ **tsp. salt**
- ¼ **tsp. sugar**
- ⅛ **tsp. cayenne pepper**

1. Combine flour and salt; cut in butter until crumbly. Gradually add 3-5 Tbsp. ice water, tossing with a fork until dough holds together when pressed. Wrap and refrigerate 1 hour.
2. Preheat oven to 450°. On a lightly floured surface, roll dough to an ⅛-in.-thick circle; transfer to a 9-in. pie plate. Trim crust to ½ in. beyond rim of plate; flute edge. Line unpricked crust with a double thickness of heavy-duty foil. Bake 5 minutes; remove foil. Bake for 5 minutes longer; remove from oven and cool on a wire rack. Reduce heat to 375°.
3. Sprinkle bacon, cheeses and onion over crust. Beat remaining ingredients until blended; pour over top. Bake until a knife inserted in center comes out clean, 30-35 minutes. Let stand 10 minutes before cutting.
1 PIECE: 709 cal., 60g fat (35g sat. fat), 290mg chol., 980mg sod., 24g carb. (3g sugars, 1g fiber), 19g pro.

HARD-BOILED EGGS

Here's a foolproof technique for making hard-boiled eggs to eat plain or to use in various recipes.
—Taste of Home Test Kitchen

- -

Prep: 20 min. + cooling • **Makes:** 12 servings

- 12 **large eggs**
  Cold water

1. Place eggs in a single layer in a large saucepan; add enough cold water to cover by 1 in. Cover and quickly bring to a boil. Remove from the heat. Let stand for 15 minutes for large eggs (18 minutes for extra-large eggs and 12 minutes for medium eggs).
2. Rinse eggs in cold water and place in ice water until completely cooled. Drain and refrigerate.
1 EGG: 75 cal., 5g fat (2g sat. fat), 213mg chol., 63mg sod., 1g carb. (1g sugars, 0 fiber), 6g pro.
DIABETIC EXCHANGES: 1 medium-fat meat.

HOME FRIES

When I was little, my dad and I would get up early on Sundays and make these for the family. The rest of the gang would be awakened by the tempting aroma.
—Teresa Koide, Manchester, CT

- -

Prep: 25 min. • **Cook:** 15 min./batch.
Makes: 8 servings

- 1 **lb. bacon, chopped**
- 8 **medium potatoes (about 3 lbs.), peeled and cut into ½-in. pieces**
- 1 **large onion, chopped**
- 1 **tsp. salt**
- ½ **tsp. pepper**

1. In a large skillet, cook chopped bacon over medium-low heat until crisp. Remove bacon from pan with slotted spoon and drain on paper towels. Remove bacon drippings from pan and reserve.
2. Working in batches, add ¼ cup bacon drippings, potatoes, onion, salt and pepper to pan; toss to coat. Cook and stir over medium-low heat until potatoes are golden brown and tender, 15-20 minutes, adding more drippings as needed. Stir in cooked bacon; serve home fries immediately.
1 CUP: 349 cal., 21g fat (8g sat. fat), 33mg chol., 681mg sod., 31g carb. (3g sugars, 2g fiber), 10g pro.

BUTTERMILK PANCAKES

You just can't beat a basic buttermilk pancake for a down-home hearty breakfast. Pair it with sausage and fresh fruit for a mouthwatering morning meal.
—*Betty Abrey, Imperial, SK*

- -

Prep: 10 min. • **Cook:** 5 min./batch
Makes: 2½ dozen

4	cups all-purpose flour
¼	cup sugar
2	tsp. baking soda
2	tsp. salt
1½	tsp. baking powder
4	large eggs, room temperature
4	cups buttermilk

1. In a large bowl, combine the flour, sugar, baking soda, salt and baking powder. In another bowl, whisk the eggs and buttermilk until blended; stir into dry ingredients just until moistened.

2. Pour batter by ¼ cupfuls onto a lightly greased hot griddle; turn pancakes when bubbles form on top. Cook until second side is golden brown.

3 PANCAKES: 270 cal., 3g fat (1g sat. fat), 89mg chol., 913mg sod., 48g carb. (11g sugars, 1g fiber), 11g pro.

TEST KITCHEN TIP

Take your pancakes up a notch with add-ins that enhance the flavor.
- Add a pinch of pumpkin pie spice or a splash of maple syrup to the batter for a taste of fall.
- For a sweet-and-spicy touch, sprinkle some vanilla and cinnamon into the batter.
- Add a little berry-flavored yogurt to the batter for added richness and a unique taste.
- For a change, try stirring in some chocolate chips or a little ginger, nutmeg or orange extract.

OVERNIGHT EGG & ASPARAGUS BAKE

This easy breakfast is great for holiday mornings, especially when we have overnight guests. All it needs is a fruit salad, and breakfast is served!
—*Jane Whittaker, Pensacola, FL*

Prep: 25 min+ chilling • **Bake:** 30 min.
Makes: 8 servings

- 6 bacon strips, chopped
- 2 cups sliced fresh mushrooms
- 1 shallot, finely chopped
- 1 lb. fresh asparagus, trimmed and cut into 2-in. pieces
- 6 large eggs
- 1 cup biscuit/baking mix
- 1 cup 2% milk
- 1 cup heavy whipping cream
- ¾ cup shredded sharp cheddar cheese
- ½ cup grated Romano cheese
- 1 tsp. ground mustard
- 1 tsp. dried parsley flakes
- ½ tsp. salt
- ¼ tsp. pepper

1. In a large skillet, cook bacon over medium heat until crisp, stirring occasionally. Remove with a slotted spoon; drain on paper towels. Discard drippings, reserving 1 Tbsp. in pan.
2. Add mushrooms and shallot to drippings; cook and stir over medium-high heat until tender, 6-8 minutes. Meanwhile, in a large saucepan, place steamer basket over 1 in. of water. Place asparagus in basket. Bring water to a boil. Reduce heat to maintain a simmer; steam asparagus, covered, until crisp-tender, 3-5 minutes.
3. In a large bowl, whisk eggs, biscuit mix, milk, cream, cheeses and seasonings until blended. Stir in bacon and mushroom mixture. Pour into a greased 13x9-in. baking dish; arrange asparagus over top. Cover and refrigerate overnight.
4. Remove from refrigerator 30 minutes before baking. Preheat oven to 350°. Bake, uncovered, until top is golden brown and a knife inserted near the center comes out clean, 30-35 minutes. Let stand 10 minutes before cutting.
1 PIECE: 362 cal., 27g fat (14g sat. fat), 196mg chol., 677mg sod., 16g carb. (4g sugars, 1g fiber), 17g pro.

JANE WHITTAKER
Pensacola, FL

COCONUT TROPICAL FRUIT SALAD

Add a serving of fruit to breakfast with this delicious medley. Toasted coconut, mango, kiwi and more bring the flavor of the tropics to any menu.
—*Katie Covington, Blacksburg, SC*

Takes: 25 min. • **Makes:** 8 servings

- 1 medium mango, peeled and cubed
- 1 medium green apple, cubed
- 1 medium red apple, cubed
- 1 medium pear, cubed
- 1 medium navel orange, peeled and chopped
- 2 medium kiwifruit, peeled and chopped
- 10 seedless red grapes, halved
- 2 Tbsp. orange juice
- 1 firm medium banana, sliced
- ¼ cup sweetened shredded coconut, toasted

In a large bowl, combine first 7 ingredients. Drizzle with orange juice; toss gently to coat. Refrigerate until serving. Just before serving, fold in banana and sprinkle with coconut.
¾ CUP: 101 cal., 1g fat (1g sat. fat), 0 chol., 10mg sod., 24g carb. (17g sugars, 3g fiber), 1g pro. **DIABETIC EXCHANGES:** 1½ fruit.

BANANAS FOSTER OATMEAL

This oatmeal tastes like bananas Foster, my favorite dessert. If you can't find rum extract, double the vanilla.
—*Carol Touchton, Seffner, FL*

Takes: 30 min. • **Makes:** 4 servings

- 2 cups water
- 1½ cups 2% milk
- ½ tsp. salt
- 2 cups old-fashioned oats
- ½ cup butter, cubed
- ½ cup packed brown sugar
- ½ tsp. ground cinnamon
-    Dash ground ginger
-    Dash ground nutmeg
- 2 medium firm ripe bananas, sliced
- ½ tsp. vanilla extract
- ½ tsp. rum extract

Optional toppings: Cinnamon sugar, sliced ripe bananas and sweetened whipped cream

1. In a large saucepan, bring water, milk and salt to a boil. Stir in oats; cook 5 minutes over medium heat, stirring occasionally. Cover and let stand.
2. In a small heavy saucepan, melt the butter over medium heat. Stir in brown sugar and spices; bring to a boil. Reduce heat; simmer, uncovered, for 5 minutes or until slightly thickened. Add bananas; cook, stirring gently, 1-2 minutes or until bananas are glazed and slightly softened.
3. Remove from heat; stir in vanilla and rum extracts. Stir banana mixture into oatmeal. Spoon oatmeal into serving bowls; add the toppings of your choice.
1⅓ CUPS: 561 cal., 28g fat (16g sat. fat), 68mg chol., 529mg sod., 72g carb. (39g sugars, 6g fiber), 9g pro.

AIR-FRYER CHEESY BREAKFAST EGG ROLLS

Whether you have to run out the door in the morning or take a few minutes to relax at the table, these breakfast egg rolls will hit the spot. The filling can be made the night before, so in the morning you can just roll, fry and go!
—*Anne Ormond, Dover, NH*

Prep: 30 min. • **Cook:** 10 min./batch
Makes: 12 servings

- ½ lb. bulk pork sausage
- ½ cup shredded sharp cheddar cheese
- ½ cup shredded Monterey Jack cheese
- 1 Tbsp. chopped green onions
- 4 large eggs
- 1 Tbsp. 2% milk
- ¼ tsp. salt
- ⅛ tsp. pepper
- 1 Tbsp. butter
- 12 egg roll wrappers
  Cooking spray
  Maple syrup or salsa, optional

1. In a small nonstick skillet, cook the pork sausage over medium heat until no longer pink, 4-6 minutes, breaking into crumbles; drain. Stir in cheeses and green onions; set aside. Wipe skillet clean.
2. In a small bowl, whisk eggs, milk, salt and pepper until blended. In the same skillet, heat butter over medium heat. Pour in egg mixture; cook and stir until eggs are thickened and no liquid egg remains. Stir in sausage mixture.
3. Preheat air fryer to 400°. With 1 corner of an egg roll wrapper facing you, place ¼ cup filling just below center of wrapper. (Cover remaining wrappers with a damp paper towel until ready to use.) Fold bottom corner over filling; moisten remaining wrapper edges with water. Fold side corners toward center over filling. Roll egg roll up tightly, pressing at tip to seal. Repeat.
4. In batches, arrange egg rolls in a single layer on greased tray in air-fryer basket; spritz with cooking spray. Cook until lightly browned, 3-4 minutes. Turn; spritz with cooking spray. Cook until golden brown and crisp, another 3-4 minutes. If desired, serve with maple syrup or salsa.

1 EGG ROLL: 209 cal., 10g fat (4g sat. fat), 87mg chol., 438mg sod., 19g carb. (0 sugars, 1g fiber), 10g pro.

BLOODY MARY

Horseradish makes this one of the best Bloody Mary recipes in the world. Without the horseradish, you'll have a more traditional drink, and without the alcohol, you'll have a Virgin Mary. Serve with a stalk of celery, dill pickle spear or olives.
—*Taste of Home Test Kitchen*

Takes: 10 min. • **Makes:** 1 serving

- ¼ tsp. plus ⅛ tsp. celery salt, divided
- 1½ to 2 cups ice cubes, divided
- 2 oz. vodka
- 1 cup tomato juice, chilled
- 1 Tbsp. lemon juice
- 1½ tsp. lime juice
- ¾ tsp. Worcestershire sauce
- ½ tsp. prepared horseradish, optional
- ⅛ tsp. pepper
- ⅛ tsp. hot pepper sauce

OPTIONAL GARNISHES
  Celery rib, pickle spear, green and ripe olives, cucumber slice and/or cocktail shrimp

1. Using water, moisten rim of a highball glass. Sprinkle ¼ tsp. celery salt on a small plate; dip rim into salt. Discard remaining celery salt from plate. Fill a shaker three-fourths full with ice. Place remaining ice in prepared glass.
2. Add vodka, juices, Worcestershire sauce, horseradish if desired, pepper, remaining celery salt and hot pepper sauce to shaker; cover and shake until condensation forms on exterior, 10-15 seconds. Strain into prepared glass. Garnish as desired.

1½ CUPS: 180 cal., 1g fat (0 sat. fat), 0 chol., 1110mg sod., 12g carb. (7g sugars, 1g fiber), 2g pro.

TOMATO QUICHE

I first tried this recipe at a family gathering and loved it! It's a great meatless dish, served hot or cold. This is my most-requested dish for parties and brunches, and it's simple to make.
—*Heidi Anne Quinn, West Kingston, RI*

Prep: 20 min. • **Bake:** 50 min.
Makes: 8 servings

- 1 cup chopped onion
- 2 Tbsp. butter
- 4 large tomatoes, peeled, seeded, chopped and drained
- 1 tsp. salt
- ¼ tsp. pepper
- ¼ tsp. dried thyme
- 2 cups Monterey Jack cheese, divided
- 1 unbaked pastry shell (10 in.)
- 4 large eggs, room temperature
- 1½ cups half-and-half cream

1. In a large skillet over medium-high heat, saute onion in butter until tender. Add the tomatoes, salt, pepper and thyme. Cook over medium-high heat until the liquid is almost evaporated, 10-15 minutes. Remove from the heat.

2. Sprinkle 1 cup cheese into bottom of pie shell. Cover with tomato mixture; sprinkle with remaining cheese.

3. In a small bowl, beat eggs until foamy. Beat in cream. Pour into pie shell.

4. Bake at 425° for 10 minutes. Reduce heat to 325°; bake 40 minutes longer or until top begins to brown and a knife inserted in the center comes out clean. Let stand 10 minutes before cutting.

1 PIECE: 375 cal., 26g fat (14g sat. fat), 167mg chol., 638mg sod., 21g carb. (7g sugars, 1g fiber), 14g pro.

READER REVIEW

"I made this recipe almost exactly as written. Only thing I did different was add some fresh basil and garlic. Loved this recipe. I will be adding this to my collection!"

CATBIRD513, TASTEOFHOME.COM

BLUEBERRY CRUNCH BREAKFAST BAKE

Fresh blueberries in season make this a special breakfast, but I find that frozen berries work just as well. My grandmother used to make this with strawberries, and I always loved to eat it at her house.

—*Marsha Ketaner, Henderson, NV*

Prep: 15 min. • **Bake:** 30 min.
Makes: 12 servings

- 1 **loaf (16 oz.) day-old French bread, cut into 1-in. slices**
- 8 **large eggs**
- 1 **cup half-and-half cream**
- ½ **tsp. vanilla extract**
- 1 **cup old-fashioned oats**
- 1 **cup packed brown sugar**
- ¼ **cup all-purpose flour**
- ½ **cup cold butter**
- 2 **cups fresh or frozen blueberries**
- 1 **cup chopped walnuts**

1. Arrange half of the bread slices in a greased 13x9-in. baking dish.

2. In a large bowl, whisk the eggs, cream and vanilla. Slowly pour half of the cream mixture over the bread. Top with remaining bread and egg mixture. Let stand until liquid is absorbed, about 5 minutes.

3. Meanwhile, in a small bowl, combine the oats, brown sugar and flour; cut in cold butter until crumbly. Sprinkle over top. Top with blueberries and walnuts.

4. Bake, uncovered, at 375° until a knife inserted in the center comes out clean, 30-35 minutes. Let stand for 5 minutes before serving.

1 SERVING: 427 cal., 21g fat (8g sat. fat), 154mg chol., 351mg sod., 50g carb. (23g sugars, 3g fiber), 12g pro.

EGGS FLORENTINE CASSEROLE

I turn eggs, sausage, mushrooms and spinach into a cheesy casserole for our Christmas brunch. Sometimes I mix in fresh peppers or green chiles. Feel free to get creative.
—*Karen Weekley, Washington, WV*

- -

Prep: 20 min. • **Bake:** 30 min. + standing
Makes: 12 servings

- 1 **lb. bulk pork sausage**
- 2 **Tbsp. butter**
- 1 **large onion, chopped**
- 1 **cup sliced fresh mushrooms**
- 1 **pkg. (10 oz.) frozen chopped spinach, thawed and squeezed dry**
- 12 **large eggs**
- 2 **cups 2% milk**
- 1 **cup shredded Swiss cheese**
- 1 **cup shredded sharp cheddar cheese**
- ¼ **tsp. paprika**

1. Preheat oven to 350°. In a large skillet, cook the pork sausage over medium heat until no longer pink, 6-8 minutes, breaking meat into crumbles; drain and transfer to a greased 13x9-in. baking dish.

2. In same skillet, heat butter over medium-high heat. Add onion and mushrooms; cook and stir 3-5 minutes or until tender. Stir in the spinach. Spoon the vegetable mixture over the sausage.

3. In a large bowl, whisk eggs and milk until blended; pour egg mixture over vegetables. Sprinkle with cheeses and paprika. Bake, uncovered, 30-35 minutes or until the center is set and a thermometer inserted in center reads 165°. Let casserole stand 10 minutes before serving.

1 PIECE: 271 cal., 20g fat (9g sat. fat), 226mg chol., 344mg sod., 6g carb. (4g sugars, 1g fiber), 16g pro.

⑤ APRICOT FLUFF

When we were young mothers, I asked my best friend if she had a recipe for an easy ambrosia salad that I could take to a cookout. She shared this recipe with me and it's become a must-have at every barbecue I attend. It also tastes great with peaches and peach gelatin.
—*Melissa Meinke, Fawn Grove, PA*

- -

Prep: 10 min. + chilling
Makes: 10 servings

- 1 **cup apricot or peach yogurt**
- 1 **pkg. (3 oz.) apricot gelatin**
- 1 **carton (8 oz.) frozen reduced-fat whipped topping, thawed**
- 1 **pkg. (10 oz.) miniature marshmallows**
- 3 **cups cubed peeled fresh apricots**

In a large bowl, add yogurt to gelatin; stir 2 minutes to completely dissolve. Gently stir in whipped topping, then marshmallows and apricots. Refrigerate salad until firm, at least 4 hours.

¾ CUP: 225 cal., 3g fat (3g sat. fat), 1mg chol., 57mg sod., 44g carb. (36g sugars, 1g fiber), 3g pro.

CORNFLAKE-COATED CRISPY BACON

I've loved my aunt's crispy coated bacon since I was a child. Now I've shared the super simple recipe with my own children. We still enjoy a big panful every Christmas morning—and on many other days throughout the year.
—*Brenda Severson, Norman, OK*

- -

Prep: 20 min. • **Bake:** 25 min.
Makes: 9 servings

½ cup evaporated milk
2 Tbsp. ketchup
1 Tbsp. Worcestershire sauce
  Dash pepper
18 bacon strips (1 lb.)
3 cups crushed cornflakes

Preheat oven to 375°. In a large bowl, combine the milk, ketchup, Worcestershire sauce and pepper. Add bacon strips, turning to coat. Dip strips in crushed cornflakes, patting to help coating adhere. Place bacon on 2 racks; place each rack on an ungreased 15x10x1-in. baking pan. Bake until golden and crisp, rotating pans halfway through baking, 25-30 minutes.
2 BACON STRIPS: 198 cal., 7g fat (3g sat. fat), 20mg chol., 547mg sod., 26g carb. (4g sugars, trace fiber), 8g pro.

CHEESY SAUSAGE POTATOES

Add these tender potato slices with lots of sausage and cheese to your next brunch menu. Everyone loves them, and afterward the pan is always empty.
—*Linda Hill, Marseilles, IL*

- -

Takes: 25 min. • **Makes:** 10 servings

3 lbs. potatoes, peeled and cut into ¼-in. slices
1 lb. bulk pork sausage
1 medium onion, chopped
¼ cup butter, melted
2 cups shredded cheddar cheese

1. Place the potatoes in a large saucepan and cover with water. Bring to a boil. Reduce heat; simmer, uncovered, until tender, 8-10 minutes. Meanwhile, crumble the sausage into a large skillet; add onion. Cook over medium heat until meat is no longer pink; drain if necessary.
2. Drain potatoes; arrange in an ungreased 13x9-in. baking dish. Drizzle with butter. Add sausage mixture and stir gently. Sprinkle with cheddar cheese.
3. Bake, uncovered, at 350° until cheese is melted, 5-7 minutes.
¾ CUP: 252 cal., 13g fat (8g sat. fat), 37mg chol., 220mg sod., 26g carb. (2g sugars, 3g fiber), 9g pro.

LIGHT & FLUFFY WAFFLES

These melt-in-your-mouth waffles are so tender. Keep them simple with butter and maple syrup or try one of these tasty toppers.
—*James Schend, Pleasant Prairie, WI*

Prep: 15 min. + standing
Cook: 5 min./batch
Makes: 12 waffles

    2 large eggs
 1½ cups all-purpose flour
   ½ cup cornstarch
    1 tsp. baking powder
   ½ tsp. baking soda
   ½ tsp. salt
   ½ cup 2% milk
    5 Tbsp. canola oil
    2 tsp. vanilla extract
    1 tsp. white vinegar
    2 Tbsp. sugar
   ½ cup club soda, chilled
       Optional: Butter and maple syrup

1. Separate eggs. Place egg whites in a clean, dry bowl; let stand at room temperature for 30 minutes.

2. In another bowl, whisk together the next 5 ingredients. In a small bowl, whisk egg yolks, milk, oil, vanilla and vinegar until blended. Beat egg whites until soft peaks form. Gradually add the sugar; continue beating until stiff peaks form.

3. Preheat waffle iron. Stir together flour mixture, egg mixture and club soda just until combined. Fold egg whites into batter. Bake waffles according to manufacturer's directions until golden brown. Serve with butter and maple syrup if desired.

2 WAFFLES: 312 cal., 14g fat (2g sat. fat), 64mg chol., 421mg sod., 39g carb. (5g sugars, 1g fiber), 6g pro.

1 FAVORITE
10 WAYS
Waffle Toppers

1. BANANAS FOSTER WAFFLES

I eat my waffles topped Bananas Foster style with the four B's (sliced bananas, butter, brown sugar and booze). I also like to fold crumbled bacon bits into the batter.
—*Rashanda Cobbins, Milwaukee, WI*

2. COFFEE BUTTER WAFFLES

The best waffle I've ever had was topped with caramelized bacon, maple syrup and coffee butter.
—*Maggie Knoebel, Hartland, WI*

6. LEMON & BLUEBERRY WAFFLES

I eat my waffles with lemon curd and blueberry sauce. (Lightly crush the blueberries and simmer with a little water, sugar and a sprig of thyme. Remove from heat and stir in a tablespoon or two of butter.) Then I top it all with whipped cream and a shower of lemon zest.
—*Jeanne Ambrose, Des Moines, IA*

7. NUTELLA WAFFLES

I top my waffles with peanut butter, Nutella, bananas and a sprinkling of crushed peanuts. *Mmm.*
—*Beth Tomkiw, Milwaukee, WI*

3. SPICED WAFFLES

I add cinnamon, nutmeg, cardamom, vanilla and almond extract to the batter. For the topping, I make a strawberry, rhubarb and orange sauce every spring and freeze it in small containers. I warm one of those up in the microwave, and serve with maple, blueberry, raspberry and apple-cinnamon syrups.
—*Linda Kast, Cedar Rapids, IA*

4. CHURRO WAFFLES

I knew someone who made waffles topped with cubed maple bacon rolled in chili powder-sugar with whipped cream. Personally, I like to make churro waffles with horchata whipped cream and dulce de leche sauce. Before that, my go-to was a habanero-apricot preserve topping and whipped cream.
—*Sarah Farmer, Waukesha, WI*

5. CHOCOLATE CHIP WAFFLES

I add chocolate chips to my batter, top the waffles with banana slices and add a dollop of a peanut butter mixture (equal parts peanut butter and marshmallow fluff and a dash of honey). It's by far one of the least nutritionally sound breakfasts that I make, but I love it too much to stop.
—*Rachel Maidl, Milwaukee, WI*

8. OVER-EASY WAFFLES

The only way I eat waffles is with a supersized over-easy egg (one whole egg, one egg white) on top, sprinkled with salt and freshly ground pepper, plus a generous splash of maple syrup over the whole thing. Sublime!
—*Deb Mulvey, Shorewood, WI*

9. PB&J WAFFLES

I like to spread waffles with peanut butter or almond butter for some protein. Then I top them with fresh berries—kind of like a PB&J.
—*Shannon Norris, Cudahy, WI*

10. CROQUE-MADAME WAFFLES

One of my favorite combos ever was a savory croque-madame waffle—egg, ham and bechamel sauce.
—*Joe Hrdina, Milwaukee, WI*

Soups & Sandwiches

Whether you dip your spoon into a steaming cup of soup or take a big bite out of a sizzling burger or robust sandwich, you will love the hearty goodness these recipes have to offer.

ITALIAN TURKEY BURGERS

Seasoned with oregano and Parmesan cheese, these plump burgers are a delicious change-of-pace entree. I like to serve them on crusty Italian bread with warmed spaghetti sauce, but you can also use hamburger buns.
—*Mary Tallman, Arbor Vitae, WI*

Takes: 30 min. • **Makes:** 4 servings

- ¼ cup canned crushed tomatoes
- 2 Tbsp. grated Parmesan cheese
- ½ tsp. garlic powder
- ½ tsp. dried oregano
- ¼ tsp. salt
- ¼ tsp. pepper
- 1 lb. ground turkey
- 8 slices Italian bread, toasted
- ½ cup meatless spaghetti sauce, warmed

1. In a large bowl, gently combine the first 6 ingredients. Crumble turkey over mixture and mix well. Shape into four ¾-in.-thick oval-shaped patties.

2. Grill patties on an oiled rack, uncovered, over medium heat or broil 4 in. from the heat on each side until a thermometer reaches 165° and juices run clear, 6-8 minutes.

3. Place a patty on each of 4 slices of bread. Drizzle with spaghetti sauce; top with the remaining bread.

1 BURGER: 306 cal., 12g fat (3g sat. fat), 92mg chol., 680mg sod., 24g carb. (0 sugars, 2g fiber), 25g pro. **DIABETIC EXCHANGES:** 3 lean meat, 1½ starch, 1 fat.

READER REVIEW

"I have been using this recipe for years, but I shape the meat into meatballs and bake them in the oven. They're perfect for a turkey meatball sub."

MOMINTHEKITCHEN, TASTEOFHOME.COM

CRUNCHY TUNA WRAPS

Packed with protein-rich tuna and fresh, crunchy veggies, these colorful wraps have sensational flavor—and they're good for you, too.
—*Edie Farm, Farmington, NM*

Takes: 10 min. • **Makes:** 2 servings

- 1 pouch (6.4 oz.) light tuna in water
- ¼ cup finely chopped celery
- ¼ cup chopped green onions
- ¼ cup sliced water chestnuts, chopped
- 3 Tbsp. chopped sweet red pepper
- 2 Tbsp. reduced-fat mayonnaise
- 2 tsp. prepared mustard
- 2 spinach tortillas (8 in.), room temperature
- 1 cup shredded lettuce

In a small bowl, mix the first 7 ingredients until blended. Spread over tortillas; sprinkle with lettuce. Roll up tightly jelly-roll style.

1 WRAP: 312 cal., 10g fat (2g sat. fat), 38mg chol., 628mg sod., 34g carb. (2g sugars, 3g fiber), 23g pro. **DIABETIC EXCHANGES:** 3 lean meat, 2 starch, ½ fat.

QUICK TOMATO SOUP

My family often requests my sweet homemade tomato soup on cold days. It's terrific with a sandwich and nearly as quick to fix as the canned variety.
—*Jane Ward, Churchville, MD*

Takes: 15 min. • **Makes:** 6 servings (1½ qt.)

- ¼ cup butter
- ¼ cup all-purpose flour
- 1 tsp. curry powder
- ¼ tsp. onion powder
- 1 can (46 oz.) tomato juice
- ¼ cup sugar
  Optional: Oyster crackers or croutons

In a large saucepan, melt butter. Stir in flour, curry powder and onion powder until smooth. Gradually add the tomato juice and sugar. Cook, uncovered, until thickened and heated through, about 5 minutes. If desired, serve with crackers or croutons.

1 CUP: 156 cal., 8g fat (5g sat. fat), 20mg chol., 862mg sod., 22g carb. (15g sugars, 1g fiber), 2g pro.

CABBAGE & BEEF SOUP

When I was young, I helped my parents work the fields of their small farm. Lunchtime was always a treat when my mom picked fresh vegetables from her garden and simmered them in her big soup pot. Now I enjoy making this soup with produce from my own garden.
—*Ethel Ledbetter, Canton, NC*

Prep: 10 min. • **Cook:** 70 min.
Makes: 12 servings (3 qt.)

- 1 lb. lean ground beef (90% lean)
- ½ tsp. garlic salt
- ¼ tsp. garlic powder
- ¼ tsp. pepper
- 2 celery ribs, chopped
- 1 can (16 oz.) kidney beans, rinsed and drained
- ½ medium head cabbage, chopped
- 1 can (28 oz.) diced tomatoes, undrained
- 3½ cups water
- 4 tsp. beef bouillon granules
  Minced fresh parsley

1. In a Dutch oven, cook and crumble beef over medium heat until no longer pink; drain. Stir in remaining ingredients except parsley.
2. Bring to a boil. Reduce heat; cover and simmer for 1 hour. Garnish with parsley.

1 CUP: 116 cal., 3g fat (1g sat. fat), 19mg chol., 582mg sod., 11g carb. (3g sugars, 3g fiber), 11g pro. **DIABETIC EXCHANGES:** 1 starch, 1 lean meat.

READER REVIEW

"Love this soup! I make a huge batch and freeze it for workday lunches. It's low in calories but not short on flavor. I also add onion and Worcestershire to the beef, plus shredded carrots and whatever other vegetables I have on hand. A keeper."

NKELLORI114, TASTEOFHOME.COM

CRANBERRY BBQ PULLED PORK

Cranberry sauce adds a yummy twist to pulled pork, and my family can't get enough of it. The pork cooks to tender perfection in the slow cooker, which also makes this dish conveniently portable.
—*Carrie Wiegand, Mount Pleasant, IA*

Prep: 20 min. • **Cook:** 9 hours
Makes: 14 servings

- 1 boneless pork shoulder roast (4 to 6 lbs.)
- ⅓ cup cranberry juice
- 1 tsp. salt

SAUCE
- 1 can (14 oz.) whole-berry cranberry sauce
- 1 cup ketchup
- ⅓ cup cranberry juice
- 3 Tbsp. brown sugar
- 4½ tsp. chili powder
- 2 tsp. garlic powder
- 1 tsp. onion powder
- ½ tsp. salt
- ¼ tsp. ground chipotle pepper
- ½ tsp. liquid smoke, optional
- 14 hamburger buns, split

1. Cut the roast in half. Place in a 4-qt. slow cooker. Add the cranberry juice and salt. Cover and cook on low 8-10 hours or until meat is tender.

2. Remove the roast and set aside. In a small saucepan, combine the cranberry sauce, ketchup, cranberry juice, brown sugar, seasonings and liquid smoke if desired. Cook and stir over medium heat until slightly thickened, about 5 minutes.

3. Skim the fat from cooking juices; set aside ½ cup juices. Discard remaining juices. When cool enough to handle, shred the pork with 2 forks and return to slow cooker.

4. Stir in sauce mixture and reserved cooking juices. Cover and cook on low about 1 hour or until heated through. Serve on buns.

FREEZE OPTION: Freeze cooled meat mixture in freezer containers. To use, partially thaw in refrigerator overnight. Heat through in a saucepan, stirring occasionally; add a little water if necessary.

1 SANDWICH: 409 cal., 15g fat (5g sat. fat), 77mg chol., 772mg sod., 42g carb. (19g sugars, 2g fiber), 26g pro.

BUFFALO CHICKEN WING SOUP

We love Buffalo chicken wings, so we created a soup with the same zippy flavor. Start with a small amount of hot sauce—you can always add more to suit your family's tastes.
—*Pat Farmer, Falconer, NY*

Prep: 5 min. • **Cook:** 4 hours
Makes: 8 servings

- 5 cups 2% milk
- 3 cans (10¾ oz. each) condensed cream of chicken soup, undiluted
- 3 cups shredded cooked chicken (about 1 lb.)
- 1 cup sour cream
- ¼ to ½ cup Louisiana-style hot sauce
  Optional: Sliced celery and additional hot sauce

In a 5-qt. slow cooker, mix the first 5 ingredients. Cook, covered, on low until heated through and the flavors are blended, 4-5 hours. If desired, top servings with celery and additional hot sauce.

1⅓ CUPS: 572 cal., 29g fat (11g sat. fat), 180mg chol., 1308mg sod., 18g carb. (9g sugars, 2g fiber), 57g pro.

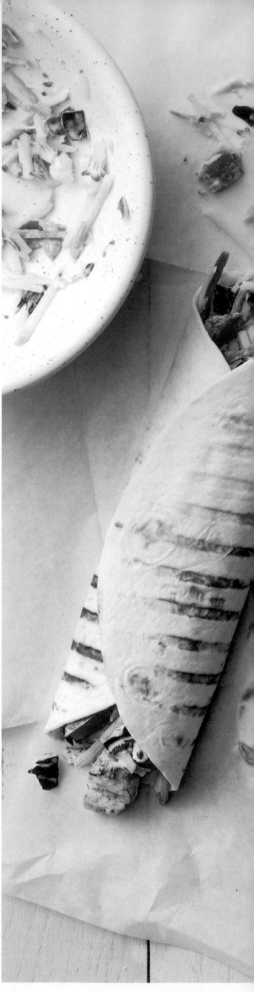

CORN CHOWDER WITH DUMPLINGS

Here's a spiced-up version of my favorite corn chowder. Dumplings give a familiar soup that extra-special surprise!
—*Shannon Kohn, Simpsonville, SC*

- -

Prep: 15 min. • **Cook:** 20 min.
Makes: 4 servings

- 2 **large onions, chopped**
- 2 **tsp. canola oil**
- 4 **cups chicken broth**
- 3 **cups frozen corn**
- 2 **cups cubed peeled potatoes**
- 1 **cup heavy whipping cream**
- 1 **to 3 tsp. minced chipotle pepper in adobo sauce**
- ¼ **tsp. salt**

CHEDDAR CORNMEAL DUMPLINGS
- ½ **cup all-purpose flour**
- ¼ **cup yellow cornmeal**
- 1 **tsp. baking powder**
- ¼ **tsp. salt**
- ½ **cup 2% milk**
- ¼ **cup shredded cheddar cheese**

1. In a large saucepan, saute onions in oil until tender. Add the broth, corn, potatoes, cream, chipotle pepper and salt. Bring to a boil. Reduce heat; simmer, uncovered, for 3-5 minutes.

2. For dumplings, in a small bowl, combine the flour, cornmeal, baking powder and salt. Stir in the milk and cheese just until moistened. Drop by tablespoonfuls onto simmering chowder.

3. Cover and simmer for 20 minutes or until a toothpick inserted in the center of a dumpling comes out clean (do not lift the cover while simmering).

1¼ CUPS: 577 cal., 29g fat (16g sat. fat), 93mg chol., 1424mg sod., 71g carb. (12g sugars, 7g fiber), 14g pro.

JAMAICAN JERK TURKEY WRAPS

After tasting these spicy wraps at a party, I got the recipe. The grilled turkey tenderloin and light jalapeno dressing make them a hit.
—*Mary Ann Dell, Phoenixville, PA*

Prep: 20 min. • **Grill:** 20 min. • **Makes:** 4 wraps

- 2 cups broccoli coleslaw mix
- 1 medium tomato, seeded and chopped
- 3 Tbsp. reduced-fat coleslaw dressing
- 1 jalapeno pepper, seeded and chopped
- 1 Tbsp. prepared mustard
- 1½ tsp. Caribbean jerk seasoning
- 2 turkey breast tenderloins (8 oz. each)
- 4 flour tortillas (8 in.)

1. In a large bowl, toss the coleslaw mix, tomato, coleslaw dressing, jalapeno and mustard; set aside.

2. Rub the seasoning over the turkey tenderloins. On a greased grill, cook the turkey, covered, over medium heat or broil 4 in. from heat 8-10 minutes on each side or until a thermometer reads 165°. Let stand 5 minutes.

3. Grill tortillas, uncovered, over medium heat 45-55 seconds on each side or until warmed. Thinly slice turkey; place down the center of tortillas. Top with coleslaw mixture and roll up.

1 WRAP: 343 cal., 8g fat (1g sat. fat), 48mg chol., 654mg sod., 37g carb. (7g sugars, 3g fiber), 34g pro. **DIABETIC EXCHANGES:** 3 lean meat, 2 starch, 1 vegetable, ½ fat.

DID YOU KNOW?
Jamaican, or Caribbean, jerk seasoning is traditionally a mix of chiles, thyme, spices (cinnamon, ginger, allspice, cloves, etc.), garlic and onions. The dry blend is used on grilled meats.

BEEF & CHEESE WRAPS

These make-ahead wraps are scrumptious, portable and ideal for picnics and tailgates. Enjoy them whole or slice them into 1-inch pieces to serve them as an appetizer. They also make an excellent lunch on the go.
—Sue Sibson, Howard, SC

- -

Prep: 10 min. + chilling • **Makes:** 4 servings

- 4 flour tortillas (10 in.), warmed
- 1 carton (8 oz.) spreadable chive and onion cream cheese
- 1 cup shredded carrots
- 1 cup shredded Monterey Jack cheese
- 1 lb. thinly sliced cooked roast beef
   Leaf lettuce

Spread 1 side of each tortilla with the cream cheese; layer with the carrots, Monterey Jack cheese, beef and lettuce. Roll up tightly and cover. Refrigerate for at least 30 minutes. Cut in half or into 1-in. slices.

1 SERVING: 657 cal., 35g fat (20g sat. fat), 143mg chol., 1431mg sod., 38g carb. (6g sugars, 7g fiber), 38g pro.

READER REVIEW

"Fantastic! I made a huge platter of these to take to a New Year's Eve party and they were a hit."

DAWNLOCKHART, TASTEOFHOME.COM

TURKEY SOUP

I make this soup around the holidays after a big turkey dinner. It is especially good on cold winter nights when it's snowing—which happens a lot where I live!
—Carol Brethauer, Denver, CO

- -

Prep: 30 min. • **Cook:** 4 hours
Makes: 12 servings (5 qt.)

- 1 leftover turkey carcass (from a 14 lb. turkey)
- 3 qt. water
- 2 cans (14½ oz. each) reduced-sodium chicken broth
- ½ cup uncooked long-grain rice
- 1 medium onion, finely chopped
- 4 celery ribs, finely chopped
- 2 medium carrots, grated
- 1 bay leaf
   Dash poultry seasoning
- ½ tsp. onion powder
- ½ tsp. garlic powder
- ¼ tsp. pepper
   Salt, optional

1. In a stock pot, place turkey carcass, water and broth. Bring to a boil. Reduce heat; cover and simmer for 4-5 hours.
2. Remove carcass from stock. Remove any meat and dice. Return to stock along with rice, onion, celery, carrots, bay leaf and poultry seasoning. Add remaining seasonings to taste. Cover and simmer over medium-low heat until the rice is cooked. Discard bay leaf.

1⅔ CUPS: 147 cal., 2g fat (0 sat. fat), 28mg chol., 412mg sod., 15g carb. (3g sugars, 1g fiber), 12g pro. **DIABETIC EXCHANGES:** 1 starch, 1 lean meat.

CURLY NOODLE CHICKEN SOUP

I created this recipe to serve at a dinner I hosted for a group of friends. The main course was Italian, and I needed a good soup, so I converted a favorite tortilla soup recipe by substituting pasta and adding different seasonings.
—*Maxine Pierson, San Ramon, CA*

Prep: 10 min. • **Cook:** 1 hour 25 min.
Makes: 9 servings (about 2 qt.)

- 1 lb. boneless skinless chicken breasts, cut into ½-in. pieces
- 1 large onion, chopped
- 4 celery ribs, sliced
- 2 medium carrots, sliced
- 4 garlic cloves, minced
- 2 Tbsp. butter
- 2 Tbsp. olive oil
- 1 tsp. dried basil
- ½ tsp. dried oregano
- ⅛ tsp. pepper
- 3 cans (14½ oz. each) reduced-sodium chicken broth, divided
- 1 can (14½ oz.) diced tomatoes, undrained
- 6 oz. uncooked tricolor spiral pasta
- ¼ cup all-purpose flour

1. In a large saucepan, saute chicken, onion, celery, carrots and garlic in butter and oil for 5 minutes. Stir in the basil, oregano and pepper until blended.
2. Set aside 1 cup broth. Gradually add the remaining broth to the pan. Stir in tomatoes. Bring to a boil. Reduce heat; cover and simmer for 45-60 minutes.
3. Return to a boil; stir in the pasta. Reduce heat; simmer, uncovered, for 10-13 minutes or until pasta is almost tender. Combine flour and reserved broth until smooth. Stir into pan. Bring to a boil; cook and stir for 2 minutes or until thickened.
1 CUP: 223 cal., 7g fat (2g sat. fat), 35mg chol., 537mg sod., 24g carb. (4g sugars, 2g fiber), 16g pro. **DIABETIC EXCHANGES:** 1½ starch, 1 lean meat, 1 vegetable, 1 fat.

TANGY BARBECUE SANDWICHES

Since the beef for these robust sandwiches is prepared in the slow cooker, it's easy to fix a meal for a hungry bunch. Everyone loves the savory homemade sauce. Rest assured, you won't have any leftovers.
—*Debbi Smith, Crossett, AR*

Prep: 10 min. • **Cook:** 8 hours
Makes: 18 servings

- 3 cups chopped celery
- 1 cup chopped onion
- 1 cup ketchup
- 1 cup barbecue sauce
- 1 cup water
- 2 Tbsp. white vinegar
- 2 Tbsp. Worcestershire sauce
- 2 Tbsp. brown sugar
- 1 tsp. chili powder
- 1 tsp. salt
- ½ tsp. pepper
- ½ tsp. garlic powder
- 1 boneless beef chuck roast (3 to 4 lbs.), trimmed and cut in half
- 18 hamburger buns, split

1. In a 5-qt. slow cooker, combine the first 12 ingredients. Add roast. Cover and cook on high for 1 hour. Reduce heat to low and cook 6-8 hours longer or until meat is tender.
2. Remove roast; cool. Shred the meat and return to sauce, heat through. Using a slotted spoon, fill each bun with about ½ cup of the meat mixture.
1 SANDWICH: 262 cal., 9g fat (3g sat. fat), 49mg chol., 659mg sod., 26g carb. (8g sugars, 2g fiber), 18g pro.

PRESSURE COOKER CHICKEN TORTILLA SOUP

Don't be shy about loading up the spices and shredded chicken into your pressure cooker. Chicken tortilla soup tastes amazing as leftovers the next day. Your family will thank you for this one!
—*Karen Kelly, Germantown, MD*

Prep: 10 min. • **Cook:** 30 min.
Makes: 10 servings

- 1   Tbsp. canola oil
- 1   medium onion, chopped
- 3   garlic cloves, minced
- 1   lb. boneless skinless chicken breasts
- 1   carton (32 oz.) reduced-sodium chicken broth
- 1   can (15 oz.) black beans, rinsed and drained
- 1   can (14 oz.) fire-roasted diced tomatoes
- 1½ cups frozen corn
- 1   Tbsp. chili powder
- 1   Tbsp. ground cumin
- 1   tsp. paprika
- ½   tsp. salt
- ¼   tsp. pepper
- ¼   cup minced fresh cilantro
     Optional: Chopped avocado, jalapeno and lime wedges

1. Select the saute setting on a 6-qt. electric pressure cooker and adjust for high heat; add oil. Add onion; cook and stir 6-8 minutes or until tender. Add garlic; cook 1 minute longer. Add the next 10 ingredients. Stir. Lock lid; close pressure-release valve.
2. Adjust to pressure-cook on high for 8 minutes. Allow pressure to naturally release for 12 minutes, then quick-release any remaining pressure.
3. Remove chicken from the pressure cooker. Shred with 2 forks; return to pressure cooker. Stir in cilantro. If desired, serve with toppings.
1 CUP: 141 cal., 3g fat (0 sat. fat), 25mg chol., 580mg sod., 15g carb. (3g sugars, 3g fiber), 14g pro. **DIABETIC EXCHANGES:** 2 lean meat, 1 starch.

GROUND BEEF & PEPPERONI STROMBOLI

I've made this delicious Stromboli many times. It is perfect when folks get together on game day and always satisfies big appetites.
—*Shelley Banzhaf, Maywood, NE*

Prep: 25 min. + rising • **Bake:** 30 min.
Makes: 2 Stromboli (8 servings each)

- 2   loaves (1 lb. each) frozen bread dough, thawed
- 2   large eggs, lightly beaten
- ⅓   cup olive oil
- ½   tsp. garlic powder
- ½   tsp. salt
- ½   tsp. pepper
- ½   tsp. ground mustard
- ½   tsp. dried oregano
- 1   lb. ground beef, cooked and drained
- 1   pkg. (3½ oz.) sliced pepperoni
- 2   cups shredded part-skim mozzarella cheese
- 1   cup shredded cheddar cheese
- 1   small onion, chopped

1. Place each loaf of bread dough in a large greased bowl, turning once to grease top. Cover and let rise in a warm place until doubled, about 45 minutes.
2. Preheat oven to 375°. Punch dough down. Roll each loaf into a 15x12-in. rectangle.
3. In a small bowl, combine the eggs, oil and seasonings. Brush over each dough to within ½ in. of edges; set the remaining egg mixture aside. Layer the beef, pepperoni, cheeses and onion on each dough to within ½ in. of edges. Roll up each, jelly-roll style, beginning with a long side. Tuck ends underneath; seal the edges well.
4. Place each, seam side down, on a greased baking sheet. Brush with egg mixture. Bake until lightly browned, 30-35 minutes, brushing with egg mixture midway through baking. Let stand 5-10 minutes before cutting.
1 SERVING: 268 cal., 17g fat (6g sat. fat), 64mg chol., 467mg sod., 16g carb. (2g sugars, 1g fiber), 14g pro.

MEXICAN SHRIMP BISQUE

I enjoy both Cajun and Mexican cuisines, and this rich, elegant soup combines the best of both. I serve it with a crispy green salad and a glass of white wine.
—*Karen Harris, Littleton, CO*

Takes: 30 min. • **Makes:** 3 servings

- 1   small onion, chopped
- 1   Tbsp. olive oil
- 2   garlic cloves, minced
- 1   Tbsp. all-purpose flour
- 1   cup water
- ½   cup heavy whipping cream
- 2   tsp. chicken bouillon granules
- 1   Tbsp. chili powder
- ½   tsp. ground cumin
- ½   tsp. ground coriander
- ½   lb. uncooked medium shrimp, peeled and deveined
- ½   cup sour cream
      Optional: Chopped fresh cilantro and sliced avocado

1. In a small saucepan, saute onion in oil until tender. Add garlic; cook 1 minute longer. Stir in flour until blended. Stir in water, cream, bouillon and seasonings; bring to a boil. Reduce heat; cover and simmer for 5 minutes.
2. Cut shrimp into bite-sized pieces if desired; add shrimp to soup. Simmer 5-10 minutes longer or until shrimp turn pink. Place the sour cream in a small bowl; gradually stir in ½ cup hot soup. Return all to the pan, stirring constantly. Heat through (do not boil). Top with cilantro and avocado if desired.
1 CUP: 357 cal., 28g fat (15g sat. fat), 173mg chol., 706mg sod., 10g carb. (3g sugars, 2g fiber), 16g pro.

HEARTY ITALIAN SANDWICHES

I've been making this sweet and spicy sandwich filling for many years. The Italian-flavored meat mixture smells just as good as it tastes.
—*Elaine Krupsky, Las Vegas, NV*

Prep: 20 min. • **Cook:** 3 hours
Makes: 8 servings

- 1½ lbs. lean ground beef (90% lean)
- 1½ lbs. bulk Italian sausage
- 2   large onions, sliced
- 2   large green peppers, sliced
- 2   large sweet red peppers, sliced
- 1   tsp. salt
- 1   tsp. pepper
- ¼   tsp. crushed red pepper flakes
- 8   sandwich rolls, split and toasted
     Shredded Monterey Jack cheese, optional

1. In a Dutch oven, cook beef and sausage over medium heat until no longer pink, breaking both into crumbles; drain. Place a third of the onions and peppers in a 5-qt. slow cooker; top with half the meat mixture. Repeat layers; top with remaining vegetables. Sprinkle with salt, pepper and pepper flakes.
2. Cover and cook on low for 3-4 hours or until vegetables are tender. With a slotted spoon, serve about 1 cup of meat and vegetables on each roll. Top with cheese if desired. Use pan juices for dipping if desired.
1 SANDWICH: 587 cal., 30g fat (10g sat. fat), 99mg chol., 1251mg sod., 44g carb. (9g sugars, 3g fiber), 35g pro.

FAST REFRIED BEAN SOUP

This recipe combines the ease of canned ingredients with the heartiness of chili. It'll fill you up on cold afternoons or make a wonderful last-minute lunch. If you like it spicier, use medium or hot green chiles instead of mild.
—Darlene Brenden, Salem, OR

Takes: 25 min. • **Makes:** 8 servings (2 qt.)

- 1 can (16 oz.) spicy fat-free refried beans
- 1 can (15¼ oz.) whole kernel corn, drained
- 1 can (15 oz.) black beans, rinsed and drained
- 1 can (14½ oz.) chicken broth
- 1 can (14½ oz.) stewed tomatoes, cut up
- ½ cup water
- 1 can (4 oz.) chopped green chiles
- ¼ cup salsa
  Tortilla chips

In a large saucepan, combine the first 8 ingredients. Bring to a boil. Reduce heat; simmer, uncovered, until heated through, 8-10 minutes. Serve with tortilla chips.
1 CUP: 117 cal., 1g fat (0 sat. fat), 1mg chol., 720mg sod., 21g carb. (6g sugars, 4g fiber), 5g pro.

DARLENE BRENDEN
Salem, OR

HOT HAM SANDWICHES

I came up with this crowd-pleasing recipe while trying to recreate a favorite sandwich from a restaurant near my hometown. The sandwiches are easy to serve in a buffet line because they don't need condiments. They're flavorful just as they are!
—Susan Rehm, Grahamsville, NY

Prep: 10 min. • **Cook:** 4 hours
Makes: 12 servings

- 3 lbs. thinly sliced deli ham (about 40 slices)
- 2 cups apple juice
- ⅔ cup packed brown sugar
- ½ cup sweet pickle relish
- 2 tsp. prepared mustard
- 1 tsp. paprika
- 12 kaiser rolls, split
  Additional sweet pickle relish, optional

1. Separate deli ham slices and place in a 3-qt. slow cooker. In a small bowl, combine the apple juice, brown sugar, relish, mustard and paprika. Pour over ham.
2. Cover and cook on low for 4-5 hours or until heated through. Place 3-4 slices of ham on each roll. Serve with additional pickle relish if desired.
1 SANDWICH: 432 cal., 13g fat (4g sat. fat), 62mg chol., 1974mg sod., 52g carb. (23g sugars, 2g fiber), 27g pro.

PRESSURE COOKER FRENCH ONION SOUP

I love French onion soup on a cold night, but I don't love the time it takes. This is my quick version for when we're short on time.
—*Teri Rasey, Cadillac, MI*

Prep: 20 min. • **Cook:** 15 min.
Makes: 16 servings (4 qt.)

- ⅓ cup butter
- 3 lbs. onions, thinly sliced (10 cups)
- 2 garlic cloves, minced
- 2 Tbsp. sugar
- 4 cups beef stock
- 4 cups chicken stock
- ¾ cup white wine
- 1 tsp. salt
  Optional: Salad croutons and grated Parmesan cheese

1. Select saute setting on a 6-qt. electric pressure cooker and adjust for medium heat; add butter. Add the onion; cook and stir until tender, 6-8 minutes. Add the garlic and sugar; cook 6 minutes longer. Stir in the stocks, wine and salt. Press cancel. Lock lid; close pressure-release valve. Adjust to pressure-cook on high for 8 minutes.

2. Let pressure release naturally for 3 minutes; quick-release any remaining pressure. If desired, serve with croutons and Parmesan.

1 CUP: 87 cal., 4g fat (2g sat. fat), 10mg chol., 724mg sod., 9g carb. (6g sugars, 1g fiber), 2g pro.

TEST KITCHEN TIP
When using a pressure cooker, always maintain at least 1 cup of liquid to create and maintain pressure. Pressure cookers work by sealing in steam, which raises the liquid above the boiling point and creates pressure to cook. If there is no liquid, there is no steam. Experiment with flavorful cooking liquids like chicken stock, vegetable stock or cooking wine.

CUBAN SANDWICH BURGERS

My mom would make these Cuban burgers when we would visit her in Florida. They are a take on the real Cuban sandwich. My kids love them. The boys could eat two of these monsters in one sitting!
—*Marina Castle Kelley, Canyon Country, CA*

- -

Prep: 20 min. • **Bake:** 15 min.
Makes: 4 servings

- ½ **lb. ground beef**
- ½ **lb. ground pork**
- 1 **Tbsp. lemon juice**
- 1 **tsp. garlic salt, divided**
- ½ **tsp. pepper, divided**
- ½ **cup mayonnaise**
- ¼ **cup Dijon mustard**
- 4 **hamburger buns, split**
- 8 **thin slices Swiss cheese**
- 4 **thin slices deli ham**
- 4 **thin sandwich pickle slices**

1. Prepare grill for medium heat. Place a large cast-iron skillet on grill grates.

2. In a large bowl, combine beef, pork, lemon juice, ½ tsp. garlic salt and ¼ tsp. pepper, mixing lightly but thoroughly. Shape into four ½-in.-thick patties. Grill burgers, covered, over medium heat until a thermometer reads 160°, 5-7 minutes on each side.

3. Combine mayonnaise, mustard, remaining ½ tsp. garlic salt and ¼ tsp. pepper; spread over cut sides of buns. Place a burger on each bun bottom; top each with Swiss cheese, ham, pickles and bun top. Using oven mitts, carefully place preheated skillet on sandwiches. Grill sandwiches, covered, until buns are browned and cheese is melted, 5-8 minutes.

1 SANDWICH: 690 cal., 44g fat (12g sat. fat), 104mg chol., 1706mg sod., 32g carb. (2g sugars, 1g fiber), 36g pro.

ENCHILADA CHICKEN SOUP

Canned soups, enchilada sauce and a few other convenience items make this recipe one of my fast-to-fix favorites. Use mild green chiles if they suit your taste, or try a spicier kind to give the soup more kick.

Cristin Fischer, Bellevue, NE

Takes: 10 min. • **Makes:** 7 servings

- 1 can (10¾ oz.) condensed nacho cheese soup, undiluted
- 1 can (10½ oz.) condensed cream of chicken soup, undiluted
- 2⅔ cups whole milk
- 1 can (10 oz.) chunk white chicken, drained
- 1 can (10 oz.) enchilada sauce
- 1 can (4 oz.) chopped green chiles
  Sour cream

In a large saucepan, combine the soups, milk, chicken, enchilada sauce and chiles. Cook and stir over medium heat until heated through. Serve with sour cream.

1 CUP: 207 cal., 10g fat (4g sat. fat), 41mg chol., 992mg sod., 15g carb. (7g sugars, 2g fiber), 14g pro.

MEAT LOAF BURGERS

These hearty meat loaf sandwiches are terrific for potluck dinners. Served on hamburger buns, the beefy patties get extra flavor when topped with the seasoned tomato sauce.

—*Peggy Burdick, Burlington, MI*

Prep: 15 min. • **Cook:** 7 hours
Makes: 6 servings

- 1 large onion, sliced
- 1 celery rib, chopped
- 2 lbs. lean ground beef (90% lean)
- 1½ tsp. salt, divided
- ¼ tsp. pepper
- 2 cups tomato juice
- 4 garlic cloves, minced
- 1 Tbsp. ketchup
- 1 tsp. Italian seasoning
- 1 bay leaf
- 6 hamburger buns, split

1. Place onion and celery in a 3-qt. slow cooker. Combine the beef, 1 tsp. salt and the pepper; shape into 6 patties. Place over onion mixture. Combine the tomato juice, garlic, ketchup, Italian seasoning, bay leaf and remaining salt. Pour over the patties.
2. Cover and cook on low for 7-9 hours or until meat is no longer pink. Discard bay leaf. Separate patties with a spatula if necessary; serve on buns.

1 BURGER: 385 cal., 14g fat (5g sat. fat), 94mg chol., 1123mg sod., 28g carb. (7g sugars, 2g fiber), 34g pro.

CREAMY SWEET POTATO & VEGGIE SOUP

I tasted a fabulous soup in a restaurant but couldn't persuade the chef to share the recipe, so I began to experiment on my own. Finally, I came up with this blend, which is very close to what I tasted—maybe even better!
—Audrey Nemeth, Mount Vernon, ME

Takes: 30 min. • Makes: 16 servings (4 qt.)

- 1 large onion, chopped
- ¼ cup butter
- 3 medium sweet potatoes, peeled and chopped
- 3 medium zucchini, chopped
- 1 bunch broccoli, chopped
- 2 cartons (32 oz. each) chicken broth
- 2 medium potatoes, peeled and shredded
- 1 tsp. celery seed
- 1 to 2 tsp. ground cumin
- 2 tsp. salt
- 1 tsp. pepper
- 2 cups half-and-half cream

In a stockpot, saute the onion in butter until transparent but not browned. Add the sweet potatoes, zucchini and broccoli; saute lightly for 5 minutes or until crisp-tender. Stir in broth; simmer for a few minutes. Add the potatoes and seasonings; cook another 10 minutes or until vegetables are tender. Stir in cream and heat through.

1 CUP: 137 cal., 6g fat (4g sat. fat), 25mg chol., 839mg sod., 16g carb. (6g sugars, 3g fiber), 4g pro.

AIR-FRYER SALSA BLACK BEAN BURGERS

Meatless meals are so tasty when these hearty bean burgers are on the menu. Top them with guacamole and sour cream for a touch of decadence.
—Jill Reichardt, Saint Louis, MO

Takes: 30 min. • Makes: 4 servings

- 1 can (15 oz.) black beans, rinsed and drained
- ⅔ cup dry bread crumbs
- 1 small tomato, seeded and finely chopped
- 1 jalapeno pepper, seeded and finely chopped
- 1 large egg
- 1 tsp. minced fresh cilantro
- 1 garlic clove, minced
- 4 whole wheat hamburger buns, split
  Optional: Reduced-fat sour cream and guacamole

1. Preheat air fryer to 375°. Place beans in a food processor; cover and process until blended. Transfer to a large bowl. Add bread crumbs, tomato, jalapeno, egg, cilantro and garlic. Mix until combined. Shape mixture into 4 patties.
2. In batches, place patties on greased tray in air-fryer basket. Cook until lightly browned, 3-4 minutes. Turn; cook until lightly browned, 3-4 minutes longer. Serve on buns. If desired, top with sour cream and guacamole.

1 BURGER: 323 cal., 8g fat (1g sat. fat), 47mg chol., 576mg sod., 51g carb. (6g sugars, 9g fiber), 13g pro.

TACO TWIST SOUP

The fun, family-friendly twist in this taco soup is the spiral pasta. I lightened this recipe by substituting black beans for ground beef.
—*Colleen Zertler, Menomonie, WI*

- -

Takes: 30 min. • **Makes:** 6 servings

- 2 **tsp. olive oil**
- 1 **medium onion, chopped**
- 2 **garlic cloves, minced**
- 3 **cups vegetable broth or reduced-sodium beef broth**
- 1 **can (15 oz.) black beans, rinsed and drained**
- 1 **can (14½ oz.) diced tomatoes, undrained**
- 1½ **cups picante sauce**
- 1 **cup uncooked spiral pasta**
- 1 **small green pepper, chopped**
- 2 **tsp. chili powder**
- 1 **tsp. ground cumin**
  Optional toppings: Shredded cheddar cheese, sour cream and cilantro

1. In a large saucepan, heat oil over medium-high heat. Add onion and garlic; cook and stir until crisp-tender, 3-4 minutes.
2. Stir in the broth, beans, tomatoes, picante sauce, pasta, green pepper and seasonings. Bring to a boil, stirring frequently. Reduce heat; cover and simmer until pasta is tender, 10-12 minutes, stirring occasionally. If desired, serve with optional toppings.
1 CUP: 176 cal., 2g fat (0 sat. fat), 0 chol., 1044mg sod., 32g carb. (7g sugars, 5g fiber), 7g pro.

SMASH BURGERS

Now is not the time to cut calories or skimp on salt. Go for ground chuck that is at least 80% lean and 20% fat. If you can find a blend with ground brisket or short rib, all the better. The best burger comes with being liberal with kosher salt — it is beef's best friend.
—*James Schend, Pleasant Prairie, WI*

- -

Takes: 15 min. • **Makes:** 4 servings

- 1 **lb. ground beef (preferably 80% lean)**
- 1 **tsp. canola oil**
- 1 **tsp. kosher salt, divided**
- ½ **tsp. coarsely ground pepper, divided**
- 4 **hamburger buns, split**
  Optional: Mayonnaise, sliced American cheese, sliced tomato, dill pickle slices, lettuce, ketchup and yellow mustard

1. Place a 9-in. cast-iron skillet over medium heat. Meanwhile, gently shape the beef into 4 balls, shaping just enough to keep together (do not compact).
2. Increase burner temperature to medium-high; add oil. Working in batches, add beef. With a heavy metal spatula, flatten to ¼- to ½-in. thickness; sprinkle each with ⅛ tsp. salt and pepper. Cook until edges start to brown, about 1½ minutes. Turn burgers and sprinkle each with additional ⅛ tsp. salt and pepper. Cook until well browned and a thermometer reads at least 160°, 1 minute. Repeat with the remaining beef.
3. Serve the burgers on buns with toppings as desired.
1 BURGER: 339 cal., 16g fat (5g sat. fat), 70mg chol., 760mg sod., 22g carb. (3g sugars, 1g fiber), 24g pro.

CHEESY HAM CHOWDER

My five children all agree that this soothing recipe is fantastic. The soup is full of potatoes, carrots and ham. The best part is that I can get it on the table in only a half hour of hands-on time.
—Jennifer Trenhaile, Emerson, NE

Prep: 30 min. • **Cook:** 30 min.
Makes: 10 servings

- 10 bacon strips, diced
- 1 large onion, chopped
- 1 cup diced carrots
- 3 Tbsp. all-purpose flour
- 3 cups whole milk
- 1½ cups water
- 2½ cups cubed potatoes
- 1 can (15¼ oz.) whole kernel corn, drained
- 2 tsp. chicken bouillon granules
  Pepper to taste
- 3 cups shredded cheddar cheese
- 2 cups cubed fully cooked ham

1. In a Dutch oven, cook the bacon over medium heat until crisp. Using a slotted spoon, remove to paper towels to drain. In the drippings, saute onion and carrots until tender. Stir in the flour until blended. Gradually add milk and water. Bring to a boil; cook and stir for 2 minutes or until thickened.
2. Add potatoes, corn, bouillon and pepper. Reduce the heat; simmer, uncovered, for 20 minutes or until potatoes are tender. Add cheese and ham; heat until cheese is melted. Stir in bacon.

1 CUP: 418 cal., 28g fat (14g sat. fat), 76mg chol., 1056mg sod., 21g carb. (8g sugars, 2g fiber), 19g pro.

BIG SANDWICH

One look at this impressive sandwich and your family and friends will know they're in for a treat. I've served it many times for casual lunches and suppers. The tall layers prompt people to ask how they're supposed to eat it. I encourage them to simply dig in and enjoy!
—Margaret Yost, Tipp City, OH

Prep: 20 min. • **Bake:** 15 min.
Makes: 8 servings

- 1 unsliced round loaf of bread (8 in.)
- 2 Tbsp. horseradish
- ½ lb. thinly sliced cooked roast beef
- 2 Tbsp. prepared mustard
- ½ lb. thinly sliced fully cooked ham or turkey
- 4 slices Swiss cheese
- 2 Tbsp. mayonnaise
- 1 small tomato, thinly sliced
- 6 bacon strips, cooked
- 4 slices American cheese
- 1 small onion, thinly sliced
- ¼ cup butter, melted
- 1 Tbsp. sesame seeds
- ½ tsp. onion salt

Slice bread horizontally into 5 equal layers. Spread bottom layer with horseradish; top with roast beef. Place the next slice of bread over beef; spread with mustard and top with ham or turkey and Swiss cheese. Add the next slice of bread; spread with mayonnaise and top with tomato and bacon. Add the next slice of bread; top with American cheese and onion. Cover with remaining bread. Combine butter, sesame seeds and onion salt; brush over top and sides of loaf. Place on a baking sheet; loosely tent with heavy-duty foil. Bake at 400° for 15-20 minutes or until heated through. Carefully slice into 8 wedges.
1 SERVING: 408 cal., 21g fat (10g sat. fat), 66mg chol., 1162mg sod., 32g carb. (4g sugars, 2g fiber), 22g pro.

JENNIFER TRENHAILE
Emerson, NE

VEGETABLE LENTIL SOUP

Here's a healthy soup that's ideal for both vegetarians and those watching their weight. Butternut squash and lentils make it filling, while herbs and other vegetables round out the flavor.
—*Mark Morgan, Waterford, WI*

Prep: 15 min. • **Cook:** 4½ hours
Makes: 6 servings (about 2 qt.)

- 3 cups cubed peeled butternut squash
- 1 cup chopped carrots
- 1 cup chopped onion
- 1 cup dried lentils, rinsed
- 2 garlic cloves, minced
- 1 tsp. dried oregano
- 1 tsp. dried basil
- 4 cups vegetable broth
- 1 can (14½ oz.) Italian diced tomatoes, undrained
- 2 cups frozen cut green beans (about 8 oz.)

1. Place the first 8 ingredients in a 5-qt. slow cooker. Cook, covered, on low until lentils are tender, about 4 hours.
2. Stir in the tomatoes and beans. Cook, covered, on high until heated through, about 30 minutes.
1⅓ CUPS: 217 cal., 1g fat (0 sat. fat), 0 chol., 685mg sod., 45g carb. (11g sugars, 8g fiber), 11g pro.

SLOW-COOKER SLOPPY JOES

On hot summer days, this dish cooks without heating up the kitchen while I work on the rest of the meal. The recipe is easy to double or triple for crowds, and if there are any leftovers, you can freeze them to enjoy later!
—*Carol Losier, Baldwinsville, NY*

Prep: 20 min. • **Cook:** 3 hours
Makes: 8 servings

- 1½ lbs. ground beef
- 2 celery ribs, chopped
- 1 small onion, chopped
- 1 bottle (12 oz.) chili sauce
- 2 Tbsp. brown sugar
- 2 Tbsp. sweet pickle relish
- 1 Tbsp. Worcestershire sauce
- 1 tsp. salt
- ⅛ tsp. pepper
- 8 hamburger buns, split

1. In a large skillet, cook the beef, celery and onion over medium-high heat 8-10 minutes or until beef is no longer pink, breaking the beef into crumbles; drain. Transfer to a 3-qt. slow cooker.
2. Stir in chili sauce, brown sugar, pickle relish, Worcestershire sauce, salt and pepper. Cook, covered, on low 3-4 hours or until heated through and flavors are blended. Spoon meat mixture onto bun bottoms. Replace tops.
1 SANDWICH: 324 cal., 10g fat (4g sat. fat), 42mg chol., 1313mg sod., 40g carb. (16g sugars, 1g fiber), 19g pro.

Veggie Chili

Beefy Sweet Potato Chili

Pork and Green Chile Stew

1 FAVORITE 5 WAYS *Chili*

CHUNKY VEGETARIAN CHILI

This robust chili teams rice, kidney and pinto beans, and a variety of colorful vegetables for a hearty meatless meal.

—Taste of Home *Test Kitchen*

Prep: 20 min. • **Cook:** 25 min.
Makes: 11 servings (2¾ qt.)

- 1   medium green pepper, chopped
- 1   medium onion, chopped
- 3   garlic cloves, minced
- 1   Tbsp. canola oil
- 2   cans (14½ oz. each) Mexican-style stewed tomatoes, undrained
- 1   can (16 oz.) kidney beans, rinsed and drained
- 1   can (15 oz.) pinto beans, rinsed and drained
- 1   can (11 oz.) whole kernel corn, drained
- 2½ cups water
- 1   cup uncooked long grain rice
- 1   to 2 Tbsp. chili powder
- 1½ tsp. ground cumin

In a Dutch oven, saute the green pepper, onion and garlic in oil until tender. Stir in all remaining ingredients; bring to a boil. Reduce heat; cover and simmer until rice is cooked, stirring occasionally, 25-30 minutes. If thinner chili is desired, add more water.

1 CUP: 196 cal., 2g fat (0 sat. fat), 0 chol., 424mg sod., 37g carb. (6g sugars, 6g fiber), 7g pro. **DIABETIC EXCHANGES:** 2½ starch.

1

PORK & GREEN CHILE STEW

As an easily adaptable slow-cooker stew, this dish is ready in 4 hours if cooked on high or 8 hours if cooked on low.
—*Paul Sedillo, Plainfield, IL*

Prep: 40 min. • **Cook:** 7 hours
Makes: 8 servings (2 qt.)

- 2 lbs. boneless pork shoulder butt roast, cut into ¾-in. cubes
- 1 large onion, cut into ½-in. pieces
- 2 Tbsp. canola oil
- 1 tsp. salt
- 1 tsp. coarsely ground pepper
- 4 large potatoes, peeled and cut into ¾-in. cubes
- 3 cups water
- 1 can (16 oz.) hominy, rinsed and drained
- 2 cans (4 oz. each) chopped green chiles
- 2 Tbsp. quick-cooking tapioca
- 2 garlic cloves, minced
- ½ tsp. dried oregano
- ½ tsp. ground cumin
- 1 cup minced fresh cilantro
  Optional: Sour cream and cilantro

1. In a large skillet, brown pork and onion in oil in batches. Sprinkle with salt and pepper. Transfer to a 5-qt. slow cooker.
2. Stir in the potatoes, water, hominy, chiles, tapioca, garlic, oregano and cumin. Cover and cook on low until meat is tender, 7-9 hours. Stir in cilantro during the last 30 minutes of cooking. If desired, serve with sour cream and additional cilantro.
1 CUP: 322 cal., 15g fat (4g sat. fat), 67mg chol., 723mg sod., 25g carb. (3g sugars, 3g fiber), 21g pro. **DIABETIC EXCHANGES:** 3 medium-fat meat, 1½ starch, ½ fat.

WHITE CHILI WITH A KICK

Store-bought rotisserie chicken works easily for this spicy chili, but you could also cook your own if you prefer. We like to top our bowls with sour cream, green onions, cheese or salsa.
—*Emmajean Anderson, Mendota Heights, MN*

Prep: 20 min. • **Cook:** 15 min.
Makes: 9 servings (2¼ qt.)

- 1 large onion, chopped
- 6 Tbsp. butter, cubed
- 2 Tbsp. all-purpose flour
- 2 cups chicken broth
- ¾ cup half-and-half cream
- 1 rotisserie chicken, cut into bite-sized pieces
- 2 cans (15 oz. each) cannellini beans, rinsed and drained
- 1 can (11 oz.) white corn, drained
- 2 cans (4 oz. each) chopped green chiles
- 2 tsp. ground cumin
- 1 tsp. chili powder
- ½ tsp. salt
- ½ tsp. white pepper
- ½ tsp. hot pepper sauce
- 1½ cups shredded pepper jack cheese
  Optional: Salsa and chopped green onions

1. In a Dutch oven, saute onion in butter. Stir in the flour until blended; cook and stir until golden brown, about 3 minutes. Gradually add broth and cream. Bring to a boil; cook and stir until thickened, about 2 minutes.
2. Add the chicken, beans, corn, chiles, cumin, chili powder, salt, pepper and pepper sauce; heat through. Stir in cheese until melted.
3. If desired, garnish each serving with salsa and green onions.
1 CUP: 424 cal., 21g fat (11g sat. fat), 113mg chol., 896mg sod., 26g carb. (3g sugars, 5g fiber), 31g pro.

BEEFY SWEET POTATO CHILI

There's no better way to warm up than with a bowl of this chili. We created this recipe with friends when we lived in Seattle, where cold and rainy days are plentiful. Sweet potatoes are the secret ingredient, but even if you leave them out, you'll still have a tasty basic chili.
—*Jonell Tempero, Omaha, NE*

Prep: 45 min. • **Cook:** 40 min.
Makes: 6 servings (2¼ qt.)

- 2 medium sweet potatoes, peeled and cubed
- 2 lbs. ground beef
- 2 celery ribs, chopped
- 1 large onion, chopped
- 1 medium green pepper, chopped
- 4 garlic cloves, minced
- 1 jalapeno pepper, seeded and minced
- 2 cans (14½ oz. each) reduced-sodium chicken broth
- 1 can (14½ oz.) diced tomatoes, undrained
- 2 Tbsp. chili powder
- 2 Tbsp. tomato paste
- ¾ tsp. ground cumin
- ½ tsp. salt
- ½ tsp. pepper
- ¼ tsp. cayenne pepper
- 1 can (16 oz.) kidney beans, rinsed and drained
- 2 Tbsp. butter

1. Place potatoes in a greased 15x10x1-in. baking pan. Bake, uncovered, at 400° until tender, stirring once, 20-25 minutes.
2. Meanwhile, in a Dutch oven, cook beef, celery, onion, green pepper, garlic and jalapeno over medium heat until meat is no longer pink and vegetables are tender, breaking beef into crumbles; drain.
3. Stir in next 8 ingredients. Bring to a boil. Reduce heat; cover and simmer 30 minutes. Add the sweet potatoes, kidney beans and butter; heat through.

1½ CUPS: 471 cal., 22g fat (9g sat. fat), 104mg chol., 956mg sod., 32g carb. (10g sugars, 8g fiber), 36g pro.

PUMPKIN TURKEY CHILI

I love pumpkin and my husband loves chili, so I combined them into a dish we would both be happy about it. It's also become a big hit with the rest of my family.
—*Catherine Walmsley, Phoenix, AZ*

Prep: 20 min. • **Cook:** 1¾ hours
Makes: 6 servings (2¼ qt.)

- 1 lb. ground turkey
- 1 medium sweet yellow pepper, chopped
- 1 medium onion, chopped
- 3 garlic cloves, minced
- 2 tsp. olive oil
- 2 cups chicken broth
- 1 can (15 oz.) kidney beans, rinsed and drained
- 1 can (15 oz.) black beans, rinsed and drained
- 1 can (15 oz.) pumpkin
- 1 can (15 oz.) tomato sauce
- 4 medium tomatoes, chopped
- ⅔ cup chili sauce
- 3 Tbsp. brown sugar
- 1 Tbsp. dried oregano
- 1 Tbsp. dried parsley flakes
- 1 tsp. dried tarragon
- ¾ tsp. salt
- ¾ tsp. pepper
- Dash crushed red pepper flakes
- Dash cayenne pepper

In a Dutch oven, cook turkey, yellow pepper, onion and garlic in oil over medium heat until meat is no longer pink, breaking turkey into crumbles; drain. Stir in remaining ingredients. Bring to a boil. Reduce the heat; simmer, uncovered, for 1½ hours or until the chili reaches desired thickness.

1½ CUPS: 422 cal., 13g fat (4g sat. fat), 53mg chol., 1695mg sod., 54g carb. (22g sugars, 12g fiber), 24g pro.

TEST KITCHEN TIP
When making chili, always bloom your spices. It's not always about what spices you use but rather how you use them. Adding salt and chili spices at the end won't infuse the dish with true depth of flavor. Instead, bring out the flavor of the spices by adding them when you brown the meat or soften the onions. This "blooming" process releases each spice's essential oils.

Sides, Salads & More

When answering the big "What's for dinner?" question, a cook must consider side dishes, too. This chapter features our most popular meal accompaniments—each one boasting fresh flavors and lively textures.

SPINACH SALAD WITH POPPY SEED DRESSING

I bring this salad to parties or serve it as a healthy lunch. It's been a family favorite for quite some time. The easy homemade vinaigrette is the best part.
—*Nikki Barton, Providence, UT*

NIKKI BARTON
Providence, UT

Takes: 25 min.
Makes: 6 servings (1 cup dressing)

- 4 **cups fresh baby spinach**
- 4 **cups torn iceberg lettuce**
- 1½ **cups sliced fresh mushrooms**
- ½ **lb. bacon strips, cooked and crumbled**

DRESSING
- ¼ **cup red wine vinegar**
- ¼ **cup chopped red onion**
- 3 **Tbsp. sugar**
- ¾ **tsp. salt**
- ¼ **tsp. ground mustard**
- ½ **cup canola oil**
- 1½ **tsp. poppy seeds**

1. In a large bowl, combine the spinach, lettuce, mushrooms and bacon. Place vinegar, onion, sugar, salt and mustard in blender. While processing, gradually add oil in a steady stream. Transfer to a bowl; stir in poppy seeds.

2. Divide salad among 6 plates; drizzle with dressing.

1½ CUPS WITH ABOUT 2 TBSP. DRESSING: 280 cal., 24g fat (3g sat. fat), 14mg chol., 557mg sod., 10g carb. (8g sugars, 1g fiber), 6g pro.

TEST KITCHEN TIP
When made well, vinaigrette is a perfectly balanced dressing that spruces up any salad or vegetable. As long as you follow a ratio of 3 parts oil to 1 part vinegar, your vinaigrette will have the perfect balance of fat and acid. Add spices and seasonings to taste. If you're cooking for kids, they may prefer a less vinegary dressing. Just add a pinch of sugar to lighten the acidity. Leftovers will keep refrigerated for a few days. Before serving, shake the jar to reemulsify the dressing.

CRANBERRY PINEAPPLE SALAD

Impress dinner guests with this delightfully different take on traditional cranberry sauce. The nuts add a tasty crunch.

—Dorothy Angley, Carver, MA

- -

Prep: 15 min. + chilling • **Makes:** 12 servings

- 1¾ cups boiling water
- 2 pkg. (3 oz. each) raspberry gelatin
- 1 can (14 oz.) jellied cranberry sauce
- 1 can (8 oz.) crushed pineapple, undrained
- ¾ cup orange juice
- 1 Tbsp. lemon juice
- ½ cup chopped walnuts
  Lettuce leaves, optional
  Miracle Whip, optional

Add boiling water to the gelatin; stir until dissolved, about 2 minutes. Stir in cranberry sauce. Add the pineapple, orange juice and lemon juice. Refrigerate until thickened, about 30 minutes. Stir in nuts. Pour into an 11x7-in. dish. Refrigerate until set. Cut into 12 squares; if desired, serve each with a lettuce leaf and a dollop of Miracle Whip.

1 PIECE: 149 cal., 3g fat (0 sat. fat), 0 chol., 49mg sod., 30g carb. (25g sugars, 1g fiber), 2g pro.

CALICO BEANS

Packed full of beef, beans and bacon, this calico beans recipe is one of my favorites. Serve it as a hearty side or main dish.

—Betty Claycomb, Alverton, PA

- -

Prep: 25 min. • **Bake:** 45 min.
Makes: 10 servings

- 1 lb. lean ground beef (90% lean)
- 1 small onion, chopped
- 1 can (21 oz.) pork and beans
- 1 can (16 oz.) kidney beans, rinsed and drained
- 1 can (16 oz.) butter beans, rinsed and drained
- ½ cup packed brown sugar
- ½ cup ketchup
- 4 bacon strips, cooked and crumbled
- 1 Tbsp. cider vinegar
- 1 tsp. prepared mustard
- 1 tsp. salt

1. Preheat oven to 325°. In a large skillet, cook ground beef and onion over medium heat until beef is no longer pink, 5-7 minutes, breaking up beef into crumbles; drain. Stir in remaining ingredients. Transfer to a greased 2-qt. cast-iron pan or baking dish.

2. Bake, uncovered, until the beans are as thick as desired, 45-60 minutes.

1 SERVING: 260 cal., 5g fat (2g sat. fat), 32mg chol., 826mg sod., 39g carb. (19g sugars, 7g fiber), 18g pro.

BROCCOLI SLAW

Here's my favorite twist on broccoli salad. It's easy to make and has a tangy crunch.
—*Konny Thomas, Citrus Heights, CA*

Prep: 15 min. + chilling • **Makes:** 6 servings

4 cups broccoli florets
2 cups shredded red cabbage
1 small sweet onion, finely chopped
1 medium carrot, shredded
½ cup raisins
1 cup coleslaw salad dressing

In a large bowl, combine all ingredients and toss. Refrigerate, covered, at least 2 hours. Stir before serving.
1 CUP: 225 cal., 12g fat (2g sat. fat), 4mg chol., 325mg sod., 25g carb. (19g sugars, 3g fiber), 3g pro.

ALMOND STRAWBERRY SALAD

It's easy to love this pretty salad topped with strawberries and sliced almonds. With just a few ingredients, it's loaded with flavor.
—*Renae Rossow, Union, KY*

Takes: 10 min. • **Makes:** 4 servings

3 cups fresh baby spinach
½ cup sliced fresh strawberries
¼ cup honey-roasted sliced almonds
1 Tbsp. cider vinegar
1 Tbsp. honey
1½ tsp. sugar

Place spinach, strawberries and almonds in a large bowl. Mix vinegar, honey and sugar until blended; toss with salad.
¾ CUP: 75 cal., 4g fat (0 sat. fat), 0 chol., 98mg sod., 9g carb. (8g sugars, 1g fiber), 2g pro.
DIABETIC EXCHANGES: 1 vegetable, 1 fat.

BACON CHEESE POTATOES

I received this recipe from a friend who's a wonderful cook. This goes great with any main course, but it's especially good with ham.
—*Bertha Jensen, Mooresville, IN*

Prep: 30 min. • **Bake:** 30 min.
Makes: 10 servings

3 lbs. potatoes (about 6 medium), peeled and cubed
½ cup finely chopped onion
1 lb. cubed Velveeta
1 cup mayonnaise
½ lb. sliced bacon, cooked and crumbled
¾ cup sliced ripe olives
Chopped fresh parsley, optional
Paprika, optional

1. Place potatoes in a large saucepan and cover with water. Bring to a boil. Reduce heat; cover and cook for 10-15 minutes or until tender. Drain. In a large bowl, mix potatoes with onion, cheese and mayonnaise.
2. Transfer to an ungreased 13x9-in. baking dish. Sprinkle with bacon and olives. Cover and bake at 350° for 30 minutes or until heated through. Sprinkle with parsley and paprika if desired.
¾ CUP: 430 cal., 32g fat (11g sat. fat), 52mg chol., 891mg sod., 24g carb. (4g sugars, 2g fiber), 12g pro.

CORN PUDDING WITH BACON & CHEDDAR

This corn pudding can be prepared ahead and refrigerated overnight. Remove from the refrigerator for 30 minutes before baking.
—*Lynn Albright, Fremont, NE*

Prep: 25 min. • **Bake:** 40 min. + standing
Makes: 6 servings

- 1 Tbsp. olive oil
- ¾ cup chopped sweet onion
- ¾ cup chopped sweet red pepper
- 4 large eggs, room temperature
- 1 cup heavy whipping cream
- 1 tsp. baking soda
- 1 tsp. hot pepper sauce
- ½ tsp. salt
- 2 cups fresh or frozen corn
- 2 cups crushed cornbread stuffing
- ½ lb. bacon strips, cooked and crumbled
- 1½ cups shredded sharp cheddar cheese, divided

Preheat oven to 350°. In a 10-in. cast-iron or other ovenproof skillet, heat oil over medium heat. Add onion and red pepper; cook and stir until crisp-tender, 6-8 minutes. Remove from skillet; set aside. In a large bowl, whisk eggs, cream, baking soda, hot pepper sauce and salt. Stir in corn, stuffing, bacon, 1 cup cheese and onion mixture. Transfer to skillet. Bake,

uncovered, 35 minutes. Sprinkle with remaining ½ cup cheese. Bake until puffed and golden brown, 5-10 minutes longer. Let stand 10 minutes before serving.
¾ CUP: 516 cal., 36g fat (18g sat. fat), 211mg chol., 1117mg sod., 29g carb. (7g sugars, 3g fiber), 20g pro.

ITALIAN TOMATO CUCUMBER SALAD

My yummy medley of vegetables is a cool complement to zesty dishes such as seasoned fish, poultry and barbecued meats.
—*Florine Bruns, Fredericksburg, TX*

Takes: 10 min. • **Makes:** 4 servings

- 2 medium cucumbers, sliced
- 1 large tomato, cut into wedges
- 1 small red onion, cut into thin strips
- ¼ cup Italian salad dressing or salad dressing of your choice

In a large bowl, combine the vegetables. Add dressing; toss to coat.
½ CUP: 93 cal., 6g fat (1g sat. fat), 0 chol., 257mg sod., 9g carb. (6g sugars, 2g fiber), 2g pro. **DIABETIC EXCHANGES:** 1 vegetable, 1 fat.

RICE DRESSING

This savory rice mixture is a scrumptious change from our traditional cornbread dressing. To make it a meal, I sometimes add finely chopped cooked chicken and a little more broth before baking.
—Linda Emery, Bearden, AR

- -

Prep: 35 min. • **Bake:** 30 min.
Makes: 10 servings

4	cups chicken broth, divided
1½	cups uncooked long grain rice
2	cups chopped onion
2	cups chopped celery
½	cup butter, cubed
2	cans (4 oz. each) mushroom stems and pieces, drained
3	Tbsp. minced fresh parsley
1½ to 2	tsp. poultry seasoning
¾	tsp. salt
½	tsp. pepper
	Fresh sage and thyme, optional

1. In a saucepan, bring 3½ cups broth and rice to a boil. Reduce heat; cover and simmer until tender, about 20 minutes.

2. Meanwhile, in a skillet, saute onion and celery in butter until tender. Stir in rice, mushrooms, parsley, poultry seasoning, salt, pepper and the remaining broth. Pour into a greased 13x9-in. baking dish. Bake, uncovered, at 350° for 30 minutes. Garnish with sage and thyme if desired.

¾ CUP: 221 cal., 10g fat (6g sat. fat), 26mg chol., 727mg sod., 29g carb. (2g sugars, 1g fiber), 4g pro.

READER REVIEW

"Delicious! I wasn't sure 1½ cups rice would make enough to fit into a 9x13 but it did! Will make this again and again."

LISADAY, TASTEOFHOME.COM

BERRY NECTARINE SALAD

This salad makes an appearance at all of our summer gatherings. The fruits look beautiful together, and the topping is the perfect accent.
—*Mindee Myers, Lincoln, NE*

Prep: 15 min. + chilling • **Makes:** 8 servings

- 4 medium nectarines, sliced
- ¼ cup sugar
- 1 tsp. lemon juice
- ½ tsp. ground ginger
- 3 oz. reduced-fat cream cheese
- 2 cups fresh raspberries
- 1 cup fresh blueberries

1. In a large bowl, toss nectarines with sugar, lemon juice and ginger. Refrigerate, covered, 1 hour, stirring once.
2. Drain nectarines, reserving juices. Gradually beat reserved juices into cream cheese. Gently combine nectarines and berries; serve with cream cheese mixture.

1 SERVING: 109 cal., 3g fat (2g sat. fat), 8mg chol., 46mg sod., 21g carb. (15g sugars, 4g fiber), 2g pro.

⑤ⓘ APPLESAUCE SWEET POTATOES

During the holidays, using your slow cooker not only frees up oven space, but time, too! Sweet potatoes are a must on our family menu, and this no-fuss version will have everyone thinking you spent hours in the kitchen.
—*Pamela Allen, Marysville, OH*

Prep: 15 min. • **Cook:** 4 hours
Makes: 8 servings

- 3 lbs. sweet potatoes (about 5 medium), peeled and sliced
- 1½ cups unsweetened applesauce
- ⅔ cup packed brown sugar
- 3 Tbsp. butter, melted
- 1 tsp. ground cinnamon
- ½ cup glazed pecans, chopped, optional

1. Place sweet potatoes in a 4-qt. slow cooker. In a small bowl, mix the applesauce, brown sugar, melted butter and cinnamon; pour over potatoes.
2. Cook, covered, on low 4-5 hours or until potatoes are tender. If desired, sprinkle with glazed pecans before serving. Serve with a slotted spoon.

¾ CUP: 303 cal., 5g fat (3g sat. fat), 11mg chol., 57mg sod., 65g carb. (39g sugars, 6g fiber), 3g pro.

BACON SPINACH SALAD

Even our kids—who normally don't care for spinach—can't resist this salad with it's rich dressing and crumbled bacon. Of course, you can use other greens instead of spinach.
—*Gretchen Kuipers, Platte, SD*

Takes: 20 min. • **Makes:** 8 servings

- 6 bacon strips, chopped
- 6 cups torn spinach leaves
- ½ small head iceberg lettuce, torn
- 6 green onions, thinly sliced
- ½ cup canola oil
- ¼ cup white vinegar
- 1 Tbsp. sugar
- 1 tsp. salt
- 1 tsp. ground mustard

In a small skillet, cook the bacon over medium heat until crisp, stirring occasionally. Drain on paper towels. Refrigerate greens and onions in a salad bowl until serving. Combine remaining ingredients in a jar with a tight-fitting lid; shake well. Just before serving, pour dressing over greens; toss to coat. Serve with bacon.
1 CUP: 176 cal., 17g fat (2g sat. fat), 6mg chol., 427mg sod., 4g carb. (3g sugars, 1g fiber), 3g pro.

HAM, BROCCOLI & ORZO CASSEROLE

This comforting casserole is a complete meal in one. I make mine in my favorite casserole dish from my Grandma Laverne.
—*Heather Arndt Anderson, Portland, OR*

Prep: 30 min. • **Bake:** 20 min.
Makes: 8 servings

- 4 cups chicken stock
- 2 cups uncooked orzo pasta
- 3 Tbsp. butter
- ¼ cup all-purpose flour
- 2 cups 2% milk
- ½ tsp. salt
- ½ tsp. pepper
- 2 cups shredded sharp cheddar cheese, divided
- 1½ cups cubed fully cooked ham
- 2 cups chopped fresh broccoli
- 2 cups chopped fresh kale
- 1 cup french-fried onions

1. Preheat oven to 350°. In a large saucepan, bring chicken stock to a boil; stir in orzo. Cook, uncovered, until orzo is al dente and broth is absorbed, 8-10 minutes .
2. Meanwhile, in a large saucepan, heat butter over medium heat. Stir in flour until blended; cook and stir until lightly browned, 4-5 minutes. Gradually whisk in milk, salt and pepper. Bring to a boil, stirring constantly; cook and stir until thickened, 1-2 minutes. Stir in 1½ cups cheese; cook until the cheese is melted.
3. Add orzo, ham, broccoli and kale. Transfer to a greased 13x9-in. baking dish; sprinkle with onions and remaining cheese. Bake, uncovered, until bubbly, 20-25 minutes.
1⅓ CUPS: 637 cal., 27g fat (14g sat. fat), 80mg chol., 1386mg sod., 66g carb. (8g sugars, 3g fiber), 32g pro.

OVEN PARMESAN CHIPS

My husband and I avoid fried foods, but potatoes are part of our menu almost every day. These delectable sliced potatoes get nice and crispy and give our meals a likable lift.
—*Mary Lou Kelly, Scottdale, PA*

Takes: 25 min. • **Makes:** 2 servings

- 2 medium potatoes
- ¼ cup butter, melted
- 1 Tbsp. finely chopped onion
- ½ tsp. salt
- ⅛ tsp. pepper
  Dash paprika
- 2 Tbsp. grated Parmesan cheese

1. Preheat oven to 425°. Cut potatoes into ¼-in. slices; arrange in a single layer on 2 greased baking sheets. In a small bowl, mix butter, onion, salt, pepper and paprika; brush over both sides of potatoes.
2. Roast until potato slices are tender and golden, 15-20 minutes, turning occasionally. Sprinkle with cheese.

1 CUP: 393 cal., 25g fat (15g sat. fat), 65mg chol., 876mg sod., 39g carb. (2g sugars, 5g fiber), 6g pro.

LIME VINAIGRETTE

My family and I have been enjoying this recipe for so long, I don't even remember where I got it from. Sometimes I add dried basil and anchovy paste for a little variation.
—*Marian Brown, Mississauga, ON*

Prep: 10 min. • **Makes:** ½ cup

- ¼ cup lime juice
- 2 garlic cloves
- ¼ tsp. Dijon mustard
- 1 tsp. honey
- ¼ tsp. salt
  Dash pepper
- ¼ cup olive oil

Place first 6 ingredients in blender. While processing, gradually add olive oil in a steady stream.

2 TBSP.: 131 cal., 14g fat (2g sat. fat), 0 chol., 156mg sod., 3g carb. (2g sugars, 0 fiber), 0 pro. **DIABETIC EXCHANGES:** 3 fat.

RED & SWEET POTATO SALAD

Two types of potatoes help this creamy side dish stand out at warm weather get-togethers. People love the spicy mustard dressing.
—*Mary Relyea, Canastota, NY*

Prep: 25 min. • **Cook:** 30 min.
Makes: 12 servings

- 2 lbs. red potatoes (about 7 medium), cut into 1-in. cubes
- 1 lb. sweet potatoes (about 2 medium), peeled and cut into 1-in. cubes
- ¼ cup red wine vinegar
- 1 Tbsp. spicy brown mustard
- 1¼ tsp. salt
- ½ tsp. pepper
- ½ cup reduced-fat mayonnaise
- ¼ cup 2% milk
- 2 celery ribs, chopped
- 1 small red onion, chopped
- ⅓ cup minced fresh parsley

1. Place red potatoes in a large saucepan; add water to cover. Bring to a boil. Reduce heat; cook, uncovered, until tender, 10-15 minutes. Drain; place in a large bowl. Repeat with sweet potatoes; add to red potatoes.
2. Whisk together vinegar, mustard, salt and pepper; toss with potatoes. Cool slightly.
3. In a small bowl, whisk together mayonnaise and milk; stir in celery, onion and parsley. Stir gently into potato mixture. Serve immediately or refrigerate and serve cold.

⅔ CUP: 136 cal., 4g fat (1g sat. fat), 4mg chol., 339mg sod., 24g carb. (6g sugars, 3g fiber), 2g pro. **DIABETIC EXCHANGES:** 1½ starch, ½ fat.

ITALIAN PASTA SALAD

My zesty Italian pasta salad recipe combines vegetables and pasta in a creamy dressing. It's always popular at picnics and potlucks.
—*Tina Dierking, Skowhegan, ME*

Prep: 15 min. + chilling • **Cook:** 10 min.
Makes: 6 servings

- 1 cup uncooked spiral pasta
- 1½ cups halved cherry tomatoes
- 1 cup sliced fresh mushrooms
- ¼ cup chopped sweet red pepper
- ¼ cup chopped green pepper
- 3 Tbsp. thinly sliced green onions
- 1 cup zesty Italian salad dressing
- ¾ cup mayonnaise
- ½ cup grated Parmesan cheese
- ⅓ cup cubed provolone cheese
- 1 can (2¼ oz.) sliced ripe olives, drained

1. Cook pasta according to package directions; rinse with cold water and drain. Place in a large bowl; add the tomatoes, mushrooms, peppers, onions and salad dressing. Cover and refrigerate at least 4 hours or overnight; drain.

2. In a small bowl, combine the mayonnaise and Parmesan cheese; stir in the provolone cheese and olives. Gently fold into the pasta mixture.

1 CUP: 371 cal., 30g fat (6g sat. fat), 13mg chol., 707mg sod., 17g carb. (4g sugars, 2g fiber), 7g pro.

CREAMY HASH BROWN CASSEROLE

This versatile side dish is so good and goes with almost any entree. A creamy cheese sauce and crunchy topping make this casserole a top pick for all kinds of gatherings.
—*Teresa Stutzman, Adair, OK*

Prep: 10 min. • **Bake:** 50 min.
Makes: 8 servings

- 1 pkg. (32 oz.) frozen cubed hash brown potatoes, thawed
- 1 lb. cubed Velveeta
- 2 cups sour cream
- 1 can (10¾ oz.) condensed cream of chicken soup, undiluted
- ¾ cup butter, melted, divided
- 3 Tbsp. chopped onion
- ¼ tsp. paprika
- 2 cups cornflakes, lightly crushed
  Fresh savory, optional

In a large bowl, combine the hash browns, cheese, sour cream, soup, ½ cup butter and onion. Spread into a greased 13x9-in. baking dish. Sprinkle with paprika. Combine the cornflakes and remaining butter; sprinkle on top. Bake, covered, at 350° until heated through, 40-50 minutes. Uncover, bake until top is golden brown, 10 minutes longer. If desired, garnish with savory.

FREEZE OPTION: Cover and freeze unbaked casserole. To use, partially thaw in refrigerator overnight. Remove from refrigerator about 30 minutes before baking. Preheat oven to 350°. Bake casserole as directed, increasing time as necessary to heat through and for a thermometer inserted in center to read 165°.

¾ CUP: 663 cal., 43g fat (27g sat. fat), 125mg chol., 1359mg sod., 49g carb. (9g sugars, 3g fiber), 19g pro.

CREAMY MUSHROOM-POTATO BAKE

The day I first made this, we'd invited a neighbor—a bachelor farmer—over, and I wanted to fix something hearty. It was a hit instantly. These days, our three sons enjoy it as a change from regular mashed potatoes. We've found that it's best served with beef... either with or without gravy.
—Kathy Smith, Granger, IN

Prep: 30 min. • **Bake:** 20 min.
Makes: 10 servings

2½ to 3 lbs. white potatoes, peeled and cubed
1 tsp. salt, divided
1 medium onion, finely chopped
½ lb. fresh mushrooms, chopped
3 Tbsp. butter, divided
½ cup sour cream
¼ tsp. pepper
¼ cup grated Parmesan cheese

1. Place potatoes in a large saucepan and cover with water. Add ½ tsp. salt. Bring to a boil. Reduce heat; cover and cook for 10-15 minutes or until tender. Drain and mash (do not add butter or milk).
2. In a large skillet, saute the onion and mushrooms in 2 Tbsp. butter for 3-4 minutes or until just tender. Stir into potatoes along with sour cream, pepper and remaining salt.
3. Spoon into a greased 2-qt. baking dish. Sprinkle with Parmesan cheese; dot with remaining butter.
4. Bake, uncovered, at 400° for 20-25 minutes or until heated through and golden brown.
¾ CUP: 141 cal., 6g fat (4g sat. fat), 19mg chol., 317mg sod., 18g carb. (3g sugars, 2g fiber), 4g pro.

ONION ORANGE SALAD

People always enjoy the bold flavors in this delightful salad. It's delicious and beautiful.
—Zita Wilensky, North Miami Beach, FL

Takes: 15 min. • **Makes:** 8 servings

⅓ cup olive oil
¼ cup orange juice
3 Tbsp. vinegar
1 garlic clove, minced
1 tsp. minced fresh parsley
¼ tsp. salt
  Dash pepper
8 cups torn spinach or mixed greens
3 medium oranges, peeled and sliced
1 cup sliced red onion
½ cup crumbled blue cheese
¼ cup slivered almonds, toasted

In a small bowl, whisk the first 7 ingredients. On a serving platter or individual plates, arrange greens, oranges and onion. Drizzle with dressing. Sprinkle with cheese and toasted almonds.
1 SERVING: 162 cal., 13g fat (3g sat. fat), 6mg chol., 216mg sod., 8g carb. (6g sugars, 2g fiber), 4g pro.

SUNFLOWER STRAWBERRY SALAD

We have an annual strawberry festival in our town, so recipes with strawberries are popular here. I've served this salad at luncheons and have always received compliments.
—Betty Malone, Humboldt, TN

Prep: 10 min. + chilling • **Makes:** 6 servings

2 cups sliced fresh strawberries
1 medium apple, diced
1 cup seedless green grapes, halved
½ cup thinly sliced celery
¼ cup raisins
½ cup strawberry yogurt
2 Tbsp. sunflower kernels

In a large bowl, combine strawberries, apple, grapes, celery and raisins. Stir in the yogurt. Cover and refrigerate for at least 1 hour. Add sunflower kernels and toss.
¾ CUP: 107 cal., 2g fat (0 sat. fat), 1mg chol., 43mg sod., 22g carb. (17g sugars, 3g fiber), 2g pro. **DIABETIC EXCHANGES:** 1½ fruit, ½ fat.

CORN & BLACK BEAN SALAD

This colorful, crunchy black bean and corn salad is chock-full of ingredients that all ages will love. Try it with a variety of summer entrees, or as a wholesome salsa.
—*Krista Frank, Rhododendron, OR*

Prep: 15 min. + chilling • **Makes:** 8 servings

- 1 can (15¼ oz.) whole kernel corn, drained
- 1 can (15 oz.) black beans, rinsed and drained
- 2 large tomatoes, finely chopped
- 1 large red onion, finely chopped
- ¼ cup minced fresh cilantro
- 2 garlic cloves, minced

DRESSING
- 2 Tbsp. sugar
- 2 Tbsp. white vinegar
- 2 Tbsp. canola oil
- 1½ tsp. lime juice
- ¼ tsp. salt
- ¼ tsp. ground cumin
- ¼ tsp. pepper

In a large bowl, combine first 6 ingredients. In a small bowl, whisk dressing ingredients; pour over corn mixture and toss to coat. Cover and refrigerate at least 1 hour. Stir before serving. Serve with a slotted spoon.

⅔ CUP: 142 cal., 4g fat (0 sat. fat), 0 chol., 326mg sod., 21g carb. (8g sugars, 4g fiber), 4g pro. **DIABETIC EXCHANGES:** 1 starch, 1 fat.

CLASSIC TARTAR SAUCE

You'll never buy the jarred stuff again once you've tried my homemade tartar sauce recipe!
—*Michelle Stromko, Darlington, MD*

Takes: 10 min. • **Makes:** 1 cup

- ⅔ cup chopped dill pickles
- ½ cup mayonnaise
- 3 Tbsp. finely chopped onion
  Dash pepper

In a small bowl, combine all ingredients. Cover and refrigerate until serving.

2 TBSP.: 93 cal., 10g fat (2g sat. fat), 1mg chol., 167mg sod., 1g carb. (0 sugars, 0 fiber), 0 pro.

KAYCEE MASON
Siloam Springs, AR

AIR-FRYER GARLIC-HERB PATTYPAN SQUASH

The first time I grew a garden, I harvested summer squash and cooked it with garlic and herbs. Pattypan is one of my favorites.
— *Kaycee Mason, Siloam Springs, AR*

- -

Takes: 25 min. • **Makes:** 4 servings

- 5 cups halved small pattypan squash (about 1¼ lbs.)
- 1 Tbsp. olive oil
- 2 garlic cloves, minced
- ½ tsp. salt
- ¼ tsp. dried oregano
- ¼ tsp. dried thyme
- ¼ tsp. pepper
- 1 Tbsp. minced fresh parsley

Preheat air fryer to 375°. Place squash in a large bowl. Mix oil, garlic, salt, oregano, thyme and pepper; drizzle over squash. Toss to coat. Place squash on greased tray in air-fryer basket. Cook until tender, 10-15 minutes, stirring occasionally. Sprinkle with parsley.

⅔ CUP: 58 cal., 3g fat (0 sat. fat), 0 chol., 296mg sod., 6g carb. (3g sugars, 2g fiber), 2g pro.

DID YOU KNOW?

Pattypan, a summer squash shaped like little UFOs, comes in all colors and sizes. Place them in the crisper drawer in the refrigerator and use within 1 week. They'll last longer in a plastic bag with a corner open for air circulation. They're best sliced, chopped or quartered for grilling, roasting, air-frying or sauteing.

LEMON POPPY SEED DRESSING

I drizzle this dressing on a romaine salad with apples and pears. If you want a stronger lemon flavor, add some lemon zest.
—*Bonnie Capper-Eckstein, Maple Grove, MN*

Takes: 10 min. • **Makes:** 1 cup

- ½ cup sugar
- ⅓ cup lemon juice
- 2 tsp. grated onion
- 1 tsp. Dijon mustard
- ½ tsp. salt
- ⅔ cup canola oil
- 1 tsp. poppy seeds

In a blender, combine the first 5 ingredients. While processing, gradually add oil in a steady stream until smooth and creamy. Stir in poppy seeds. Store in the refrigerator.

2 TBSP.: 54 cal., 0 fat (0 sat. fat), 0 chol., 163mg sod., 13g carb. (13g sugars, 0 fiber), 0 pro.

HONEY-PECAN KIWI SALAD

This dish won second place in a summer salad recipe feature published in our local newspaper. But it takes first place with my family, always happy to try my new creations.
—*Marla Arbet, Kenosha, WI*

Takes: 10 min. • **Makes:** 6 servings

- 5 cups torn Boston lettuce
- 3 medium kiwifruit, peeled and sliced
- ¼ cup chopped pecans, toasted
- 2 Tbsp. vanilla yogurt
- 2 Tbsp. lemon juice
- 1 Tbsp. olive oil
- 1 Tbsp. honey

Combine the lettuce, kiwi and pecans. In a separate bowl, mix yogurt, lemon juice, oil and honey until smooth. Pour over salad and toss; serve immediately.

¾ CUP: 94 cal., 6g fat (1g sat. fat), 0 chol., 7mg sod., 11g carb. (7g sugars, 2g fiber), 2g pro. **DIABETIC EXCHANGES:** 1 vegetable, 1 fat, ½ starch.

ROASTED SWEET POTATO SALAD WITH HONEY-MAPLE VINAIGRETTE

This salad makes a beautiful presentation for the holidays with the bright colors of the sweet potatoes, cranberries and spinach.
—*Susan Bickta, Kutztown, PA*

Prep: 20 min. • **Bake:** 35 min.
Makes: 8 servings

- 2 lbs. sweet potatoes, peeled and cut into ¾-in. pieces (about 7 cups)
- 5 Tbsp. canola oil, divided
- 3 Tbsp. cider vinegar
- 2 Tbsp. honey
- 2 Tbsp. maple syrup
- 1 small garlic clove, minced
- ½ tsp. Dijon mustard
- ⅛ tsp. salt
- ⅛ tsp. pepper
- 1 pkg. (6 oz.) fresh baby spinach
- 1 medium apple, chopped
- ½ cup dried cranberries
- ½ cup chopped pecans, toasted
- ½ cup crumbled blue cheese

1. Preheat oven to 400°. Place sweet potatoes in a greased 15x10x1-in. baking pan; toss with 2 Tbsp. oil. Roast 35-40 minutes or until tender. Transfer to a large bowl; cool slightly.
2. In a small bowl, whisk the vinegar, honey, maple syrup, garlic, mustard, salt, pepper and remaining oil until blended. Add spinach, apple, cranberries and pecans to the sweet potatoes. Drizzle with vinaigrette and toss to coat. Top with cheese. Serve immediately.

1 CUP: 340 cal., 16g fat (3g sat. fat), 6mg chol., 192mg sod., 46g carb. (26g sugars, 5g fiber), 5g pro.

TURKEY ALMOND SALAD

Our congregation hosted a luncheon, and we were asked to use leftover turkey from the church's Thanksgiving supper. I created this crunchy salad based on one I'd tried years before. Everyone loved it, and I've made it many times since.
—Donna Rear, Olds, AB

- -

Prep: 20 min. + chilling • **Makes:** 6 servings

- ⅔ cup Miracle Whip
- 1 Tbsp. 2% milk
- 2 tsp. prepared mustard
- 1½ tsp. sugar
- ½ tsp. salt
- ¼ tsp. pepper
- 3 cups cubed cooked turkey
- 2 cups shredded cabbage
- ¾ cup diced celery
- ½ cup sliced green onion
- 1½ cups chow mein noodles
- ½ cup slivered almonds, toasted
- 2 Tbsp. sesame seeds, toasted

In a large bowl, combine first 6 ingredients. Add the turkey, cabbage, celery and green onions; toss to combine. Cover and chill for several hours. Just before serving, add the chow mein noodles, almonds and sesame seeds; toss to combine.

1 CUP. 388 cal., 25g fat (4g sat. fat), 62mg chol., 518mg sod., 16g carb. (5g sugars, 3g fiber), 25g pro.

MARINARA SAUCE

My mother, who was Italian American, called marinara sauce gravy. She made this sauce in big batches several times a month, so it was a staple on our dinner table. A mouthwatering aroma filled the house each time she cooked it.
—James Grimes, Frenchtown, NJ

- -

Prep: 20 min. • **Cook:** 1 hour • **Makes:** 5 cups

- 2 cans (28 oz. each) whole tomatoes
- 1 large onion, finely chopped
- 4 garlic cloves, minced
- 3 Tbsp. extra virgin olive oil
- ¼ cup chopped fresh basil
- 1½ tsp. dried oregano
- ¾ tsp. salt
- ¼ tsp. pepper

In a large saucepan, heat oil over medium-high heat. Add onions; cook and stir until tender, 3-5 minutes. Add garlic; cook and stir 1 minute longer. Stir in remaining ingredients. Bring to a boil. Reduce heat; cover and simmer until thickened and flavors are blended, 30-45 minutes, stirring occasionally and breaking up tomatoes with wooden spoon.

½ CUP. 44 cal., 4g fat (1g sat. fat), 0 chol., 178mg sod., 2g carb. (1g sugars, 0 fiber), 0 pro.

5i 🎗

ROASTED GREEN BEAN SALAD

This easy recipe turns homegrown green beans into something special. A tangy dill and Dijon vinaigrette coats them without overpowering, so the fresh-picked flavor comes through.
—*Kathy Shell, San Diego, CA*

Prep: 10 min. • **Bake:** 30 min.
Makes: 6 servings

- 2   lbs. fresh green beans, trimmed
- 3   Tbsp. olive oil, divided
- ¾   tsp. salt, divided
- 2   Tbsp. white wine vinegar
- 2   Tbsp. snipped fresh dill or
      2 tsp. dill weed
- 1½ tsp. Dijon mustard
- 1½ tsp. sugar
- ¼   tsp. pepper

1. Preheat oven to 400°. In a large bowl, toss beans with 1 Tbsp. oil and ½ tsp. salt. Transfer to 2 ungreased 15x10x1-in. baking pans.
2. Roast 30-35 minutes or until beans are tender and lightly browned, stirring occasionally.
3. In a small bowl, whisk vinegar, dill, mustard, sugar, pepper and the remaining oil and salt until blended. Transfer beans to a large bowl. Drizzle with vinaigrette and toss to coat.
1 SERVING: 108 cal., 7g fat (1g sat. fat), 0 chol., 335mg sod., 11g carb. (4g sugars, 5g fiber), 3g pro. **DIABETIC EXCHANGES:** 1½ fat, 1 vegetable.

TEST KITCHEN TIP
Don't overcrowd the pan when roasting green beans. If the beans are too close to each other, they will not brown evenly. Pop the baking pan into the oven and bake, stirring occasionally, until the beans are tender and the edges are browned. Carefully remove the pan from the oven and serve.

5i

PISTACHIO MALLOW SALAD

This fluffy salad is a real treat since it's creamy but not overly sweet. It's easy to mix up too, and the flavor gets better the longer it stands. It's perfect for St. Patrick's Day, served in a green bowl.
—*Pattie Ann Forssberg, Logan, KS*

Prep: 5 min. + chilling • **Makes:** 12 servings

- 1   carton (16 oz.) whipped topping
- 1   pkg. (3.4 oz.) instant pistachio pudding mix
- 6   to 7 drops green food coloring, optional
- 3   cups miniature marshmallows
- 1   can (20 oz.) pineapple tidbits, undrained
- ½   cup chopped pistachios or walnuts
     Additional whipped topping, optional

In a large bowl, combine whipped topping, pudding mix and food coloring if desired. Fold in the marshmallows and pineapple. Cover and refrigerate at least 2 hours. Just before serving, top with additional whipped topping if desired, sprinkle with nuts.
¾ CUP: 236 cal., 9g fat (7g sat. fat), 0 chol., 140mg sod., 35g carb. (23g sugars, 1g fiber), 2g pro.

SLOW-COOKER CREAMED CORN

I'm a teacher, and this is one of my go-to recipes for faculty potlucks. It's perfect for holidays, too, when you are looking for an simple, comforting dish that has just a little bit of bite.
—*Shelby Winters, Bonner Springs, KS*

Prep: 15 min. • **Cook:** 3 hours
Makes: 8 servings

- ½   cup butter, cubed
- 1   medium onion, finely chopped
- ¼   cup finely chopped sweet red pepper
- 6   cups frozen corn (about 30 oz.), thawed
- 1   pkg. (8 oz.) cream cheese, cubed
- 1   can (4 oz.) chopped green chiles
- 1   tsp. salt
- ½   tsp. garlic powder
- ¼   tsp. pepper

In a large skillet, heat butter over medium-high heat. Add the onion and red pepper; cook and stir 3-4 minutes or until tender. Transfer to a greased 3-qt. slow cooker. Stir in remaining ingredients. Cook, covered, on low until heated through, 3-4 hours. Stir just before serving.
⅔ CUP: 302 cal., 22g fat (13g sat. fat), 59mg chol., 536mg sod., 25g carb. (4g sugars, 3g fiber), 5g pro.

STEAKHOUSE BAKED POTATOES

On weekends, we often have salad, steak and a baked potato. This fun twist on that classic steakhouse dinner combines all three into one easy dish.
—*Debbie Glasscock, Conway, AR*

- -

Prep: 20 min. + standing • **Bake:** 1¼ hours
Makes: 4 servings

- 4 **large baking potatoes**
- 2 **boneless beef ribeye steaks (6 oz. each)**
- ½ **tsp. kosher salt**
- ½ **tsp. pepper**
- 1 **Tbsp. olive oil**
- 2 **Tbsp. butter, melted**
  Toppings: Fresh arugula, blue cheese salad dressing, sour cream and crumbled blue cheese

1. Preheat oven to 400°. Scrub potatoes; pierce several times with a fork. Bake until tender, 50-75 minutes.
2. Meanwhile, sprinkle steak with salt and pepper. In a large skillet, heat olive oil over medium-high heat. Add the steaks; cook until meat reaches desired doneness, 5-8 minutes on each side (for medium-rare, a thermometer should read 135°; medium, 140°; medium-well, 145°). Let stand for 10 minutes; cut into bite-sized pieces. Transfer to a bowl. Drizzle with butter; toss to coat.
3. With a sharp knife, cut an X in each potato. Fluff pulp with a fork; season with salt and pepper. Divide steak evenly over potatoes. Top with arugula, salad dressing, sour cream and blue cheese.
1 STUFFED POTATO: 550 cal., 23g fat (10g sat. fat), 65mg chol., 347mg sod., 65g carb. (3g sugars, 8g fiber), 23g pro.

1 FAVORITE 7 WAYS Baked Potatoes

HUNGRY MAN'S BAKED POTATOES

Baked potatoes are topped with bacon, veggies, pulled pork and goat cheese in this unique take on a baked potato dinner.
—Taste of Home *Test Kitchen*

Takes: 30 min. • **Makes:** 4 servings

- 4 **large sweet or Russet potatoes**
- 3 **thick-sliced bacon strips, cut into quarters**
- 1 **cup fresh or frozen corn**
- 1 **medium red onion, halved and thinly sliced**
- 2 **cups refrigerated fully cooked barbecued shredded pork**
- ¼ **cup crumbled goat cheese**
- ¼ **cup minced fresh cilantro**

1. Scrub and pierce potatoes; place on a microwave-safe plate. Microwave, uncovered, on high for 12-15 minutes or until tender, turning once.
2. In a large skillet, cook bacon over medium heat until crisp. Remove to paper towels with a slotted spoon; drain, reserving 1 Tbsp. drippings. Saute corn and onion in drippings until tender.
3. With a sharp knife, cut an X in each potato and fluff pulp with a fork. Place pork in a microwave-safe bowl. Microwave, uncovered, for 1-2 minutes or until heated through. Top potatoes with pork, corn mixture, bacon, goat cheese and cilantro.
1 STUFFED POTATO: 435 cal., 12g fat (5g sat. fat), 49mg chol., 1044mg sod., 60g carb. (32g sugars, 5g fiber), 22g pro.

HAM & BROCCOLI BAKED POTATOES

This loaded baked potato dish is a spin on a favorite family recipe I have made for years: ham and potato casserole. It's great when you have a tight food budget, and it tastes amazing. The potatoes and filling can be prepared ahead of time, then assembled prior to serving.
—*Patricia Prescott, Manchester, NH*

Prep: 20 min. • **Bake:** 55 min
Makes: 4 servings

- 4 **large baking potatoes**
- 1 **cup frozen chopped broccoli**
- 1 **can (10½ oz.) condensed cream of mushroom soup, undiluted**
- ¼ **cup 2% milk**
- ¼ **tsp. pepper**
- 2 **cups chopped fully cooked ham**
- 2 **cups shredded cheddar cheese, divided**
- ½ **cup sour cream**
- 1 **cup soft bread crumbs**
- 2 **Tbsp. butter, melted**
- 2 **Tbsp. minced fresh chives or chopped green onion**

1. Preheat oven to 400°. Scrub potatoes; pierce several times with a fork. Bake until tender, 50-75 minutes. Meanwhile, cook the broccoli according to package directions; drain.
2. In a small saucepan, combine soup, milk and pepper. Cook and stir over medium-low heat until smooth, about 3 minutes. Add ham, 1½ cups cheese and broccoli; cook and stir until cheese is melted, 3-5 minutes. Remove from heat; stir in sour cream.
3. With a sharp knife, cut an X in each potato. Fluff pulp with a fork. If desired, season with salt and additional pepper. Place potatoes on a baking sheet. Spoon ham mixture over top; sprinkle with remaining ½ cup cheese. Combine bread crumbs and butter; sprinkle over top. Bake until cheese is melted and crumbs are browned, 5-7 minutes. Sprinkle with chives.
1 STUFFED POTATO: 820 cal., 38g fat (20g sat. fat), 124mg chol., 1904mg sod., 81g carb. (7g sugars, 11g fiber), 40g pro.

4

5

BUENOS DIAS BAKED POTATOES

Convenience products take the heavy labor out of this Tex-Mex side dish. You know it's going to a good day when you get the chance to gobble up this hearty baked potato.
—*Taste of Home Test Kitchen*

Takes: 30 min. • **Makes:** 4 servings

- 4 **large baking potatoes**
- 1½ **cups frozen pepper strips**
- 1 **medium onion, halved and thinly sliced**
- 1 **Tbsp. butter**
- 2 **pkg. (6 oz. each) ready-to-use Southwestern chicken strips**
- 1 **cup salsa con queso dip**
- 2 **Tbsp. canned chopped green chiles**
- 1 **chipotle pepper in adobo sauce, minced**
  Optional toppings: Salsa, sliced avocado and french-fried onions

1. Scrub and pierce potatoes; place on a microwave-safe plate. Microwave potatoes, uncovered, on high for 15 minutes or until tender, turning once.
2. In a large skillet, saute pepper strips and onion in butter until crisp tender. Stir in the chicken strips, queso dip, chiles, and chipotle pepper. Heat through.
3. With a sharp knife, cut an X in each potato; fluff pulp with a fork. Spoon chicken mixture over the potatoes and serve with toppings of your choice.
1 STUFFED POTATO: 524 cal., 11g fat (5g sat. fat), 73mg chol., 1055mg sod., 80g carb. (8g sugars, 9g fiber), 29g pro.

EGGS BENEDICT BAKED POTATOES

Here's a new way to do breakfast potatoes. This baked potato dish would be eggs-cellent for brunch or a breakfast-for-dinner evening. The options are endless, but one thing's for sure: Once you get a taste, you'll want more!
—*Becky Carver, North Royalton, OH*

Prep: 20 min. • **Bake:** 1¼ hours.
Makes: 4 servings

- 4 **large baking potatoes**
- 4 **large eggs**
- ½ **tsp. salt**
- ½ **tsp. pepper**
- 8 **slices halved Canadian bacon, warmed**
- ¼ **cup prepared hollandaise sauce**
  Minced fresh parsley, optional

1. Preheat oven to 400°. Scrub potatoes; pierce several times with a fork. Bake until tender, 50-75 minutes.
2. Meanwhile, place 2-3 in. of water in a large saucepan or skillet with high sides. Bring to a boil; adjust heat to maintain a gentle simmer. Break cold eggs, 1 at a time, into a small bowl; holding bowl close to surface of water, slip egg into water.
3. Cook, uncovered, until the whites are completely set and yolks begin to thicken but are not hard, 3-5 minutes. Using a slotted spoon, lift eggs out of water. With a sharp knife, cut an X in each potato. Fluff pulp with a fork; season with salt and pepper. Top the potatoes with Canadian bacon, poached eggs and hollandaise sauce. If desired, sprinkle with minced parsley.
1 STUFFED POTATO: 444 cal., 11g fat (5g sat. fat), 212mg chol., 535mg sod., 66g carb. (4g sugars, 8g fiber), 20g pro.

THAT'S AMORE BAKED POTATOES

We add a touch of Italy to these baked potatoes with beefed up spaghetti sauce, pepperoni and more. Now, that's amore!
—Taste of Home *Test Kitchen*

Prep: 20 min. • **Cook:** 15 min.
Makes: 4 servings

- 4 large baking potatoes
- ½ lb. ground beef
- 1 medium green pepper, chopped
- 1 medium carrot, shredded
- 1 small onion, chopped
- 2 garlic cloves, minced
- 1 jar (24 oz.) spaghetti sauce with mushrooms
- 5 oz. pepperoni, chopped
- ¼ cup dry red wine or reduced-sodium beef broth
- 2 tsp. minced fresh oregano
- ½ tsp. salt
- 1 cup shredded reduced-fat Colby-Monterey Jack cheese

1. Scrub and pierce potatoes; place on a microwave-safe plate. Microwave potatoes, uncovered, on high for 15 minutes or until tender, turning once.
2. In a Dutch oven, cook the ground beef, green pepper, carrot, onion and garlic over medium heat until meat is no longer pink; drain. Add the spaghetti sauce, pepperoni, wine, oregano and salt. Bring to a boil. Reduce heat; simmer, uncovered, for 10 minutes.
3. With a sharp knife, cut an X in each potato; fluff pulp with a fork. Spoon sauce over potatoes and sprinkle with cheese. Microwave until cheese is melted.

1 STUFFED POTATO: 794 cal., 35g fat (15g sat. fat), 115mg chol., 1279mg sod., 73g carb. (8g sugars, 7g fiber), 42g pro.

VERY VEGGIE BAKED POTATOES

Take a break from the typical meat-and-potato pairing with these veggie-filled spuds. They're a perfect way to use your homegrown harvest.
—Taste of Home *Test Kitchen*

Prep: 25 min. • **Grill:** 10 min.
Makes: 4 servings

- 4 large baking potatoes
- 2 medium yellow summer squash, sliced
- 2 small zucchini, sliced
- 1 small eggplant, sliced
- 2 medium leeks (white portion only), sliced lengthwise into quarters
- 2 Tbsp. reduced-fat Italian salad dressing
- ⅛ tsp. salt
- 1 pkg. (6½ oz.) garlic-herb spreadable cheese
- ¼ cup reduced-fat sour cream
- ¼ cup fresh basil leaves, thinly sliced

1. Scrub and pierce potatoes; place on a microwave-safe plate. Microwave the potatoes, uncovered, on high until tender, about 15 minutes, turning once.
2. In a large bowl, combine the squash, zucchini, eggplant and leeks. Add the salad dressing and toss to coat. Transfer vegetables to a grill wok or basket. Grill, uncovered, over medium heat until tender, 8-12 minutes, stirring frequently. Sprinkle potatoes with salt and keep warm.
3. Combine spreadable cheese and sour cream. With a sharp knife, cut an X in each potato. Fluff pulp with a fork. Spoon grilled vegetables over potatoes; dollop with cheese mixture. Garnish with basil.

1 STUFFED POTATO: 586 cal., 23g fat (15g sat. fat), 59mg chol., 458mg sod., 87g carb. (14g sugars, 12g fiber), 15g pro.

Hearty Main Dishes

Here's a sampling of our top-rated main dishes. Whether you serve beef, pork, chicken or fish, it will be easy to summon your family to the table with these dinnertime faves!

TACORITOS

This mild and meaty southwestern dish combines the delicious flavor of tacos with the heartiness of burritos. Your family's going to love 'em!
— *Monica Flatford, Knoxville, TN*

Prep: 40 min. • **Bake:** 20 min.
Makes: 8 servings

¼ cup butter, cubed
¼ cup all-purpose flour
4 cups water
3 Tbsp. chili powder
1 tsp. garlic salt
1 lb. ground beef
1 lb. bulk pork sausage
¼ cup chopped onion
1 cup refried beans
8 flour tortillas (8 in.), warmed
3 cups shredded Monterey Jack cheese
  Optional toppings: Shredded lettuce, chopped tomatoes, sliced ripe olives and sour cream

1. In a large saucepan, melt butter. Stir in the flour until smooth; gradually add water. Bring to a boil; cook and stir for 1 minute or until thickened. Stir in chili powder and garlic salt. Bring to a boil. Reduce the heat; simmer, uncovered, for 10 minutes.

2. In a large skillet over medium heat, cook beef, sausage and onion until the meat is no longer pink; drain. Stir in the refried beans; heat through.

3. Spread ¼ cup sauce in a greased 13x9-in. baking dish. Spread 1 Tbsp. sauce over each tortilla; place ⅔ cup meat mixture down the center of each. Top each with ¼ cup cheese. Roll up and place seam side down in baking dish. Pour remaining sauce over the top; sprinkle with remaining cheese.

4. Bake, uncovered, at 350° for 18-22 minutes or until bubbly and the cheese is melted. Serve with optional toppings as desired.

1 TACORITO: 627 cal., 40g fat (19g sat. fat), 111mg chol., 1131mg sod., 36g carb. (2g sugars, 3g fiber), 31g pro.

MONICA FLATFORD
Knoxville, TN

SHRIMP ORZO WITH FETA

This stovetop specialty is one of my favorites. The dish is tender and flavorful, and garlic and a splash of lemon add to the fresh taste and heart-healthy benefits of shrimp.
—*Sarah Hummel, Moon Township, PA*

Takes: 25 min. • **Makes:** 4 servings

- 1¼ cups uncooked whole wheat orzo pasta
- 2 Tbsp. olive oil
- 2 garlic cloves, minced
- 2 medium tomatoes, chopped
- 2 Tbsp. lemon juice
- 1¼ lbs. uncooked shrimp (26-30 per lb.), peeled and deveined
- 2 Tbsp. minced fresh cilantro
- ¼ tsp. pepper
- ½ cup crumbled feta cheese

1. Cook orzo according to package directions. Meanwhile, in a large skillet, heat the oil over medium heat. Add the garlic; cook and stir 1 minute. Add tomatoes and lemon juice. Bring to a boil. Stir in shrimp. Reduce heat; simmer, uncovered, until shrimp turn pink, 4-5 minutes.

2. Drain orzo. Add orzo, cilantro and pepper to shrimp mixture; heat through. Sprinkle with feta cheese.

1 CUP: 406 cal., 12g fat (3g sat. fat), 180mg chol., 307mg sod., 40g carb. (2g sugars, 9g fiber), 33g pro. **DIABETIC EXCHANGES:** 4 lean meat, 2 starch, 1 fat.

SHEET-PAN CAESAR CHICKEN & POTATOES

In our area we have an abundance of fresh lemons year-round. When I had a few extra on hand, I put together a quick marinade and ended up with a tasty meal with a burst of flavor. I baked it so I could add potatoes, but you can grill the chicken if you prefer.
—*Kallee Krong-McCreery, Escondido, CA*

Prep: 15 min. + marinating • **Bake:** 30 min.
Makes: 4 servings

- ¼ cup lemon juice
- ¼ cup Caesar vinaigrette
- 4 bone-in chicken thighs (about 1½ lbs.)
- 3 medium red potatoes (about 1¼ lbs.), each cut into 8 wedges
- ½ lb. medium carrots, cut into 1½-in. pieces
- 1 tsp. garlic salt
- ½ tsp. dill weed
- ¼ tsp. pepper

1. For the marinade, in a large bowl, mix lemon juice and dressing; remove 2 Tbsp. mixture for potatoes. Add chicken to remaining marinade; turn to coat. Cover and refrigerate chicken and reserved marinade 4 hours or overnight.

2. Preheat oven to 400°. Place chicken on center of a foil-lined 15x10x1-in. baking pan; discard chicken marinade. Toss the potatoes and carrots with the reserved marinade and seasonings; arrange around chicken.

3. Roast until a thermometer inserted in chicken reads 170°-175° and potatoes are tender, 30-40 minutes.

1 CHICKEN THIGH WITH 1 CUP VEGETABLES: 348 cal., 18g fat (5g sat. fat), 80mg chol., 698mg sod., 20g carb. (4g sugars, 3g fiber), 25g pro.

TOMATO-HERB GRILLED TILAPIA

This super tilapia with ginger and lemon takes dinner over the top and, even better, requires minimal prep. Grilling the fish in foil is about as easy as it gets.
—*Trisha Kruse, Eagle, ID*

Takes: 30 min. • **Makes:** 4 servings

- 1 cup fresh cilantro leaves
- 1 cup fresh parsley leaves
- 2 Tbsp. olive oil
- 2 tsp. grated lemon zest
- 2 Tbsp. lemon juice
- 1 Tbsp. coarsely chopped fresh gingerroot
- ¾ tsp. sea salt or kosher salt, divided
- 2 cups grape tomatoes, halved lengthwise
- 1½ cups fresh or frozen corn (about 8 oz.), thawed
- 4 tilapia fillets (6 oz. each)

1. Place the first 6 ingredients in a food processor; add ½ tsp. salt. Pulse until the mixture is finely chopped.
2. In a bowl, combine the tomatoes and corn; stir in 1 Tbsp. herb mixture and remaining salt.
3. Place each fillet on a piece of heavy-duty foil (about 12 in. square). Top with herb mixture; spoon tomato mixture alongside fish. Fold foil around fish and vegetables, sealing tightly.
4. Grill, covered, over medium-high heat until the fish just begins to flake easily with a fork, 6-8 minutes. Open foil carefully to allow steam to escape.

1 SERVING: 270 cal., 9g fat (2g sat. fat), 83mg chol., 443mg sod., 15g carb. (6g sugars, 3g fiber), 35g pro. **DIABETIC EXCHANGES:** 5 lean meat, 1½ fat, 1 vegetable, ½ starch.

TURKEY BISCUIT SKILLET

My mother always made this while we were growing up. Now I make it for my own husband and kids. I cut the biscuits into smaller pieces so they will brown up nicely on top. I also add mushrooms to this recipe sometimes because my family likes them so much.
—*Keri Boffeli, Monticello, IA*

Takes: 30 min. • **Makes:** 6 servings

- 1 Tbsp. butter
- ⅓ cup chopped onion
- ¼ cup all-purpose flour
- 1 can (10½ oz.) condensed chicken broth, undiluted
- ¼ cup fat-free milk
- ⅛ tsp. pepper
- 2 cups cubed cooked turkey breast
- 2 cups frozen peas and carrots (about 10 oz.), thawed
- 1 tube (12 oz.) refrigerated buttermilk biscuits, quartered

1. Preheat oven to 400°. Melt the butter in a 10-in. cast-iron or other ovenproof skillet over medium-high heat. Add onion; cook and stir until tender, 2-3 minutes.
2. In a small bowl, mix flour, broth, milk and pepper until smooth; stir into pan. Bring to a boil, stirring constantly; cook and stir until thickened, 1-2 minutes. Add the turkey and frozen vegetables; heat through. Arrange biscuits over stew. Bake until biscuits are golden brown, 15-20 minutes.

1 SERVING: 319 cal., 10g fat (4g sat. fat), 43mg chol., 878mg sod., 36g carb. (4g sugars, 2g fiber), 22g pro.

SLOW-COOKER SPAGHETTI & MEATBALLS

I've been cooking for over 50 years, and this classic is still one that guests ask for frequently. It also makes amazing meatball sandwiches, and the sauce works for any type of pasta.
—*Jane Whittaker, Pensacola, FL*

Prep: 50 min. • **Cook:** 5 hours
Makes: 12 servings

- 1 cup seasoned bread crumbs
- 2 Tbsp. grated Parmesan and Romano cheese blend
- 1 tsp. pepper
- ½ tsp. salt
- 2 large eggs, lightly beaten
- 2 lbs. ground beef

SAUCE
- 1 large onion, finely chopped
- 1 medium green pepper, finely chopped
- 3 cans (15 oz. each) tomato sauce
- 2 cans (14½ oz. each) diced tomatoes, undrained
- 1 can (6 oz.) tomato paste
- 6 garlic cloves, minced
- 2 bay leaves
- 1 tsp. each dried basil, oregano and parsley flakes
- 1 tsp. salt
- ½ tsp. pepper
- ¼ tsp. crushed red pepper flakes
  Hot cooked spaghetti

1. In a large bowl, mix bread crumbs, cheese, pepper and salt; stir in eggs. Add beef; mix lightly but thoroughly. Shape into 1½-in. balls. In a large skillet, brown meatballs in batches over medium heat; drain.

2. Place the first 5 sauce ingredients in a 6-qt. slow cooker; stir in garlic and seasonings. Add the meatballs, stirring gently to coat. Cook, covered, on low 5-6 hours or until meatballs are cooked through.

3. Remove bay leaves. Serve meatballs and sauce with spaghetti.

ABOUT 3 MEATBALLS WITH ¾ CUP SAUCE: 254 cal., 11g fat (4g sat. fat), 79mg chol., 1133mg sod., 20g carb. (7g sugars, 3g fiber), 20g pro.

JANE WHITTAKER
Pensacola, FL

CONTEST-WINNING PEANUT CHICKEN STIR-FRY

Here's a colorful and comforting peanut chicken dish with just a touch of heat from crushed red pepper. If you want even more color, add frozen stir-fry veggies.
—*Lisa Erickson*, *Ripon*, *WI*

- -

Takes: 30 min. • **Makes:** 6 servings

8	oz. uncooked thick rice noodles
⅓	cup water
¼	cup reduced-sodium soy sauce
¼	cup peanut butter
4½	tsp. brown sugar
1	Tbsp. lemon juice
2	garlic cloves, minced
½	tsp. crushed red pepper flakes
2	Tbsp. canola oil, divided
1	lb. boneless skinless chicken breasts, cut into ½-in. strips
1	bunch broccoli, cut into florets
½	cup shredded carrot
	Sesame seeds, optional

1. Cook noodles according to the package directions. Meanwhile, in a small bowl, combine the water, soy sauce, peanut butter, brown sugar, lemon juice, garlic and pepper flakes; set aside.

2. In a large skillet, heat 1 Tbsp. oil over medium-high heat. Add chicken; stir-fry until no longer pink, 3-4 minutes. Remove from pan.

3. Stir-fry broccoli and carrot in remaining oil until crisp-tender, 4-6 minutes. Add soy sauce mixture; bring to a boil. Cook and stir until sauce is thickened, 1-2 minutes. Return chicken to pan; heat through. Drain noodles; toss with chicken mixture in pan. If desired, sprinkle with sesame seeds.

1⅓ CUPS: 384 cal., 13g fat (2g sat. fat), 42mg chol., 575mg sod., 45g carb. (7g sugars, 4g fiber), 24g pro. **DIABETIC EXCHANGES:** 3 starch, 3 lean meat, 2 fat.

SHEET-PAN CHIPOTLE-LIME SHRIMP BAKE

I like to make this seafood dinner for company because it tastes amazing but takes very little effort to throw together. Use asparagus, Broccolini or a mix of the two. It's all about what's available for a decent price.
—*Colleen Delawder, Herndon, VA*

- -

Prep: 10 min. • **Bake:** 40 min.
Makes: 4 servings

1½ lbs. baby red potatoes,
    cut into ¾-in. cubes
1   Tbsp. extra virgin olive oil
¾   tsp. sea salt, divided
3   medium limes
¼   cup unsalted butter, melted
1   tsp. ground chipotle pepper
½   lb. fresh asparagus, trimmed
½   lb. Broccolini or broccoli, cut into
    small florets
1   lb. uncooked shrimp (16-20 per lb.),
    peeled and deveined
2   Tbsp. minced fresh cilantro

1. Preheat oven to 400°. Place potatoes in a greased 15x10x1-in. baking pan; drizzle with the olive oil. Sprinkle with ¼ tsp. sea salt; stir to combine. Bake 30 minutes. Meanwhile, squeeze ⅓ cup juice from limes, reserving fruit. Combine lime juice, melted butter, chipotle and remaining sea salt.
2. Remove sheet pan from oven; stir potatoes. Arrange the asparagus, Broccolini, shrimp and reserved limes on top of potatoes. Pour lime juice mixture over vegetables and shrimp.
3. Bake until the shrimp turn pink and the vegetables are tender, about 10 minutes longer. Sprinkle with cilantro.
1 SERVING: 394 cal., 17g fat (8g sat. fat), 168mg chol., 535mg sod., 41g carb. (4g sugars, 6g fiber), 25g pro.

AIR-FRYER NASHVILLE HOT CHICKEN

I live in Tennessee and love our state's famous Nashville hot chicken. In an attempt to make it easier to prepare, I cooked it in my air fryer. I'm so glad I did—this version is almost better than the original!
—*April Lane, Greeneville, TN*

- -

Prep: 30 min. • **Cook:** 10 min./batch
Makes: 6 servings

2   Tbsp. dill pickle juice, divided
2   Tbsp. hot pepper sauce, divided
1   tsp. salt, divided
2   lbs. chicken tenderloins
1   cup all-purpose flour
½   tsp. pepper
1   large egg
½   cup buttermilk
    Cooking spray
½   cup olive oil
2   Tbsp. cayenne pepper
2   Tbsp. dark brown sugar
1   tsp. paprika
1   tsp. chili powder
½   tsp. garlic powder
    Dill pickle slices

1. In a bowl or shallow dish, combine 1 Tbsp. pickle juice, 1 Tbsp. hot sauce and ½ tsp. salt. Add the chicken and turn to coat. Refrigerate, covered, for at least 1 hour. Drain, discarding any marinade.
2. Preheat air fryer to 375°. In a shallow bowl, mix flour, remaining ½ tsp. salt and the pepper. In another shallow bowl, whisk egg, buttermilk, and the remaining 1 Tbsp. pickle juice and 1 Tbsp. hot sauce. Dip chicken in flour to coat both sides; shake off excess. Dip in egg mixture, then again in flour mixture.
3. In batches, arrange chicken in a single layer on well-greased tray in air-fryer basket; spritz with cooking spray. Cook until golden brown, 5-6 minutes. Turn; spritz with cooking spray. Cook until golden brown, 5-6 minutes longer.
4. Whisk together oil, cayenne pepper, brown sugar and seasonings; pour over hot chicken and toss to coat. Serve with pickles.
5 OZ. COOKED CHICKEN: 413 cal., 21g fat (3g sat. fat), 96mg chol., 170mg sod., 20g carb. (5g sugars, 1g fiber), 39g pro.

CHICKEN POTPIE WITH CHEDDAR BISCUIT TOPPING

With chunks of chicken, veggies and a golden biscuit topping, this potpie makes a hearty meal that's as homey as the ones Mom made.
—*Sala Houtzer, Goldsboro, NC*

- -

Prep: 20 min. • **Bake:** 45 min. + standing
Makes: 9 servings

- 4 cups cubed cooked chicken
- 1 pkg. (12 oz.) frozen broccoli with cheese sauce
- 1 can (10¾ oz.) condensed cream of chicken and mushroom soup, undiluted
- 1 can (10¾ oz.) condensed cream of chicken soup, undiluted
- 2 medium potatoes, cubed
- ¾ cup chicken broth
- ⅔ cup sour cream
- ½ cup frozen peas
- ¼ tsp. pepper

TOPPING
- 1½ cups biscuit/baking mix
- ¾ cup shredded sharp cheddar cheese
- ¾ cup 2% milk
- 3 Tbsp. butter, melted

1. In a Dutch oven, combine the first 9 ingredients; bring to a boil. Transfer to a greased 13x9-in. baking dish.
2. In a bowl, combine topping ingredients; spoon over top. Bake, uncovered, at 350° for 40-45 minutes or until bubbly and the topping is golden brown. Let stand for 10 minutes before serving.

1 SERVING: 457 cal., 24g fat (11g sat. fat), 98mg chol., 1181mg sod., 32g carb. (4g sugars, 2g fiber), 27g pro.

READER REVIEW

"This was a family favorite! Three generations of happy customers. Given the busy day we had, rotisserie chickens were the way to go for the 4 cups in this recipe...super moist and tender."

GG5575, TASTEOFHOME.COM

ITALIAN SPIRAL MEAT LOAF

Take a classic comfort food to fantastic new heights with this impressive recipe. Sausage, pizza sauce and mozzarella give meat loaf an Italian accent.
—*Megan Krumm, Schererville, IN*

- -

Prep: 40 min. • **Bake:** 1¼ hours
Makes: 12 servings

- 2 large eggs, lightly beaten
- 1 cup pizza sauce, divided
- 1 cup seasoned bread crumbs
- 1 medium onion, chopped
- 1 medium green pepper, chopped
- 1 tsp. dried oregano
- 1 garlic clove, minced
- ½ tsp. salt
- ¼ tsp. pepper
- 2 lbs. lean ground beef (90% lean)
- 1 lb. bulk Italian sausage
- ½ lb. sliced deli ham
- 2 cups shredded part-skim mozzarella cheese, divided
- 1 jar (6 oz.) sliced mushrooms, drained

1. Preheat oven to 375°. In a large bowl, combine the eggs, ¾ cup pizza sauce, bread crumbs, onion, green pepper, oregano, garlic, salt and pepper. Crumble beef and sausage over mixture and mix lightly but thoroughly.
2. On a piece of parchment, pat beef mixture into a 12x10-in. rectangle. Layer the ham, 1½ cups cheese and mushrooms over the beef mixture to within 1 in. of edges. Roll up jelly-roll style, starting with a short side and peeling parchment away as you roll. Seal seam and ends. Place seam side down in a greased 13x9-in. baking dish; brush with remaining pizza sauce.
3. Bake, uncovered, 1 hour. Sprinkle with the remaining cheese. Bake until no pink remains and a thermometer reads 160°, 15-20 minutes longer. Using 2 large spatulas, carefully transfer meat loaf to a serving platter.

FREEZE OPTION: Securely wrap and freeze cooled baked meat loaf in foil. To use, partially thaw in refrigerator overnight. Unwrap meat loaf; reheat on a greased shallow baking pan in a preheated 350° oven until heated through and a thermometer inserted in the center reads 165°.

1 SLICE: 386 cal., 23g fat (9g sat. fat), 130mg chol., 981mg sod., 12g carb. (4g sugars, 1g fiber), 31g pro.

SHEET-PAN TILAPIA & VEGETABLE MEDLEY

Unlike some one-pan dinners that require precooking in a skillet or pot, this one uses just the sheet pan, period. How easy is that?
—Judy Batson, Tampa, FL

- -

Prep: 15 min. • **Bake:** 25 min.
Makes: 2 servings

- 2 medium Yukon Gold potatoes, cut into wedges
- 3 large fresh Brussels sprouts, thinly sliced
- 3 large radishes, thinly sliced
- 1 cup fresh sugar snap peas, cut into ½-in. pieces
- 1 small carrot, thinly sliced
- 2 Tbsp. butter, melted
- ½ tsp. garlic salt
- ½ tsp. pepper
- 2 tilapia fillets (6 oz. each)
- 2 tsp. minced fresh tarragon or ½ tsp. dried tarragon
- ⅛ tsp. salt
- 1 Tbsp. butter, softened
  Optional: Lemon wedges and tartar sauce

1. Preheat oven to 450°. Line a 15x10x1-in. baking pan with foil; grease foil.
2. In a large bowl, combine the first 5 ingredients. Add melted butter, garlic salt and pepper; toss to coat. Place vegetables in a single layer in prepared pan; bake until potatoes are tender, about 20 minutes.
3. Remove from oven; preheat broiler. Arrange vegetables on 1 side of sheet pan. Add fish to other side. Sprinkle fillets with tarragon and salt; dot with softened butter. Broil 4-5 in. from heat until fish flakes easily with a fork, about 5 minutes. If desired, serve with lemon wedges and tartar sauce.
1 SERVING: 555 cal., 20g fat (12g sat. fat), 129mg chol., 892mg sod., 56g carb. (8g sugars, 8g fiber), 41g pro.

TEST KITCHEN TIP
If food is burned on one side of the pan and undercooked on the other, it could be due to hot spots in your oven. Invest in an oven thermometer to test different areas of the oven to determine the hot spots and rotate the pan accordingly. Also, cut foods that take longer to cook into very small pieces while leaving quicker cooking ingredients in larger sizes.

GRILLED STEAK TACOS

Spicy aioli brings a zesty kick to steak tacos, and the ribeye is a nice upgrade from typical ground beef. Grab one and enjoy the burst of flavor in each bite!
—Michael Compean, Los Angeles, CA

- -

Prep: 25 min. • **Grill:** 15 min.
Makes: 4 servings

SPICY AIOLI
- ¼ cup mayonnaise
- 2 tsp. Sriracha chili sauce or 1 tsp. hot pepper sauce
- ⅛ tsp. sesame oil

AVOCADO-CORN SALSA
- 1 medium ripe avocado, peeled and finely chopped
- ½ medium tomato, seeded and chopped
- 3 Tbsp. sliced ripe olives
- 2 Tbsp. canned whole kernel corn
- 2 Tbsp. chopped sweet red pepper
- 2 Tbsp. lime juice
- 4 tsp. minced fresh cilantro
- 1 tsp. kosher salt
- 1 tsp. finely chopped onion
- 1 garlic clove, minced
- ¼ tsp. ground cumin

STEAKS
- 2 tsp. pepper
- 2 tsp. olive oil
- 1 tsp. kosher salt
- 1 tsp. seafood seasoning
- 1 beef ribeye steak (1 lb.), trimmed
- 8 flour tortillas (6 in.)
  Optional toppings: Shredded lettuce, cheddar cheese and Cotija cheese

1. In a small bowl, combine the spicy aioli ingredients. In another bowl, combine the salsa ingredients. Refrigerate until serving.
2. Combine the pepper, oil, salt and seafood seasoning; rub over both sides of steak.
3. Grill, covered, over medium heat until meat reaches desired doneness (for medium-rare, a thermometer should read 135°; medium, 140°; medium-well, 145°), 6-8 minutes on each side. Let stand for 5 minutes.
4. Meanwhile, grill tortillas until warm, about 45 seconds on each side. Thinly slice steak; place on tortillas. Serve with aioli, salsa and toppings of your choice.
2 TACOS: 650 cal., 45g fat (10g sat. fat), 72mg chol., 1843mg sod., 35g carb. (2g sugars, 4g fiber), 28g pro.

SOUTHWESTERN FISH TACOS

These bright tacos take me on an instant trip to sunny Southern California. The recipe has been on my family's most-requested list for years.
—*Joan Hallford, North Richland Hills, TX*

Takes: 20 min. • **Makes:** 2 servings

- ¼ cup mayonnaise
- ¼ cup sour cream
- 2 Tbsp. minced fresh cilantro
- 4 tsp. taco seasoning
- ½ lb. cod or haddock fillets, cut into 1-in. pieces
- 1 Tbsp. lemon juice
- 1 Tbsp. canola oil
- 4 taco shells
  Optional ingredients: Shredded lettuce, chopped tomato and lime wedges

1. For sauce, mix mayonnaise, sour cream, cilantro and 2 tsp. taco seasoning. In another bowl, toss cod with lemon juice and remaining taco seasoning.

2. In a skillet, heat oil over medium-high heat; saute cod just until it begins to flake easily with a fork, 4-6 minutes (fish may break apart as it cooks). Spoon into taco shells; serve with sauce and optional ingredients as desired.

2 TACOS: 506 cal., 38g fat (8g sat. fat), 52mg chol., 852mg sod., 20g carb. (1g sugars, 1g fiber), 20g pro.

ONE-SKILLET PORK CHOP SUPPER

My husband, Clark, and I reserve this recipe for Sundays after the grandkids have gone home and we're too tired to prepare a big meal. It's comforting and quick.
—*Kathy Thompson, Port Orange, FL*

Prep: 10 min. • **Cook:** 30 min.
Makes: 4 servings

- 1 Tbsp. butter
- 4 pork loin chops (½ in. thick and 7 oz. each)
- 3 medium red potatoes, cut into small wedges
- 3 medium carrots, cut into ½-in. slices, or 2 cups fresh baby carrots
- 1 medium onion, cut into wedges
- 1 can (10¾ oz.) condensed cream of mushroom soup, undiluted
- ½ cup water
  Optional: Cracked black pepper and chopped fresh parsley

1. In a large cast-iron or other heavy skillet, heat butter over medium heat. Brown pork chops on both sides; remove from the pan, reserving drippings.

2. In same pan, saute vegetables in drippings until lightly browned. Whisk together soup and water; stir into vegetables. Bring to a boil. Reduce heat; simmer, covered, just until vegetables are tender, 15-20 minutes.

3. Add the pork chops; cook, covered, until a thermometer inserted in pork reads 145°, 8-10 minutes. Remove from heat; let stand 5 minutes. If desired, sprinkle with pepper and parsley.

1 SERVING: 390 cal., 15g fat (6g sat. fat), 97mg chol., 700mg sod., 28g carb. (6g sugars, 4g fiber), 33g pro.

READER REVIEW

"This is our ultimate comfort food. I add a green salad and rolls. So good!"

REDTEETOP, TASTEOFHOME.COM

51 GLAZED ROAST CHICKEN

A few pantry items inspired this recipe, which I've since made for small weeknight meals or for big parties. The quince jelly comes from my boss, who grows the fruit in his own backyard.
—*Victoria Miller, San Ramon, CA*

Prep: 15 min.
Bake: 1½ hours + standing
Makes: 6 servings

- 1 cup white wine or chicken broth
- 1 cup apricot preserves or quince jelly
- 1 Tbsp. stone-ground mustard
- 1 broiler/fryer chicken (3 to 4 lbs.)
- ¾ tsp. salt
- ½ tsp. pepper

1. Preheat oven to 375°. In a small saucepan, bring wine to a boil; cook until wine is reduced by half, 3-4 minutes. Stir in the preserves and mustard. Reserve half of the glaze for serving.
2. Place chicken on a rack in a shallow roasting pan, breast side up. Sprinkle chicken with salt and pepper. Tuck wings under chicken; tie drumsticks together.
3. Roast for 45 minutes; baste with glaze. Continue roasting the chicken until a thermometer inserted in thigh reads 170°-175°, basting occasionally with glaze. Cover loosely with foil if chicken browns too quickly. Remove chicken from oven; tent with foil. Let stand 15 minutes before carving. Serve with remaining reserved glaze.
1 SERVING: 437 cal., 17g fat (5g sat. fat), 104mg chol., 458mg sod., 35g carb. (23g sugars, 0 fiber), 34g pro.

COMPANY POT ROAST

The aroma of this roast slowly cooking in the oven is absolutely mouthwatering. It gives the home such a cozy feeling, even on the chilliest winter days.
—*Anita Osborne, Thomasburg, ON*

Prep: 20 min. • **Bake:** 2¾ hours
Makes: 6 servings

- 1 boneless beef chuck roast (3 to 4 lbs.)
- 2 Tbsp. olive oil
- 1 cup sherry or beef broth
- ½ cup reduced-sodium soy sauce
- ¼ cup sugar
- 2 tsp. beef bouillon granules
- 1 cinnamon stick (3 in.)
- 8 medium carrots, cut into 2-in. pieces
- 6 medium potatoes, peeled and cut into 1½-in. pieces
- 1 medium onion, sliced
- 2 Tbsp. cornstarch
- 2 Tbsp. cold water

1. Brown the roast in oil in a Dutch oven on all sides; drain. Combine the sherry, soy sauce, sugar, bouillon and cinnamon stick; pour over the roast.
2. Cover and bake at 325° for 2¾-3¼ hours or until the meat and vegetables are tender, adding carrots, potatoes and onion during the last 30 minutes of cooking.
3. Remove roast and vegetables to a serving platter; keep warm. Combine the cornstarch and water until smooth. Stir into pan. Bring to a boil; cook and stir for 2 minutes or until thickened. Serve with roast and vegetables.
6 OZ. COOKED MEAT WITH 2 CUPS VEGETABLES AND ¼ CUP GRAVY: 713 cal., 26g fat (9g sat. fat), 148mg chol., 1437mg sod., 56g carb. (17g sugars, 5g fiber), 49g pro.

LEMON-DIJON PORK SHEET-PAN SUPPER

Most nights, I need something on the table with minimal effort and maximum results. This sheet-pan supper has become an all-time favorite, not only because of its bright flavors, but also because of its speedy cleanup time.
—*Elisabeth Larsen, Pleasant Grove, UT*

Prep: 20 min. • **Bake:** 20 min.
Makes: 4 servings

- 4 tsp. Dijon mustard
- 2 tsp. grated lemon zest
- 1 garlic clove, minced
- ½ tsp. salt
- 2 Tbsp. canola oil
- 1½ lbs. sweet potatoes (about 3 medium), cut into ½-in. cubes
- 1 lb. fresh Brussels sprouts (about 4 cups), quartered
- 4 boneless pork loin chops (6 oz. each)
  Coarsely ground pepper, optional

1. Preheat oven to 425°. In a large bowl, mix first 4 ingredients; gradually whisk in the oil. Reserve 1 Tbsp. mixture. Add vegetables to remaining mixture; toss to coat.

2. Place the pork chops and vegetables in a 15x10x1-in. pan coated with cooking spray. Brush chops with reserved mustard mixture. Roast 10 minutes.

3. Turn chops and stir vegetables; roast until a thermometer inserted in the pork reads 145° and vegetables are tender, 10-15 minutes longer. If desired, sprinkle with pepper. Let stand 5 minutes before serving.

1 PORK CHOP WITH 1¼ CUPS VEGETABLES: 516 cal., 17g fat (4g sat. fat), 82mg chol., 505mg sod., 51g carb. (19g sugars, 9g fiber), 39g pro. **DIABETIC EXCHANGES:** 5 lean meat, 3 starch, 1½ fat, 1 vegetable.

SLOW-COOKED ITALIAN CHICKEN

With its nicely seasoned tomato sauce, this enticing chicken entree is especially good over pasta. My father loved this dish.
—*Deanna D'Auria, Banning, CA*

- -

Prep: 20 min. • **Cook:** 4 hours
Makes: 4 servings

- 4   boneless skinless chicken breast halves (4 oz. each)
- 1   can (14½ oz.) reduced-sodium chicken broth
- 1   can (14½ oz.) stewed tomatoes, cut up
- 1   can (8 oz.) tomato sauce
- 1   medium green pepper, chopped
- 1   green onion, chopped
- 1   garlic clove, minced
- 3   tsp. chili powder
- 1   tsp. ground mustard
- ½   tsp. pepper
- ¼   tsp. garlic powder
- ¼   tsp. onion powder
- ⅓   cup all-purpose flour
- ½   cup cold water
    Hot cooked pasta
    Optional: Grated Parmesan cheese and minced fresh basil

1. Place chicken in a 3-qt. slow cooker. In a bowl, combine the broth, tomatoes, tomato sauce, green pepper, onion, garlic and seasonings; pour over chicken. Cover and cook on low for 4-5 hours or until meat is tender. Remove chicken and keep warm.
2. Pour cooking juices into a large saucepan; skim fat. Combine flour and cold water until smooth; stir into juices. Bring to a boil; cook and stir for 2 minutes or until thickened. Serve with chicken and pasta. Top with Parmesan and basil if desired.

1 SERVING: 231 cal., 3g fat (1g sat. fat), 63mg chol., 818mg sod., 22g carb. (8g sugars, 3g fiber), 28g pro. **DIABETIC EXCHANGES:** 3 lean meat, 1 starch, 1 vegetable.

DID YOU KNOW?
When using a slow cooker, avoid overfilling the crock. The contents could start to bubble over, or, when you open the lid, you could discover that your meal is a hard mass stuck to the bottom. Since slow cookers operate best when filled halfway to three-quarters full, make sure your recipe meets that criterion.

TASTY TURKEY SKILLET

I like to use boxed rice and pasta mixes as the bases for quick meals. This colorful dish is simple to cook on the stovetop using fried rice mix, tender turkey and convenient frozen vegetables.

—Betty Kleberger, Florissant, MO

- -

Prep: 10 min. • **Cook:** 35 min.
Makes: 4 servings

- 1 lb. turkey breast tenderloins, cut into ¼-in. strips
- 1 pkg. (6.2 oz.) fried rice mix
- 1 Tbsp. butter
- 2 cups water
- ⅛ tsp. cayenne pepper
- 1½ cups frozen corn, thawed
- 1 cup frozen broccoli cuts, thawed
- 2 Tbsp. chopped sweet red pepper, optional

1. In a skillet coated with cooking spray, cook turkey over medium heat until no longer pink; drain. Remove turkey and keep warm.
2. Set aside seasoning packet from rice. In the same skillet, saute the rice in butter until lightly browned. Stir in the water, cayenne and contents of seasoning packet.
3. Bring to a boil. Reduce heat; cover and simmer for 15 minutes. Stir in the corn, broccoli, red pepper if desired and turkey. Return to a boil. Reduce heat; cover and simmer until the rice and vegetables are tender, 6-8 minutes.
1¼ CUPS: 351 cal., 6g fat (2g sat. fat), 53mg chol., 971mg sod., 43g carb. (4g sugars, 4g fiber), 35g pro.

❄ 🎀 MEAT LOAF MINIATURES

I'm not a huge fan of meat loaf, but my family and I can't get enough of these little muffins topped with a sweet ketchup sauce. The recipe requires no chopping, so it's quick and easy to make a double batch and have extras for another day. I've given them to new moms and new neighbors.

—Joyce Wegmann, Burlington, IA

- -

Prep: 20 min. • **Bake:** 30 min.
Makes: 1½ dozen

- 1 cup ketchup
- 3 to 4 Tbsp. packed brown sugar
- 1 tsp. ground mustard
- 2 large eggs, lightly beaten
- 4 tsp. Worcestershire sauce
- 3 cups Crispix cereal, crushed
- 3 tsp. onion powder
- ½ to 1 tsp. seasoned salt
- ½ tsp. garlic powder
- ½ tsp. pepper
- 3 lbs. lean ground beef (90% lean)

1. In a large bowl, combine the ketchup, brown sugar and mustard. Remove ½ cup mixture for topping; set aside. Add the eggs, Worcestershire sauce, cereal and seasonings to remaining ketchup mixture. Let stand for 5 minutes. Crumble beef over cereal mixture and mix lightly but thoroughly.
2. Press the meat mixture into 18 muffin cups (about ⅓ cup each). Bake at 375° for 18-20 minutes. Drizzle with the reserved ketchup mixture; bake 10 minutes longer or until the meat is no longer pink and a thermometer reads 160°.
3. Serve desired number of meat loaves. Refrigerate or freeze leftovers.
FREEZE OPTION: Cool the remaining loaves. Transfer to a freezer container; close and freeze for up to 3 months. Completely thaw loaves in the refrigerator. Place in a greased baking dish. Bake at 350° for 30 minutes or until heated through, or cover and microwave on high for 1 minute or until heated through.
1 SERVING: 165 cal., 6g fat (2g sat. fat), 61mg chol., 305mg sod., 11g carb. (4g sugars, 0 fiber), 16g pro.

CAST-IRON SAUSAGE PIZZA

This shortcut pizza starts with frozen dough in a cast-iron pan. Add your family's favorite toppings for variety.
—Taste of Home *Test Kitchen*

Prep: 30 min. • **Bake:** 20 min. • **Makes:** 6 slices

- 1 loaf (1 lb.) frozen bread dough, thawed
- 2 tsp. cornmeal
- 1½ cups pizza sauce
- ½ lb. bulk Italian sausage, cooked and drained
- 1½ cups shredded part-skim mozzarella cheese, divided
- 1 tsp. dried oregano
- 1 small green pepper, sliced into rings
  Crushed red pepper flakes, optional

1. Preheat oven to 425°. On a lightly floured surface, roll and stretch dough into a 10-in. circle. Cover; let rest for 10 minutes. Roll and stretch the dough into a 12-in. circle. Grease a 10-in. cast-iron or other ovenproof skillet; sprinkle with cornmeal. Press dough onto bottom and 1 in. up sides of prepared skillet.
2. Spread with pizza sauce; top with sausage, 1 cup cheese, oregano and green pepper. Sprinkle with remaining ½ cup cheese. Bake until crust is golden brown, 20-25 minutes. If desired, sprinkle with red pepper flakes.
1 SLICE: 424 cal., 18g fat (6g sat. fat), 39mg chol., 1092mg sod., 45g carb. (7g sugars, 4g fiber), 20g pro.

❄ SIMMERED TURKEY ENCHILADAS

I discovered a new way to serve economical turkey thighs. I simmer them in tomato sauce, green chiles and seasonings until they're tender and flavorful, then serve them in tortillas with our favorite fresh toppings.
—*Stella Schams, Tempe, AZ*

Prep: 10 min. • **Cook:** 6 hours
Makes: 4 servings

- 2 lbs. turkey thighs or drumsticks
- 1 can (8 oz.) tomato sauce
- 1 can (4 oz.) chopped green chiles
- ⅓ cup chopped onion
- 2 Tbsp. Worcestershire sauce
- 1 to 2 Tbsp. chili powder
- ¼ tsp. garlic powder
- 8 flour tortillas (6 in.), warmed
  Optional toppings: Chopped green onions, sliced ripe olives, chopped tomatoes, shredded cheddar cheese, sour cream and shredded lettuce

1. Remove skin from turkey; place turkey in a 5-qt. slow cooker. In a small bowl, combine tomato sauce, chiles, onion, Worcestershire sauce, chili powder and garlic powder; pour over turkey. Cover and cook on low until the turkey is tender, 6-8 hours.
2. Remove turkey; shred meat with a fork and return to the slow cooker. Heat through.
3. Spoon about ½ cup turkey mixture down the center of each tortilla. Fold the bottom of tortilla over filling and roll up. Add toppings of your choice.
FREEZE OPTION: Individually wrap cooled burritos in paper towels and foil; freeze in a freezer container. To use, remove foil; place paper towel-wrapped burrito on a microwave-safe plate. Microwave on high until heated through, 3-4 minutes, turning once. Let stand 20 seconds.
2 ENCHILADAS: 497 cal., 20g fat (4g sat. fat), 114mg chol., 1028mg sod., 34g carb. (3g sugars, 2g fiber), 45g pro.

THOMAS FAGLON
Somerset, NJ

LEMONY SCALLOPS WITH ANGEL HAIR PASTA

This delicate dish tastes so bright with a touch of lemon and tender sauteed scallops. Serve with crusty whole grain bread, and you have an impressive dinner that comes together in a flash.
—Thomas Faglon, Somerset, NJ

Takes: 25 min. • **Makes:** 4 servings

- 8 oz. uncooked multigrain angel hair pasta
- 3 Tbsp. olive oil, divided
- 1 lb. sea scallops, patted dry
- 2 cups sliced radishes (about 1 bunch)
- 2 garlic cloves, sliced
- ½ tsp. crushed red pepper flakes
- 6 green onions, thinly sliced
- ½ tsp. kosher salt
- 1 Tbsp. grated lemon zest
- ¼ cup lemon juice

1. In a 6-qt. stockpot, cook pasta according to package directions; drain and return to pot.
2. Meanwhile, in a large skillet, heat 2 Tbsp. oil over medium-high heat; sear the scallops in batches until opaque and edges are golden brown, about 2 minutes per side. Remove from skillet; keep warm.
3. In the same skillet, saute radishes, garlic and pepper flakes in remaining oil 2-3 minutes or until radishes are tender. Stir in green onions and salt; cook 1 minute. Add to pasta; toss to combine. Sprinkle with lemon zest and juice. Top with scallops to serve.

1½ CUPS: 404 cal., 13g fat (2g sat. fat), 27mg chol., 737mg sod., 48g carb. (4g sugars, 6g fiber), 25g pro.

❄ CLASSIC CHEESECLOTH TURKEY

This turkey uses a classic method, wine-soaked cheesecloth, to give you the juiciest turkey and most flavorful gravy you've ever tasted! Pair with your favorite sides for a complete meal.
—Rashanda Cobbins, Milwaukee, WI

Prep: 30 minutes
Bake: 3¾ hours + standing
Makes: 24 servings (4 cups gravy)

- 1 turkey (14 to 16 lbs.)
- ½ cup butter, softened
- 3 Tbsp. minced fresh thyme
- 3 Tbsp. minced fresh sage
- 1 tsp. salt
- 1 tsp. pepper
- 2 celery ribs, quartered
- 1 medium onion, chopped
- 1 medium carrot, quartered
- 1 cup butter, cubed
- 2 cups white wine

GRAVY
- 2 to 3 cups chicken broth
- 5 Tbsp. all-purpose flour

1. Preheat oven to 325°. Remove giblets from turkey; cover and refrigerate for gravy. Pat the turkey dry; place breast side up on a rack in a roasting pan. In a small bowl, combine softened butter, thyme and sage. With fingers, carefully loosen skin from turkey breast; rub the butter mixture under skin. Sprinkle salt and pepper over turkey and inside cavity; fill cavity with celery, onion and carrot.
2. In a large saucepan, melt cubed butter; stir in wine. Saturate a 4-layered 17-in. square of cheesecloth in butter mixture; drape over turkey. Bake turkey, uncovered, 3 hours; baste with wine mixture every 30 minutes, keeping cheesecloth moist at all times.
3. Remove and discard cheesecloth. Bake turkey until a thermometer inserted in the thigh reads 170°-175°, basting occasionally with pan drippings, 45 minutes to 1¼ hours longer. (Cover loosely with foil if turkey browns too quickly.)
4. Remove turkey to a serving platter; cover and let stand for 20 minutes before carving. Discard vegetables from cavity. Pour drippings and loosened brown bits into a measuring cup. Skim fat, reserving ⅓ cup. Add enough broth to the remaining drippings to measure 4 cups.
5. For gravy, chop reserved giblets. In a large saucepan, saute giblets in reserved fat until browned. Stir in flour until blended; gradually stir in broth mixture. Bring to a boil; cook and stir until thickened, about 2 minutes. Serve with turkey.

FREEZE OPTION: Place sliced turkey in freezer containers; top with any cooking juices. Cool and freeze. To use, partially thaw in refrigerator overnight. Heat through in a covered saucepan, stirring occasionally; add broth or water if necessary.

6 OZ. COOKED TURKEY WITH ABOUT 3 TBSP. GRAVY: 354 cal., 16g fat (5g sat. fat), 149mg chol., 302mg sod., 3g carb. (1g sugars, 0 fiber), 43g pro.

AUTUMN LAMB SKILLET

I've found that even those who do not prefer lamb will enjoy this comforting recipe. It is especially delicious on a chilly night!
—*Arlene Aughey, Saddle Brook, NJ*

Prep: 25 min. • **Cook:** 35 min.
Makes: 4 servings

- 2 Tbsp. olive oil
- 8 lamb rib or loin chops
  (about 1 in. thick and 3 oz. each)
- 1 tsp. salt, divided
- ½ tsp. pepper, divided
- 1 large onion, chopped
- 2 celery ribs, chopped
- 1 medium green pepper, chopped
- 1 garlic clove, minced
- ½ tsp. dried basil
- 1 can (14½ oz.) stewed tomatoes
- 1 cup uncooked long grain rice
- ½ tsp. ground turmeric, optional

In a large skillet, heat oil over medium heat. Sprinkle the lamb chops with ½ tsp. salt and ¼ tsp. pepper. Brown the chops in batches; remove and keep warm. Add onion, celery, green pepper, garlic, basil, and remaining ½ tsp. salt and ¼ tsp. pepper. Cook and stir until crisp-tender, 5-7 minutes. Return lamb to skillet; add tomatoes. Cook, covered, until the lamb reaches desired doneness (for medium-rare, a thermometer should read 135°; medium, 140°; medium-well, 145°), about 20 minutes longer. Meanwhile, cook rice according to package directions, adding turmeric if desired. Serve with lamb mixture.
1 SERVING: 455 cal., 14g fat (4g sat. fat), 68mg chol., 856mg sod., 54g carb. (8g sugars, 3g fiber), 27g pro.

COLORFUL BEEF STIR-FRY

If you love stir fry as much as I do, you'll go for this recipe. The easy sesame-ginger marinade and vibrant mix of vegetables make it a keeper.
—*Deb Blendermann, Boulder, CO*

Prep: 35 min. + marinating
Cook: 15 min. • **Makes:** 4 cups

- ¼ cup reduced-sodium soy sauce
- 1 Tbsp. honey
- 2 tsp. sesame oil
- 3 garlic cloves, minced
- ⅛ tsp. ground ginger
- ½ lb. boneless beef sirloin steak, thinly sliced
- 4½ tsp. cornstarch
- ½ cup reduced-sodium beef broth
- 1½ tsp. canola oil, divided
- 1 small green pepper, cut into chunks
- 1 small onion, cut into chunks
- 1 medium carrot, julienned
- ¼ cup sliced celery
- 1 small zucchini, julienned
- ½ cup fresh snow peas
- ½ cup canned bean sprouts, rinsed and drained
  Hot cooked rice or linguine, optional

1. In a small bowl, combine first 5 ingredients. Place the beef in a shallow dish; add half of the marinade. Turn to coat; cover and refrigerate for at least 2 hours. Cover and refrigerate the remaining marinade.
2. In a small bowl, combine cornstarch and broth until smooth. Stir in reserved marinade; set aside. Drain beef, discarding marinade. In a large nonstick skillet or wok coated with cooking spray, cook beef in 1 tsp. oil until no longer pink; drain. Remove and keep warm.
3. In the same pan, stir-fry green pepper and onion in remaining ½ tsp. oil for 2 minutes. Add the carrot and celery; cook 2-3 minutes longer. Add the zucchini and snow peas; stir-fry for 1 minute. Stir in the canned bean sprouts and heat through.
4. Stir broth mixture and stir into vegetable mixture. Bring to a boil; cook and stir until thickened, 1-2 minutes. Return beef to the pan; heat through. Serve over rice or linguine if desired.
1 CUP: 318 cal., 8g fat (2g sat. fat), 43mg chol., 542mg sod., 41g carb. (8g sugars, 4g fiber), 21g pro. **DIABETIC EXCHANGES:** 2 lean meat, 1 starch, ½ fat.

CHORIZO SPAGHETTI SQUASH SKILLET

Get your noodle fix minus the pasta with this spicy one-dish meal. It's a fill-you-up dinner that's low in calories—a weeknight winner!
—*Sherrill Oake, Springfield, MA*

Takes: 30 min. • **Makes:** 4 servings

- 1 small spaghetti squash (about 2 lbs.)
- 1 Tbsp. canola oil
- 1 pkg. (12 oz.) fully cooked chorizo chicken sausage links or flavor of choice, sliced
- 1 medium sweet yellow pepper, chopped
- 1 medium sweet onion, halved and sliced
- 1 cup sliced fresh mushrooms
- 1 can (14½ oz.) no-salt-added diced tomatoes, undrained
- 1 Tbsp. reduced-sodium taco seasoning
- ¼ tsp. pepper
  Chopped green onions, optional

1. Halve squash lengthwise; discard seeds. Place squash on a microwave-safe plate, cut side down; microwave on high until tender, about 15 minutes. Cool slightly.
2. Meanwhile, in a large skillet, heat oil over medium-high heat; saute sausage, yellow pepper, onion and mushrooms until onion is tender, about 5 minutes.
3. Separate strands of squash with a fork; add to skillet. Stir in the tomatoes and seasonings; bring to a boil. Reduce the heat; simmer, uncovered, until flavors are blended, about 5 minutes. If desired, top with green onions.
1½ CUPS: 299 cal., 12g fat (3g sat. fat), 65mg chol., 725mg sod., 34g carb. (12g sugars, 6g fiber), 18g pro. **DIABETIC EXCHANGES:** 2 starch, 2 lean meat, 1 vegetable, 1 fat.

AIR-FRYER FISH & CHIPS

Looking for easy recipes for an air fryer? Try this simple fish and chips. The fish fillets have a fuss-free coating that's healthier but just as crunchy and golden as the deep-fried kind. Simply seasoned, the crispy fries are perfect on the side.
—*Janice Mitchell, Aurora, CO*

Prep: 15 min. • **Cook:** 25 min.
Makes: 2 servings

- 1 medium potato
- 1 Tbsp. olive oil
- ⅛ tsp. pepper
- ⅛ tsp. salt

FISH

- 3 Tbsp. all-purpose flour
- ⅛ tsp. pepper
- 1 large egg
- 2 Tbsp. water
- ⅓ cup crushed cornflakes
- 1½ tsp. grated Parmesan cheese
  Dash cayenne pepper
- ⅛ tsp. salt
- ½ lb. haddock or cod fillets
  Tartar sauce, optional

1. Preheat air fryer to 400°. Peel and cut potato lengthwise into ½-in.-thick slices; cut slices into ½-in.-thick sticks.
2. In a large bowl, toss the potato with oil, pepper and salt. Place the potato pieces in a single layer in air fryer basket; cook until just tender, 5-10 minutes. Toss potatoes in basket to redistribute; continue to cook until lightly browned and crisp, 5-10 minutes longer.
3. Meanwhile, in a shallow bowl, mix flour and pepper. In another shallow bowl, whisk egg with water. In a third bowl, toss cornflakes with cheese and cayenne. Sprinkle fish with salt; dip into flour mixture to coat both sides, and shake off the excess. Dip fish in the egg mixture, then in the cornflake mixture, patting to help coating adhere.
4. Remove fries from basket; keep warm. Place fish in a single layer in air-fryer basket. Cook until the fish is lightly browned and just beginning to flake easily with a fork, turning halfway through cooking, 8-10 minutes. Do not overcook. Return fries to basket to heat through. Serve immediately. If desired, serve with tartar sauce.
1 SERVING: 304 cal., 9g fat (2g sat. fat), 84mg chol., 503mg sod., 33g carb. (3g sugars, 1g fiber), 23g pro. **DIABETIC EXCHANGES:** 3 lean meat, 2 starch, 1½ fat.

Casserole Entrees

Rich, creamy, cheesy, carb-y perfection is yours for the taking with this lineup of our most popular dinnertime bakes. Pull out your trusty pan and get ready to dish out comfort all year long.

POTLUCK TACO CASSEROLE

This is the dish I most often take to potlucks, and the pan comes home empty every time.
—*Kim Stoller, Smithville, OH*

Prep: 25 min. • **Bake:** 20 min.
Makes: 8 servings

2   lbs. ground beef
2   envelopes taco seasoning
4   large eggs
¾   cup 2% milk
1¼ cups biscuit/baking mix
    Dash pepper
½   cup sour cream
2   to 3 cups chopped lettuce
¾   cup chopped tomato
¼   cup chopped green pepper
2   green onions, chopped
2   cups shredded cheddar cheese

1. Preheat oven to 400°. In a large skillet, cook beef over medium heat 10-12 minutes or until no longer pink, breaking into crumbles; drain. Add the taco seasoning and prepare according to package directions. Spoon the meat into a greased 13x9-in. baking dish.
2. In a large bowl, beat the eggs and milk. Stir in the biscuit mix and pepper. Pour over the meat. Bake, uncovered, 20-25 minutes or until golden brown. Cool 5-10 minutes.
3. Spread the sour cream over top; sprinkle with lettuce, tomato, green pepper, onions and cheese.

FREEZE OPTION: Cool baked casserole; cover and freeze. To use, partially thaw in the refrigerator overnight. Remove from the refrigerator 30 minutes before baking. Preheat oven to 350°. Unwrap the casserole; reheat on a lower oven rack until heated through and a thermometer inserted in center reads 165°. Cool for 5-10 minutes, then top as directed.
1 SERVING: 472 cal., 27g fat (14g sat. fat), 205mg chol., 1360mg sod., 24g carb. (3g sugars, 1g fiber), 32g pro.

TEST KITCHEN TIP
For individual portions that kids will love, bake in greased muffin cups until golden brown, 15-20 minutes.

POPPY SEED CHICKEN

This simple yet delicious dish is terrific for dinner, but the leftovers are a bonus for lunch. It reheats well in the microwave, so you may want to double the recipe.
—Janet Zoss, Jackson, MI

Prep: 15 min. • **Bake:** 30 min.
Makes: 6 servings

- 1 cup sour cream
- 1 can (10¾ oz.) condensed cream of chicken soup, undiluted
- 1 Tbsp. poppy seeds
- 1 tsp. dill weed
- 4 cups cubed cooked chicken
- 3 cups cooked rice
- 1½ cups butter-flavored cracker crumbs
- ½ cup butter, melted

1. In a large bowl, combine the sour cream, soup, poppy seeds and dill. Stir in the chicken and rice.
2. Spread into a greased 11x7-in. baking dish. Combine crumbs and butter; sprinkle over casserole. Bake, uncovered, at 350° until bubbly, about 30 minutes.
1⅓ CUPS: 668 cal., 40g fat (18g sat. fat), 137mg chol., 771mg sod., 44g carb. (4g sugars, 2g fiber), 33g pro.

MUSHROOM SHEPHERD'S PIE

The one thing I miss most about meatless meals is, well, the meat. Except in this recipe! Hearty and satisfying, this works as a meatless entree or in smaller portions as a side dish.
—Glen Warren, Keswick, ON

Prep: 45 min. • **Bake:** 15 min.
Makes: 6 servings

- 2 Tbsp. butter
- 3 Tbsp. olive oil, divided
- 1 lb. sliced fresh button mushrooms
- ½ lb. coarsely chopped fresh oyster mushrooms
- ½ lb. coarsely chopped fresh chanterelle mushrooms
- 1 large onion, thinly sliced
- 3 garlic cloves, minced
- ½ cup dry red wine or vegetable stock
- ½ cup vegetable stock
- 2 Tbsp. minced fresh parsley
- 2 Tbsp. minced fresh thyme
- ¼ tsp. salt
- ¼ tsp. pepper
- 1 Tbsp. all-purpose flour
- 1 Tbsp. butter, softened

TOPPING
- 6 medium red potatoes, cubed
- ¼ cup 2% milk
- 2 to 4 Tbsp. butter
- 1 tsp. garlic powder
- ¾ tsp. salt
- ¼ tsp. pepper
- ¾ cup shredded cheddar cheese
  Optional: Additional thyme or parsley

1. Preheat oven to 425°. In a Dutch oven, heat butter and 2 Tbsp. oil over medium-high heat. Add mushrooms; cook and stir 4-6 minutes or until browned. Remove and set aside.
2. In the same pan, heat the remaining oil. Add onion; cook and stir 3-4 minutes or until tender. Add garlic; cook 1 minute longer. Add wine, stirring to loosen browned bits from pan. Bring to a boil; cook 2-3 minutes or until the wine is almost evaporated. Stir in stock, parsley, thyme, salt, pepper and mushrooms. Bring to a boil; cook 3-4 minutes longer or until liquid is reduced by half.
3. In a small bowl, mix flour and softened butter until blended; stir into the mushroom mixture until thickened. Transfer to a greased 11x7-in. baking dish.
4. Meanwhile, place the potatoes in a large saucepan; add water to cover. Bring to a boil. Reduce heat; cook, uncovered, 10-15 minutes or until tender. Drain; return to pan. Mash the potatoes, gradually adding milk, butter, garlic powder, salt and pepper.
5. Spread potatoes over mushroom mixture; sprinkle with the cheese. Bake 15-20 minutes or until heated through. If desired, top with additional thyme or parsley.
1½ CUPS: 354 cal., 22g fat (10g sat. fat), 40mg chol., 636mg sod., 30g carb. (6g sugars, 5g fiber), 11g pro.

VEGGIE LASAGNA

No one will miss the meat when you serve this hearty, vegetable-rich, pull-out-all-the-stops lasagna. It's fabulous for holidays with its fresh, full-bodied flavor. To save time, prepare the carrot and spinach layers in advance.
—Mary Jane Jones, Williamstown, WV

Prep: 70 min. • **Bake:** 1¼ hours + standing
Makes: 12 servings

- 1 pkg. (16 oz.) frozen sliced carrots
- ¼ cup finely chopped onion
- 2 Tbsp. butter
- 1 cup ricotta cheese
- ¼ tsp. each salt and pepper

SPINACH LAYER
- 2 shallots, chopped
- 1 Tbsp. olive oil
- 2 pkg. (10 oz. each) frozen chopped spinach, thawed and squeezed dry
- 1 cup ricotta cheese
- 1 large egg
- ¼ tsp. each salt and pepper

EGGPLANT LAYER
- 1 medium eggplant, peeled and cut into ¼-in. slices
- 3 garlic cloves, minced
- 6 Tbsp. olive oil
- ½ tsp. salt
- 2½ cups marinara sauce
- 12 lasagna noodles, cooked and drained
- ¼ cup minced fresh basil
- 4 cups part-skim shredded mozzarella cheese
- 3 cups grated Parmesan cheese

1. Cook carrots according to the package directions; drain and cool. In a small skillet, saute onion in butter until tender. In a food processor, puree the carrots, onion, ricotta, salt and pepper. In same skillet, saute the shallots in oil until tender. In a food processor, puree the shallots, spinach, ricotta, egg, salt and pepper.

2. In a large skillet, cook the eggplant and garlic in oil over medium heat in batches for 7-10 minutes or until tender; drain. Sprinkle with salt.

3. Spread ½ cup marinara sauce in a greased 13x9-in. baking dish. Layer with 4 noodles, carrot mixture, ½ cup sauce, 1 Tbsp. basil, 1 cup mozzarella and ¾ cup Parmesan. Top with 4 noodles, eggplant, ½ cup sauce, 1 Tbsp. basil, 1 cup mozzarella and ¾ cup Parmesan.

4. Layer with remaining noodles, spinach mixture, ½ cup sauce, 1 Tbsp. basil, 1 cup mozzarella and ¾ cup Parmesan. Top with the remaining sauce, basil, mozzarella and Parmesan (dish will be full).

5. Cover and bake at 350° for 1 hour. Uncover; bake 15 minutes longer or until bubbly. Let stand 15 minutes before serving.

1 PIECE: 496 cal., 27g fat (13g sat. fat), 77mg chol., 954mg sod., 37g carb. (12g sugars, 5g fiber), 29g pro.

PIZZA TATER TOT CASSEROLE

For a new spin on a classic, try my easy version. Feel free to add other favorite pizza toppings— pepperoni, black olives, tomatoes—that your family loves.
—Sharon Skildum, Maple Grove, MN

Prep: 10 min. • **Bake:** 35 min.
Makes: 8 servings

- 1½ lbs. ground beef
- 1 medium green pepper, chopped, optional
- 1 medium onion, chopped
- ½ lb. sliced fresh mushrooms
- 1 can (15 oz.) pizza sauce
- 1 tsp. dried basil
- 3 cups shredded part-skim mozzarella cheese
- 1 pkg. (32 oz.) frozen Tater Tots
- 1 cup shredded cheddar cheese

1. In a large skillet, cook the beef, green pepper if desired, onion and mushrooms over medium heat until meat is no longer pink, breaking it into crumbles; drain. Add pizza sauce and basil.

2. Transfer to a greased 3-qt. or 13x9-in. baking dish. Top with the mozzarella cheese and potatoes. Bake, uncovered, at 400° until potatoes are lightly browned, 30-35 minutes.

3. Sprinkle with cheddar cheese; bake until cheese is melted, 5 minutes.

1 SERVING: 572 cal., 32g fat (13g sat. fat), 96mg chol., 1081mg sod., 41g carb. (7g sugars, 5g fiber), 36g pro.

SLOPPY JOE VEGGIE CASSEROLE

My family adores this dynamic duo of sloppy joes and pasta, and you'll love how simple it is to prepare—all in one pan.
—Sue Schmidtke, Oro Valley, AZ

Prep: 25 min. • Bake: 30 min.
Makes: 8 servings

- 2½ cups uncooked penne pasta
- 1 lb. ground beef
- 1 small onion, chopped
- 1 pkg. (16 oz.) frozen mixed vegetables
- 1½ cups water
- 1 can (15 oz.) tomato sauce
- 1 can (6 oz.) tomato paste
- 1 envelope sloppy joe mix
- 1 Tbsp. dried parsley flakes
- ½ tsp. dried oregano
- 2 cups 2% cottage cheese
- 1½ cups shredded Colby-Monterey Jack cheese, divided

1. Cook the pasta according to the package directions.

2. Meanwhile, cook beef and onion in a large skillet over medium heat until the meat is no longer pink, breaking it into crumbles; drain. Add vegetables, water, tomato sauce, tomato paste, sloppy joe mix, parsley and oregano. Bring to a boil. Reduce the heat; simmer, uncovered, 7-9 minutes or until vegetables are crisp-tender. Drain the pasta; stir into the beef mixture.

3. Spoon half the mixture into a greased 13x9-in. baking dish. Top with cottage cheese, ¾ cup Colby-Monterey Jack cheese and the remaining pasta mixture.

4. Cover and bake at 350° for 25 minutes. Uncover; sprinkle with remaining Colby-Monterey Jack cheese. Bake 5-10 minutes longer or until bubbly and cheese is melted.

1¼ CUPS: 433 cal., 16g fat (9g sat. fat), 59mg chol., 1127mg sod., 40g carb. (11g sugars, 5g fiber), 31g pro.

READER REVIEW

"Loved it! My 7-year-old even asked for seconds, and that never happens!"

DILIGENTFROG, TASTEOFHOME.COM

EGGPLANT ROLL-UPS

We crave these easy Italian roll-ups stuffed with creamy ricotta and spinach. The fact that they are vegetarian is a bonus!
—Laura Haugen, Portland, OR

Prep: 50 min. • **Bake:** 20 min.
Makes: 6 servings

2   medium eggplants (about 2½ lbs.)
     Cooking spray
½   tsp. salt
3   cups fresh spinach leaves

SAUCE
1   Tbsp. olive oil
2   garlic cloves, minced
1   can (14½ oz.) diced tomatoes
1   can (15 oz.) tomato puree
3   Tbsp. minced fresh basil or
     3 tsp. dried basil
2   tsp. sugar
1   tsp. dried oregano
¼   tsp. salt
¼   tsp. pepper

FILLING
1   carton (15 oz.) reduced-fat
     ricotta cheese
¼   cup grated Parmesan cheese
½   tsp. dried oregano
¼   tsp. pepper
     Dash ground nutmeg

TOPPING
¼   cup grated Parmesan cheese
3   Tbsp. panko bread crumbs
     Minced fresh parsley, optional

1. Preheat oven to 400°. Cut the eggplant lengthwise into eighteen ¼-in.-thick slices, reserving leftover pieces. Line 2 baking sheets with foil. Coat both sides of the eggplant with cooking spray; place in a single layer on prepared pans. Sprinkle eggplant with ½ tsp. salt. Bake until just pliable (do not soften completely), 10-12 minutes; cool slightly.

2. Meanwhile, in a large saucepan, bring ½ in. of water to a boil. Add spinach; cover and boil 2-3 minutes or until wilted. Drain spinach and squeeze dry. Chop spinach and set aside.

3. Finely chop leftover eggplant to measure 1 cup (discard remaining or save for another use). In a large saucepan, heat oil over medium heat. Add chopped eggplant; cook and stir until tender. Add garlic; cook 1 minute longer. Stir in tomatoes, puree, basil, sugar, oregano, salt and pepper. Bring to a boil. Reduce heat; simmer, uncovered, 8-10 minutes or until flavors are blended.

4. Spread 1 cup sauce into a 13x9-in. baking dish coated with cooking spray. In a small bowl, combine filling ingredients and spinach. Place a rounded Tbsp. of filling on the wide end of each eggplant slice; carefully roll up. Place roll-ups over sauce, seam side down. Top with 1½ cups sauce. In a small bowl, mix Parmesan cheese and bread crumbs; sprinkle over the top. Bake until heated through and bubbly, 20-25 minutes. Serve with remaining sauce and, if desired, sprinkle with parsley.

3 ROLL-UPS: 257 cal., 10g fat (3g sat. fat), 23mg chol., 652mg sod., 28g carb. (14g sugars, 8g fiber), 12g pro. **DIABETIC EXCHANGES:** 2 starch, 2 medium-fat meat, ½ fat.

POTATO SAUSAGE CASSEROLE

The subtle spices in the pork sausage give this dish a distinctive flavor we have loved for years. The casserole tastes divine when served hot and fresh, but it reheats nicely, too.
—*Fred Osborn, Thayer, KS*

Prep: 20 min. • **Bake:** 65 min.
Makes: 6 servings

- 1 lb. bulk pork sausage
- 1 can (10¾ oz.) condensed cream of mushroom soup, undiluted
- ¾ cup 2% milk
- ½ cup chopped onion
- ½ tsp. salt
- ¼ tsp. pepper
- 3 cups sliced peeled potatoes
- 2 cups shredded cheddar cheese
  Minced fresh parsley, optional

1. Preheat oven to 350°. In a large skillet, cook sausage over medium heat until no longer pink, breaking into crumbles; drain and set aside. Combine soup, milk, onion, salt and pepper.
2. In a greased 2-qt. baking dish, layer half the potatoes, soup mixture and sausage. Repeat layers.
3. Cover and bake until potatoes are tender, 60-65 minutes. Sprinkle with the cheese; bake, uncovered, until cheese is melted, 2-3 minutes. If desired, garnish with parsley.
1 CUP: 430 cal., 29g fat (15g sat. fat), 77mg chol., 1130mg sod., 25g carb. (4g sugars, 2g fiber), 17g pro.

CONTEST-WINNING HOT CHICKEN SALAD

After I tasted this chicken salad at a women's luncheon, I left with the recipe in hand. I was our city clerk for several years, and on election days I brought this to serve our poll workers for lunch. It got everyone's vote of approval! I've found it is also delicious stuffed in a tomato.
—*Ruth Glabe, Oronoco, MN*

Prep: 30 min. • **Bake:** 30 min.
Makes: 8 servings

- 2 lbs. boneless skinless chicken breasts
- 2 bay leaves
- 4 cups diced celery
- 1 can (10½ oz.) condensed cream of chicken soup, undiluted
- 2 cups mayonnaise
- 2 cups sour cream
- 2 cans (8 oz. each) water chestnuts, drained
- 1 can (8 oz.) mushroom stems and pieces, drained
- 1 cup slivered almonds
- 2 Tbsp. chopped onion
- 2 Tbsp. lemon juice
- 2 tsp. salt
- ½ tsp. pepper
- 2 cups shredded cheddar cheese
- 2 cans (2.8 oz. each) french-fried onions
  Chopped green onions, optional

1. Preheat oven to 350°. Place the chicken in a Dutch oven and cover with water; add bay leaves. Bring to a boil. Cook, uncovered, until chicken juices run clear. Remove chicken and cut into ½-in. cubes; place in a large bowl. Stir in the next 11 ingredients.
2. Transfer to a 13x9-in. baking dish (dish will be full). Sprinkle with the cheese and french-fried onions. Bake, uncovered, until heated through, about 30 minutes. Garnish with green onions, if desired.
1½ CUPS: 1003 cal., 83g fat (23g sat. fat), 112mg chol., 1697mg sod., 27g carb. (6g sugars, 5g fiber), 36g pro.

ACAPULCO DELIGHT

This Mexican-inspired dish always delights my family and friends.
—*Margene Skaggs, Guinda, CA*

Prep: 25 min. • **Bake:** 25 min.
Makes: 10 servings

- 2 **lbs. ground beef**
- 1 **envelope (1¼ oz.) taco seasoning**
- ¾ **cup water**
- 1 **bottle (15 oz.) mild green taco sauce**
- 9 **flour tortillas (6 in.)**
- 2 **cups shredded cheddar cheese**
- 1 **can (16 oz.) refried beans**
- 2 **cups sour cream**
- 4 **green onions, chopped**
- 1 **can (2¼ oz.) sliced ripe olives, drained**
  Optional: Chopped tomatoes and chopped avocados

1. Preheat oven to 350°. In a large skillet, cook and crumble beef over medium heat until no longer pink; drain. Stir in taco seasoning and water. Add taco sauce; simmer until slightly thickened, 5-10 minutes.
2. Cover the bottom of a 13x9-in. baking dish with 3 tortillas, tearing them into pieces as necessary. Layer half the meat mixture over tortillas; sprinkle with half the cheese. Layer with 3 more tortillas; spread with the refried beans. Cover with sour cream; sprinkle with green onions and olives. Layer remaining tortillas over top; cover with the remaining meat mixture and cheese. Bake until heated through, 25-30 minutes. Let stand a few minutes before serving. If desired, serve with chopped tomatoes and avocados.
1 PIECE: 468 cal., 27g fat (14g sat. fat), 104mg chol., 1064mg sod., 26g carb. (3g sugars, 3g fiber), 28g pro.

LASAGNA WITH WHITE SAUCE

I'm an old-fashioned country cook and love preparing simple recipes like this lasagna. White sauce, tomatoes and beef are kitchen staples I normally keep on hand, so it's simple to make this dish on weeknights.
—*Angie Price, Bradford, TN*

Prep: 40 min. • **Bake:** 40 min.
Makes: 12 servings

- 1 **lb. ground beef**
- 1 **large onion, chopped**
- 1 **can (14½ oz.) diced tomatoes, undrained**
- 2 **Tbsp. tomato paste**
- 1 **tsp. beef bouillon granules**
- 1½ **tsp. Italian seasoning**
- 1 **tsp. salt**
- ½ **tsp. pepper**
- ¼ **tsp. cayenne pepper**

WHITE SAUCE

- 2 **Tbsp. butter**
- 3 **Tbsp. all-purpose flour**
- 1 **tsp. salt**
- ¼ **tsp. pepper**
- 2 **cups 2% milk**
- 1¼ **cups shredded mozzarella cheese, divided**
- 10 **to 12 uncooked lasagna noodles**
  Minced fresh parsley, optional

1. In a Dutch oven, cook beef and onion over medium heat until the meat is no longer pink, breaking it into crumbles; drain. Add tomatoes, tomato paste, bouillon and seasonings. Cover and cook over medium-low heat 20 minutes, stirring occasionally.
2. Meanwhile, melt butter in a large saucepan; stir in the flour, salt and pepper until blended. Gradually add milk. Bring to a boil; cook and stir until thickened, about 1 minute. Remove from heat and stir in half the cheese; set aside.
3. Pour half the meat sauce into an ungreased 13x9-in. baking dish. Layer with half the lasagna noodles and remaining meat sauce. Top with remaining noodles. Pour white sauce over noodles. Sprinkle with remaining cheese.
4. Cover and bake at 400° until bubbly and noodles are tender, 40 minutes. If desired, uncover and broil 5-6 in. from heat until lightly browned, about 2 minutes. Sprinkle with parsley as desired.
1 PIECE: 232 cal., 10g fat (5g sat. fat), 38mg chol., 639mg sod., 22g carb. (5g sugars, 1g fiber), 14g pro.

TURKEY ENCHILADA LASAGNA

Everyone will devour this layered southwestern casserole when you bring it to the table. The dish boasts familiar enchilada flavors in every mouthwatering bite. Feel free to use ground beef in place of the ground turkey if you'd like.
—*Julie Cackler, West Des Moines, IA*

Prep: 25 min. • **Bake:** 20 min. + standing
Makes: 8 servings

- 1 lb. lean ground turkey
- 1 large onion, chopped
- 1 large green pepper, chopped
- 1 small sweet red pepper, chopped
- 1 pkg. (8 oz.) fat-free cream cheese
- 1 tsp. chili powder
- 1 can (10 oz.) enchilada sauce
- 6 whole wheat flour tortillas (8 in.)
- 1 cup shredded reduced-fat Mexican cheese blend
  Optional: Salsa and sour cream

1. Preheat oven to 400°. In a large skillet, cook turkey, onion and peppers over medium-high heat until turkey is no longer pink, breaking turkey into crumbles, 5-7 minutes. Stir in cream cheese and chili powder.
2. Pour the enchilada sauce into a shallow bowl. Dip tortillas in the sauce to coat. Place 2 tortillas in a 13x9-in. baking dish coated with cooking spray; spread with half the turkey mixture. Sprinkle with 1/3 cup cheese. Repeat layers. Top casserole with remaining tortillas and cheese.
3. Bake, uncovered, until heated through and cheese is melted, 20-25 minutes. Let stand 10 minutes before serving. If desired, serve with salsa and sour cream.
FREEZE OPTION: Cover and freeze unbaked lasagna. To use, partially thaw in refrigerator overnight. Remove from the refrigerator 30 minutes before baking. Preheat oven to 400°. Bake lasagna as directed, increasing time as necessary to heat through and for a thermometer inserted in center to read 165°.
1 PIECE: 282 cal., 11g fat (3g sat. fat), 57mg chol., 697mg sod., 27g carb. (2g sugars, 2g fiber), 22g pro. **DIABETIC EXCHANGES:** 2 lean meat, 1½ starch, 1 fat.

VEGETARIAN POTATO AU GRATIN

Fill up on veggies and load up on fantastic flavor with this creamy entree. The homey bread-crumb topping and hands-free bake time are appreciated at the end of a long day.
—*Taste of Home* Test Kitchen

Prep: 15 min. • **Bake:** 50 min. + standing
Makes: 6 servings

- 3 medium carrots, thinly sliced
- 1 medium green pepper, chopped
- 4 Tbsp. butter, divided
- 3 Tbsp. all-purpose flour
- 1 tsp. dried oregano
- ½ tsp. salt
- 2½ cups 2% milk
- 1 can (15 oz.) black beans, rinsed and drained
- 3 cups shredded Swiss cheese, divided
- 4 medium Yukon Gold potatoes, thinly sliced
- ½ cup seasoned bread crumbs

1. Preheat oven to 400°. In a large saucepan, saute the carrots and pepper in 3 Tbsp. butter until tender. Stir in flour, oregano and salt until blended; gradually add milk. Bring to a boil; cook and stir 2 minutes or until thickened. Stir in beans and 2 cups cheese until cheese is melted.
2. Layer half the potatoes and sauce in a greased 13x9-in. baking dish; repeat layers. Sprinkle with the remaining cheese. In a microwave, melt the remaining butter. Stir in bread crumbs. Sprinkle over top.
3. Cover and bake 50-55 minutes. Let stand 10 minutes before serving.
1 SERVING: 557 cal., 25g fat (16g sat. fat), 77mg chol., 749mg sod., 56g carb. (12g sugars, 7g fiber), 27g pro.

> **DID YOU KNOW?**
> Rich in fiber, folate, magnesium, thiamin and phosphorous, black beans are a smart ingredient to add to any meatless casserole.

NACHO CHICKEN

I have been serving this rich and zippy chicken casserole for years, and it's a favorite of my family and friends. It disappears quickly at bring-a-dish gatherings, too.
—*Thom Britton, Three Rivers, MI*

Prep: 15 min. • **Bake:** 30 min.
Makes: 10 servings

- 4 cups cubed cooked chicken
- 1 lb. Velveeta, cubed
- 2 cans (10¾ oz. each) condensed cream of chicken soup, undiluted
- 1 can (10 oz.) diced tomatoes and green chiles, undrained
- 1 cup chopped onion
- ½ tsp. garlic salt
- ¼ tsp. pepper
- 1 pkg. (14½ oz.) nacho cheese tortilla chips
  Optional: Sliced jalapeno pepper and diced tomato

In a large bowl, combine first 7 ingredients; mix well. Crush chips; set aside 1 cup for topping. Add remaining chips to chicken mixture. Spoon into a greased 13x9-in. baking dish; sprinkle with the reserved chips. Bake, uncovered, at 350° until cheese is melted and edges are bubbly, 30 minutes. Serve with sliced jalapenos and diced tomatoes if desired.

1 CUP: 496 cal., 27g fat (11g sat. fat), 81mg chol., 1299mg sod., 32g carb. (8g sugars, 2g fiber), 29g pro.

CHILI BEEF CORNBREAD CASSEROLE

This recipe is my potluck standby. And when I hear that someone may need a comforting home-cooked meal, I bring them this casserole.
—*Lorraine Espenhain, Corpus Christi, TX*

Prep: 25 min. • **Bake:** 25 min.
Makes: 6 servings

- 1 lb. ground beef
- 1 Tbsp. cornstarch
- 1 Tbsp. dried minced onion
- 1 tsp. chili powder
- ½ tsp. garlic powder
- 1 can (15 oz.) tomato sauce
- ¾ cup all-purpose flour
- ¾ cup yellow cornmeal
- 3 Tbsp. sugar
- 2 tsp. baking powder
- 2 large eggs
- ½ cup 2% milk
- 3 Tbsp. canola oil
- 1 can (8¼ oz.) cream-style corn
- 1 cup shredded cheddar cheese
  Optional: Sour cream and salsa

1. Preheat oven to 375°. In a large skillet, cook beef over medium heat 6-8 minutes or until no longer pink, breaking into crumbles; drain. Stir in cornstarch, onion, chili powder and garlic powder. Stir in the tomato sauce. Cook and stir 2 minutes or until thickened. Remove from the heat.

2. In a large bowl, whisk flour, cornmeal, sugar and baking powder. In another bowl, whisk eggs, milk and oil until blended; stir in corn. Add to flour mixture; stir just until moistened. Stir in cheese.

3. Spread half the batter into a greased 2-qt. baking dish. Top with beef mixture. Spread remaining batter over filling.

4. Bake, uncovered, until a toothpick inserted in the cornbread portion comes out clean, 25-30 minutes. Let stand 5 minutes before serving. If desired, serve with sour cream and salsa.

1 PIECE: 482 cal., 22g fat (9g sat. fat), 130mg chol., 773mg sod., 46g carb. (10g sugars, 3g fiber), 25g pro.

BROCCOLI TUNA CASSEROLE

When I was in the Navy, a co-worker's wife shared this recipe with me. I've tweaked it over the years, but it still brings back memories of my family away from home.
—*Yvonne Cook, Haskins, OH*

Prep: 35 min.
Bake: 1 hour
Makes: 8 servings

- 5 cups uncooked whole wheat egg noodles
- 1 tsp. butter
- ¼ cup chopped onion
- ¼ cup cornstarch
- 2 cups fat-free milk
- 1 tsp. dried basil
- 1 tsp. dried thyme
- ¾ tsp. salt
- ½ tsp. pepper
- 1 cup reduced-sodium chicken broth
- 1 cup shredded Monterey Jack cheese, divided
- 4 cups frozen broccoli florets, thawed
- 2 pouches (6.4 oz. each) albacore white tuna in water
- ⅓ cup panko bread crumbs
- 1 Tbsp. butter, melted

1. Preheat oven to 350°. Cook the noodles according to the package directions; drain. Transfer to a shallow 3-qt. or 13x9-in. baking dish coated with cooking spray.
2. Meanwhile, in a large nonstick skillet, heat butter over medium-high heat. Add onion; cook and stir until tender. In a small bowl, whisk cornstarch, milk and seasonings until smooth; stir into pan. Stir in broth. Bring to a boil; cook and stir until thickened, about 2 minutes. Stir in ¾ cup cheese until melted; stir in broccoli and tuna.
3. Spoon over noodles; mix well. Sprinkle with remaining cheese. Toss bread crumbs with melted butter; sprinkle over casserole. Bake, covered, 45 minutes. Uncover and bake until cheese is melted, 15-20 minutes longer.

FREEZE OPTION: Cool unbaked casserole; cover and freeze. To use, partially thaw in the refrigerator overnight. Remove from refrigerator 30 minutes before baking. Preheat oven to 350°. Bake the casserole as directed, increasing time as necessary to heat through and for a thermometer inserted in center to read 165°.

1¼ CUPS: 271 cal., 8g fat (4g sat. fat), 38mg chol., 601mg sod., 30g carb. (4g sugars, 4g fiber), 22g pro. **DIABETIC EXCHANGES:** 2 starch, 2 lean meat, ½ fat.

CRUNCHY WHITE BAKED MACARONI & CHEESE

This creamy, bubbly, indulgent classic is down-home comfort food at its finest. The topping is made with panko bread crumbs for an extra bit of crunch.
—*Nicole Duffy, New Haven, CT*

Prep: 25 min. • **Bake:** 30 min. + standing.
Makes: 8 servings

- 1 pkg. (16 oz.) uncooked elbow macaroni
- 1 can (12 oz.) evaporated milk
- 1 cup whole milk
- 1 lb. white deli cheese, cubed
- 8 oz. cubed white cheddar cheese
- 1½ cups panko bread crumbs
- ½ cup grated Parmesan cheese
- ½ tsp. dried parsley flakes

1. In a large saucepan, cook the macaroni according to package directions. Drain and set aside.
2. In same saucepan, combine evaporated milk, whole milk, deli cheese and cheddar cheese. Cook and stir until cheeses are melted and mixture is smooth. Stir in macaroni; heat through. Transfer to a greased 13x9-in. baking dish. Combine the bread crumbs, Parmesan cheese and parsley flakes; sprinkle over the macaroni mixture. Cover and bake at 350° for 20 minutes. Uncover; bake until bubbly and golden brown, 10-15 minutes longer. Let stand 10 minutes before serving.

1 CUP: 639 cal., 31g fat (18g sat. fat), 104mg chol., 1091mg sod., 61g carb. (11g sugars, 2g fiber), 30g pro.

BEEFY EGGPLANT PARMIGIANA

I developed this recipe one summer when my husband grew eggplant. I was thrilled when it won high honors at a national beef contest.
—*Celeste Copper, Baton Rouge, LA*

- -

Prep: 50 + simmering
Bake: 35 min. + standing
Makes: 8 servings

- ⅓ cup chopped onion
- ¼ cup finely chopped celery
- ⅛ tsp. garlic powder
- 2 Tbsp. canola oil
- 1 can (14½ oz.) Italian stewed tomatoes
- ½ cup water
- ¼ cup tomato paste
- 1 tsp. dried parsley flakes
- ½ tsp. dried oregano
- 1¼ tsp. salt, divided
- ½ tsp. pepper, divided
- 1 bay leaf
- 1 lb. ground beef
- 1½ cups all-purpose flour
- 1 cup buttermilk
- 2 medium eggplants, peeled and cut into ½-in. slices
  Additional canola oil
- ½ cup grated Parmesan cheese
- 2 cups shredded part-skim mozzarella cheese, divided
  Minced fresh parsley

1. In a large saucepan, saute onion, celery and garlic powder in oil until tender. Stir in the tomatoes, water, tomato paste, parsley, oregano, ½ tsp. salt, ¼ tsp. pepper and bay leaf. Bring to a boil. Reduce heat; cover and simmer for 1 hour. Discard bay leaf.

2. In a large skillet, cook beef over medium heat until no longer pink, breaking into crumbles; drain and set aside. In a shallow dish, combine flour and remaining salt and pepper. Place the buttermilk in another shallow dish. Dip eggplant in buttermilk, then in flour mixture.

3. In a large skillet, cook eggplant in batches in ½ in. of hot oil until golden brown on each side; drain.

4. Place half the eggplant in a greased 13x9-in. baking dish. Top with half the Parmesan cheese, beef and tomato mixture. Sprinkle with 1 cup mozzarella cheese. Top with the remaining eggplant, Parmesan cheese, beef and tomato mixture.

5. Bake, uncovered, at 350° for 30 minutes or until heated through. Sprinkle with the remaining mozzarella cheese. Bake until the cheese is melted, 5-10 minutes longer. Let stand for 10 minutes before serving. Sprinkle with parsley.

1 CUP: 498 cal., 33g fat (8g sat. fat), 58mg chol., 841mg sod., 27g carb. (4g sugars, 2g fiber), 22g pro.

THAI PEANUT CHICKEN CASSEROLE

I used traditional pizza sauce and toppings in this recipe for years. After becoming a fan of Thai peanut chicken pizza, I decided to use those flavors instead. Serve this dish with stir-fried vegetables or a salad with sesame dressing for an easy, delicious meal.
—Katherine Wollgast, Troy, MO

- -

Prep: 30 min. • **Bake:** 40 min.
Makes: 10 servings

- 2 tubes (12 oz. each) refrigerated buttermilk biscuits
- 3 cups shredded cooked chicken
- 1 cup sliced fresh mushrooms
- 1 bottle (11½ oz.) Thai peanut sauce, divided
- 2 cups shredded mozzarella cheese, divided
- ½ cup chopped sweet red pepper
- ½ cup shredded carrot
- 4 green onions, sliced
- ¼ cup honey-roasted peanuts, coarsely chopped

1. Preheat oven to 350°. Cut each biscuit into 4 pieces. Place in a greased 13x9-in. baking pan.
2. In a large bowl, combine the chicken, mushrooms and 1 cup peanut sauce; spread over biscuits. Top with 1 cup cheese, the red pepper, carrot and green onions. Sprinkle with remaining cheese.
3. Bake until topping is set, cheese is melted and biscuits have cooked all the way through, about 40 minutes. Sprinkle with peanuts and serve with remaining peanut sauce.
1 SERVING: 490 cal., 25g fat (8g sat. fat), 55mg chol., 1013mg sod., 43g carb. (13g sugars, 1g fiber), 26g pro.

READER REVIEW
"Absolutely delicious and very easy to make. I followed the recipe, but it was just my wife and I so I got to enjoy leftovers all week for lunch while at work. Ten out of ten. Will make again."
MICHAEL, TASTEOFHOME.COM

CHICKEN & RICE CASSEROLE

Everyone loves this classic casserole because it's a tasty combination of hearty ingredients mixed in a creamy sauce. The crushed potato chips take it over the top!
—*Myrtle Matthews, Marietta, GA*

Prep: 15 min. • **Bake:** 1 hour
Makes: 12 servings

- 4 cups cooked white rice or a combination of wild and white rice
- 4 cups diced cooked chicken
- ½ cup slivered almonds
- 1 small onion, chopped
- 1 can (8 oz.) sliced water chestnuts, drained
- 1 pkg. (10 oz.) frozen peas, thawed
- ¾ cup chopped celery
- 1 can (10¾ oz.) condensed cream of celery soup, undiluted
- 1 can (10¾ oz.) condensed cream of chicken soup, undiluted
- 1 cup mayonnaise
- 2 tsp. lemon juice
- 1 tsp. salt
- 2 cups crushed potato chips Paprika

1. Preheat oven to 350°. In a greased 13x9-in. baking dish, combine the first 7 ingredients. In a large bowl, combine soups, mayonnaise, lemon juice and salt. Pour over the chicken mixture and toss to coat.

2. Sprinkle with potato chips and paprika. Bake until heated through, about 1 hour.

1 CUP: 439 cal., 26g fat (5g sat. fat), 51mg chol., 804mg sod., 31g carb. (3g sugars, 3g fiber), 19g pro.

❄ LAYERED BEEF CASSEROLE

On my busy days, I treasure meal-in-one recipes like this one. Toss together a salad, and dinner is ready in no time.
—*Dorothy Wiedeman, Eaton, CO*

Prep: 25 min. • **Bake:** 2 hours + standing
Makes: 8 servings

- 6 medium potatoes, peeled and thinly sliced
- 1 can (15¼ oz.) whole kernel corn, drained
- ½ cup chopped green pepper
- 1 cup chopped onion
- 2 cups sliced fresh carrots
- 1½ lbs. lean ground beef (90% lean)
- 1 can (8 oz.) tomato sauce Salt and pepper to taste
- 1 cup shredded Velveeta

1. In a greased 13x9-in. baking dish, layer the potatoes, corn, green pepper, onion and carrots. Crumble beef over vegetables. Pour tomato sauce over top. Sprinkle with salt and pepper.

2. Cover and bake at 350° for 2 hours or until the meat is no longer pink and a thermometer reads 160°. Sprinkle with cheese. Let stand for 10 minutes before serving.

FREEZE OPTION: Before baking, cover and freeze for up to 3 months. Thaw in the refrigerator overnight and bake as directed, increasing time as needed to reach 160°. Sprinkle with cheese before serving.

1 SERVING: 341 cal., 11g fat (5g sat. fat), 64mg chol., 526mg sod., 35g carb. (8g sugars, 4g fiber), 23g pro.

SPINACH LASAGNA ROLL-UPS

One night friends on a tight schedule stopped by. I invited them to stay for dinner, so I needed something I could fix in short order. I created these savory roll-ups, featuring a creamy three-cheese filling. They taste like lasagna but bake in a fraction of the time.
—*Julia Trachsel, Victoria, BC*

Prep: 30 min. • **Bake:** 25 min.
Makes: 6 servings

- 12 uncooked lasagna noodles
- 2 large eggs, lightly beaten
- 1 pkg. (10 oz.) frozen chopped spinach, thawed and squeezed dry
- 2½ cups whole-milk ricotta cheese
- 2½ cups shredded part-skim mozzarella cheese
- ½ cup grated Parmesan cheese
- ¼ tsp. salt
- ¼ tsp. pepper
- ¼ tsp. ground nutmeg
- 1 jar (24 oz.) meatless pasta sauce

1. Preheat oven to 375°. Cook the noodles according to package directions; drain. Meanwhile, mix the eggs, spinach, cheeses and seasonings.
2. Pour 1 cup pasta sauce into an ungreased 13x9-in. baking dish. Spread ⅓ cup cheese mixture over each noodle; roll up and place over sauce, seam side down. Top the rolls with the remaining sauce. Bake, covered, 20 minutes. Uncover; bake until heated through, 5-10 minutes longer.
2 ROLL-UPS: 569 cal., 22g fat (13g sat. fat), 145mg chol., 1165mg sod., 57g carb. (17g sugars, 5g fiber), 38g pro.

LEFTOVER TURKEY TETRAZZINI

This casserole turns leftover turkey into a brand new meal. We look forward to it after Christmas and Thanksgiving and any other time I roast a turkey for a family gathering.
—*Susan Payne, Corner Brook, NL*

Prep: 25 min. • **Bake:** 25 min.
Makes: 6 servings

- 1 pkg. (7 oz.) thin spaghetti, broken in half
- 2 cups cubed cooked turkey
- 1 cup sliced fresh mushrooms
- 1 small onion, chopped
- 3 Tbsp. butter
- 1 can (10¾ oz.) condensed cream of mushroom soup, undiluted
- 1 cup 2% milk
- ½ tsp. poultry seasoning
- ⅛ tsp. ground mustard
- 1 cup shredded cheddar cheese
- 1 cup shredded part-skim mozzarella cheese
- 1 Tbsp. shredded Parmesan cheese Minced fresh parsley

1. Cook the spaghetti according to package directions. Drain and place in a greased 11x7-in. baking dish. Top with the cooked turkey; set aside.
2. In a large skillet, saute mushrooms and onion in butter until tender. Whisk in soup, milk, poultry seasoning and mustard until blended. Add cheddar cheese; cook and stir over medium heat until melted. Pour over the turkey.
3. Sprinkle with mozzarella and Parmesan cheeses (dish will be full). Bake, uncovered, at 350° for 25-30 minutes or until heated through. Sprinkle with parsley.
1 SERVING: 444 cal., 21g fat (12g sat. fat), 90mg chol., 685mg sod., 33g carb. (5g sugars, 2g fiber), 30g pro.

Slow-Cooker & Instant Pot® Dinners

Time-crunched cooks know that the easiest way to satisfy hungry appetites is with a piping-hot meal from a slow cooker or an electric pressure cooker. Lift the lid on some of our readers' all-time favorites!

COUNTRY CASSOULET

This bean stew is fantastic with fresh dinner rolls and your favorite salad. It's a hearty meal that's perfect after a long day in the garden.
—*Suzanne McKinley, Lyons, GA*

Prep: 20 min. + standing • **Cook:** 6 hours
Makes: 10 servings

- 1 lb. dried great northern beans
- 2 uncooked garlic-flavored pork sausage links
- 3 bacon strips, diced
- 1½ lbs. boneless pork, cut into 1-in. cubes
- 1 lb. boneless lamb, cut into 1-in. cubes
- 1½ cups chopped onion
- 3 garlic cloves, minced
- 2 tsp. salt
- 1 tsp. dried thyme
- 4 whole cloves
- 2 bay leaves
- 2½ cups chicken broth
- 1 can (8 oz.) tomato sauce

1. Rinse and sort beans; soak according to package directions. Drain and rinse beans, discarding liquid.
2. In a large skillet over medium-high heat, brown sausage links; transfer to a 5-qt. slow cooker. Add bacon to skillet; cook until crisp. Remove with a slotted spoon to slow cooker.
3. In the bacon drippings, cook the pork and lamb until browned on all sides. Place in the slow cooker. Stir in the beans and the remaining ingredients.
4. Cover and cook on low for 6-8 hours or until beans are tender. Discard cloves and bay leaves. Remove the sausage and cut into ¼-in. slices; return to slow cooker and stir gently.
1 CUP: 375 cal., 12g fat (4g sat. fat), 74mg chol., 950mg sod., 32g carb. (5g sugars, 10g fiber), 35g pro.

READER REVIEW

"Excellent! I have made cassoulet from a gourmet cookbook that has taken 2 days to make and this rivals that recipe!"

BLARNEY1, TASTEOFHOME.COM

⏱ PRESSURE-COOKER PORK CHOPS

Everyone will enjoy these fork-tender pork chops with a light gravy.
—*Sue Bingham, Madisonville, TN*

Prep: 15 min. • **Cook:** 5 min.
Makes: 4 servings

½ cup all-purpose flour, divided
½ tsp. ground mustard
½ tsp. garlic pepper blend
¼ tsp. seasoned salt
4 boneless pork loin chops (4 oz. each)
2 Tbsp. canola oil
1 can (14½ oz.) chicken broth, divided

1. In a shallow bowl, mix ¼ cup flour, mustard, garlic pepper and seasoned salt. Add pork chops, 1 at a time, and toss to coat; shake off excess.
2. Select saute or browning setting on a 6-qt. electric pressure cooker. Adjust for medium heat; add oil. When oil is hot, brown pork in batches. Add 1½ cups broth to pressure cooker. Cook 30 seconds, stirring to loosen browned bits from pan. Press cancel. Return all pork to pressure cooker.
3. Lock lid; close the pressure-release valve. Adjust to pressure-cook on high for 3 minutes. Quick-release the pressure. A thermometer inserted in pork should read at least 145°. Remove pork to a serving plate; keep warm.
4. In a bowl, mix remaining ¼ cup flour and ¼ cup broth until smooth; stir into pressure cooker. Select saute setting and adjust for low heat. Simmer, stirring constantly, until thickened, 1-2 minutes. Serve with pork.
1 PORK CHOP WITH ⅓ CUP GRAVY: 257 cal., 14g fat (3g sat. fat), 57mg chol., 606mg sod., 8g carb. (0 sugars, 0 fiber), 23g pro.

SLOW-COOKER THAI PEANUT CHICKEN WITH NOODLES

I serve this Thai favorite with noodles mixed into the sauce, but it's also wonderful over rice. Garnish with chopped green onion or cilantro for a pop of color and fresh flavor.
—*Catherine Cebula, Littleton, MA*

Prep: 35 min. • **Cook:** 2½ hours
Makes: 6 servings

1½ lbs. boneless skinless chicken breasts, cut into ¾ in. cubes
1 medium onion, chopped
¾ cup salsa
¼ cup creamy peanut butter
2 Tbsp. black bean sauce
1 Tbsp. reduced-sodium soy sauce
8 oz. uncooked linguine
1 Tbsp. canola oil
½ lb. sliced baby portobello mushrooms
Thinly sliced green onions, optional

1. Place the chicken and onion in a 4-qt. slow cooker. Combine salsa, peanut butter, bean sauce and soy sauce; add to the slow cooker. Cook, covered, on low until chicken is tender, 2½-3½ hours.
2. Meanwhile, prepare pasta according to package directions. In a large skillet, heat oil over medium-high heat. Add mushrooms; cook and stir until tender, 6-8 minutes. Drain pasta; stir into slow cooker. Stir in the mushrooms. If desired, sprinkle with green onions.
1⅓ CUPS: 378 cal., 11g fat (2g sat. fat), 63mg chol., 436mg sod., 37g carb. (5g sugars, 2g fiber), 32g pro.

1 pkg. (14 oz.) smoked turkey kielbasa, sliced
1 small head cabbage, cut into 1-in. pieces
4 medium carrots, sliced
4 small red potatoes, peeled and halved
1 cup vegetable broth
1 small onion, chopped
½ cup sauerkraut, rinsed and well drained
3 Tbsp. butter, cubed
½ tsp. garlic powder
¼ tsp. salt

Place all ingredients in a 6-qt. electric pressure cooker. Lock lid; close pressure-release valve. Adjust to pressure-cook on high for 6 minutes. Quick-release pressure.

1 SERVING: 318 cal., 14g fat (7g sat. fat), 85mg chol., 1552mg sod., 29g carb. (12g sugars, 8g fiber), 20g pro.

TENDER & TANGY RIBS

These ribs are so simple to prepare! Just brown them in a skillet and then combine them with the sauce ingredients in your slow cooker. Serve them for lunch, or let them cook all day for fall-off-the-bone tenderness.
—*Denise Hathaway Valasek, Perrysburg, OH*

Prep: 15 min. • **Cook:** 4 hours
Makes: 3 servings

¾ to 1 cup white vinegar
½ cup ketchup
2 Tbsp. sugar
2 Tbsp. Worcestershire sauce
1 garlic clove, minced
1 tsp. ground mustard
1 tsp. paprika
½ to 1 tsp. salt
⅛ tsp. pepper
2 lbs. pork spareribs
1 Tbsp. canola oil

Combine the first 9 ingredients in a 3-qt. slow cooker. Cut the ribs into serving-sized pieces; brown in a skillet in oil. Transfer ribs to slow cooker. Cover and cook on low for 4-6 hours or until tender.

1 CUP: 689 cal., 48g fat (16g sat. fat), 170mg chol., 1110mg sod., 22g carb. (13g sugars, 1g fiber), 42g pro.

SLOW-COOKED FLANK STEAK

My slow cooker gets lots of use, especially during the summer months when I don't want to heat up the kitchen. I can fix this flank steak in the morning and forget about it until dinner. Serve with noodles and a tossed salad.
—*Michelle Armistead, Keyport, NJ*

Prep: 15 min. • **Cook:** 4 hours
Makes: 6 servings

1 flank steak (about 1¼ lbs.), cut in half
1 Tbsp. canola oil
1 large onion, sliced
⅓ cup water
1 can (4 oz.) chopped green chiles
2 Tbsp. vinegar
1¼ tsp. chili powder
1 tsp. garlic powder
½ tsp. sugar
½ tsp. salt
⅛ tsp. pepper

In a skillet, brown the steak in oil; transfer to a 5-qt. slow cooker. In the same skillet, saute the onion for 1 minute. Gradually add water, stirring to loosen browned bits from pan. Add remaining ingredients; bring to a boil. Pour over the flank steak. Cover and cook on low until the meat is tender, 4-5 hours. Slice meat; serve with onion and pan juices.

3 OZ. COOKED BEEF: 199 cal., 11g fat (4g sat. fat), 48mg chol., 327mg sod., 4g carb. (2g sugars, 1g fiber), 20g pro.
DIABETIC EXCHANGES: 3 lean meat, ½ fat.

PRESSURE-COOKER KIELBASA & CABBAGE

My grandmother was Polish and made this often. It's an excellent one-pot meal. We enjoy our veggies soft, but if you like them a bit crisp, cook them for 5 minutes. Also, you can sub any precooked sausage for the kielbasa.
—*Beverly Dolfini, Surprise, AZ*

Prep: 25 min. • **Cook:** 10 min.
Makes: 4 servings

COUNTRY-STYLE PORK LOIN

This pork roast is so moist and tender that it melts in your mouth. My son puts it at the top of his list of most-loved foods. We enjoy it with mashed potatoes.
—*Corina Flansberg, Carson City, NV*

Prep: 20 min. • **Cook:** 5 hours + standing
Makes: 8 servings

- 1   boneless pork loin roast (3 lbs.)
- ½   cup all-purpose flour
- 1   tsp. onion powder
- 1   tsp. ground mustard
- 2   Tbsp. canola oil
- 2   cups reduced-sodium chicken broth
- ¼   cup cornstarch
- ¼   cup cold water
  Hot mashed potatoes, optional

1. Cut the roast in half. In a large shallow dish, combine the flour, onion powder and mustard. Add pork, 1 portion at a time, and turn to coat. In a large skillet, brown pork in oil on all sides.

2. Transfer to a 5-qt. slow cooker. Pour the broth over pork. Cover and cook on low for 5-6 hours or until tender. Remove pork and keep warm. Let pork stand for 10-15 minutes before slicing.

3. Strain cooking juices, reserving 2½ cups juices; skim fat from reserved juices. Transfer to a small saucepan. Bring the liquid to a boil. Combine cornstarch and water until smooth; gradually stir into the pan. Bring to a boil; cook and stir for 2 minutes or until thickened. Serve the pork and gravy with mashed potatoes if desired.

FREEZE OPTION: Cool pork and gravy. Freeze sliced pork and gravy in freezer containers. To use, partially thaw in refrigerator overnight. Heat through slowly in a covered skillet until heated through, stirring occasionally; add broth or water if necessary. Serve as directed.

5 OZ. COOKED MEAT WITH ¼ CUP GRAVY: 291 cal., 11g fat (3g sat. fat), 85mg chol., 204mg sod., 10g carb. (0 sugars, 0 fiber), 34g pro. **DIABETIC EXCHANGES:** 5 lean meat, ½ starch, ½ fat.

SLOW-COOKED BEEF BURRITOS WITH GREEN CHILES

I created this recipe years ago, and it has become such a favorite that the delightful aroma of it cooking makes my family instantly happy. It is hearty, flavorful and easy to prepare, and it uses the long, slow cook that truly defines comfort food.
—*Sally Pahler, Palisade, CO*

- -

Prep: 20 min. • **Cook:** 7 hours
Makes: 14 servings

- 2 garlic cloves, minced
- 1 tsp. salt
- 2 tsp. ground cumin
- 1 tsp. cayenne pepper
- 1 boneless beef chuck roast (4 lbs.)
- 1 can (28 oz.) diced tomatoes
- 4 cans (7 oz. each) whole green chiles, drained and coarsely chopped
- 1 large onion, diced
- 14 whole wheat tortillas (8 in.), warmed
  Optional toppings: Shredded cheddar cheese, salsa, sour cream, sliced ripe olives

1. Combine garlic, salt, cumin and cayenne; rub over roast. Place in a 5- or 6-qt. slow cooker. Add the tomatoes, chiles and onion. Cook, covered, on low 7-8 hours or until meat is tender.

2. Remove the roast from slow cooker; shred with 2 forks. Remove the vegetables with a slotted spoon; discard the cooking juices. Return the beef and vegetables to slow cooker and heat through. Serve in tortillas, with toppings as desired.

1 BURRITO: 355 cal., 13g fat (5g sat. fat), 84mg chol., 499mg sod., 28g carb. (4g sugars, 4g fiber), 30g pro. **DIABETIC EXCHANGES:** 4 lean meat, 2 starch.

SLOW-COOKER MAC & CHEESE

This classic casserole is a rich and cheesy meatless main dish. I've never met anyone who didn't ask for a second helping.
—*Bernice Glascoe, Roxboro, NC*

Prep: 15 min. • **Cook:** 3¾ hours
Makes: 10 servings

- 1 pkg. (16 oz.) elbow macaroni
- ½ cup butter, melted
- 4 cups shredded cheddar cheese, divided
- 1 can (12 oz.) evaporated milk
- 1 can (10¾ oz.) condensed cheddar cheese soup, undiluted
- 1 cup 2% milk
- 2 large eggs, beaten
- ⅛ tsp. paprika

1. Cook macaroni according to the package directions; drain. Place in a 5-qt. slow cooker; add butter. In a large bowl, mix 3 cups cheese, evaporated milk, condensed soup, 2% milk and eggs. Pour over the macaroni mixture; stir to combine. Cook, covered, on low for 3½-4 hours or until a thermometer reads at least 160°.

2. Sprinkle with remaining cheese. Cook, covered, on low until the cheese is melted, 15-20 minutes longer. Sprinkle with paprika.

1 SERVING: 502 cal., 28g fat (18g sat. fat), 131mg chol., 638mg sod., 42g carb. (7g sugars, 2g fiber), 21g pro.

LADONNA REED
Ponca City, OK

SLOW-COOKED BEEF & VEGGIES

My husband and I came up with this soothing slow-cooker recipe. It's simple and filling with lots of flavor.
—*LaDonna Reed, Ponca City, OK*

Prep: 15 min. + marinating • **Cook:** 8 hours
Makes: 2 servings

- 1 boneless beef top round steak (½ lb.), cut into 2 pieces
  Dash seasoned salt, optional
  Dash pepper
  Dash garlic powder
- 1 cup Italian salad dressing
- ½ cup water
- 1 Tbsp. browning sauce, optional
- 2 medium carrots, cut into 2-in. pieces
- 2 medium red potatoes, cubed
- 1 small onion, sliced
- ½ small green pepper, cut into small chunks

1. For each piece of steak, sprinkle 1 side with seasoned salt if desired and pepper; sprinkle the other side with garlic powder. Cover and refrigerate for 2-3 hours or overnight.

2. In a 3-qt. slow cooker, combine the salad dressing, water and, if desired, browning sauce. Add carrots and potatoes; toss to coat. Add steak and coat with sauce. Top with onion and green pepper.

3. Cover and cook on low until the meat is tender, 8-9 hours.

1 SERVING: 505 cal., 22g fat (3g sat. fat), 63mg chol., 1283mg sod., 36g carb. (14g sugars, 5g fiber), 29g pro.

TEST KITCHEN TIP
If there are any leftovers, allow them to cool, then refrigerate. Slow cookers should not be used to reheat leftovers. Instead, use a microwave, stovetop burner or oven to reheat foods to 165°. This ensures the food is safe to eat.

PRESSURE-COOKER SPICY LIME CHICKEN

This tender chicken with light lime flavor is a natural filling for tacos, but my son Austin also loves it spooned over cooked rice and sprinkled with his favorite taco toppings.
—*Christine Hair, Odessa, FL*

Prep: 10 min. • **Cook:** 10 min.
Makes: 6 servings

- 4 boneless skinless chicken breast halves (6 oz. each)
- 2 cups chicken broth
- 3 Tbsp. lime juice
- 1 Tbsp. chili powder
- 1 tsp. grated lime zest
  Fresh cilantro leaves, optional

1. Place chicken in a 6-qt. electric pressure cooker. Combine broth, lime juice and chili powder; pour over chicken. Lock lid; close pressure-release valve. Adjust to pressure-cook on high for 6 minutes.

2. Quick-release pressure. A thermometer inserted in chicken should read at least 165°.

3. Remove chicken. When cool enough to handle, shred meat with 2 forks; return to pressure cooker. Stir in lime zest. If desired, serve with cilantro.

FREEZE OPTION: Freeze cooled meat mixture in freezer containers. To use, partially thaw in refrigerator overnight. Microwave, covered, on high in a microwave-safe dish until heated through, stirring occasionally; add a little broth if necessary.

1 SERVING: 132 cal., 3g fat (1g sat. fat), 64mg chol., 420mg sod., 2g carb. (1g sugars, 1g fiber), 23g pro. **DIABETIC EXCHANGES:** 3 lean meat.

SWEET & SOUR RIBS

Looking for a change from typical barbecue ribs? You'll enjoy this recipe my mom always prepared on birthdays and special occasions. The tender ribs have a slight sweet-and-sour taste that my family adores. Serve them with garlic mashed potatoes and a salad or coleslaw.
—*Dorothy Voelz, Champaign, IL*

Prep: 10 min. • **Cook:** 8 hours
Makes: 8 servings

- 3 to 4 lbs. boneless country-style pork ribs
- 1 can (20 oz.) pineapple tidbits, undrained
- 2 cans (8 oz. each) tomato sauce
- ½ cup thinly sliced onion
- ½ cup thinly sliced green pepper
- ½ cup packed brown sugar
- ¼ cup cider vinegar
- ¼ cup tomato paste
- 2 Tbsp. Worcestershire sauce
- 1 garlic clove, minced
- ½ tsp. salt
- ½ tsp. pepper
- 1 Tbsp. cornstarch
- 1 Tbsp. cold water

1. Place ribs in an ungreased 5-qt. slow cooker. Combine the next 11 ingredients; pour over ribs. Cook, covered, on low until meat is tender, 8-10 hours.

2. To make sauce, transfer cooking juices to a small saucepan; bring to a boil. Meanwhile, in a small bowl, combine the cornstarch and water until smooth; stir into juices. Return to a boil, stirring constantly; cook and stir until thickened, 1-2 minutes. Serve with ribs.

1 SERVING: 392 cal., 16g fat (6g sat. fat), 98mg chol., 532mg sod., 30g carb. (25g sugars, 2g fiber), 32g pro.

1. Place vegetables and broth in a 6-qt. electric pressure cooker. Brush turkey with oil; sprinkle with seasonings. Place over vegetables.

2. Lock lid; close the pressure-release valve. Adjust to pressure-cook on high for 25 minutes. Let pressure release naturally for 10 minutes; quick-release any remaining pressure. A thermometer inserted in turkey breast should read at least 170°. Remove turkey from pressure cooker; tent with foil. Let stand 10 minutes before slicing.

1 SERVING: 308 cal., 13g fat (3g sat. fat), 106mg chol., 409mg sod., 5g carb. (2g sugars, 1g fiber), 41g pro. **DIABETIC EXCHANGES:** 5 lean meat, ½ fat.

PEAR & POMEGRANATE LAMB TAGINE

Pomegranate, pear and orange go together so well that I decided to use them to prepare a Middle Eastern-themed tagine with lamb. This tastes delicious served over couscous, polenta or cauliflower mashed with some feta cheese.
—*Arlene Erlbach, Morton Grove, IL*

Prep: 20 min. • **Cook:** 6 hours
Makes: 4 servings

- 2½ lbs. lamb shanks
- 2 large pears, finely chopped
- 3 cups thinly sliced shallots
- ½ cup orange juice, divided
- ½ cup pomegranate juice, divided
- 1 Tbsp. honey
- 1½ tsp. ground cinnamon
- 1 tsp. salt
- 1 tsp. ground allspice
- 1 tsp. ground cardamom
- ¼ cup pomegranate seeds
- ¼ cup minced fresh parsley
  Cooked couscous, optional

1. Place lamb in a 5- or 6-qt. oval slow cooker. Add the pears and shallots. Combine ¼ cup orange juice, ¼ cup pomegranate juice, the honey and seasonings; pour over shallots.

2. Cook, covered, on low 6-8 hours or until the meat is tender. Remove lamb to a rimmed serving platter; keep warm. Stir remaining orange and pomegranate juices into cooking liquid; pour over lamb. Sprinkle with the pomegranate seeds and parsley. If desired, serve over couscous.

½ LAMB SHANK WITH 1 CUP VEGETABLES: 438 cal., 13g fat (5g sat. fat), 99mg chol., 680mg sod., 52g carb. (28g sugars, 5g fiber), 31g pro.

CHICKEN IN SOUR CREAM SAUCE

Tender chicken is deliciously dressed up in a flavorful cream sauce with fresh mushrooms. This is an excellent entree when your family craves classic comfort food.
—*Jane Carlovsky, Sebring, FL*

Prep: 15 min. • **Cook:** 4 hours
Makes: 6 servings

- 1½ tsp. salt
- ¼ tsp. pepper
- ¼ tsp. paprika
- ¼ tsp. lemon-pepper seasoning
- 6 bone-in chicken breast halves, skin removed (7 oz. each)
- 1 can (10¾ oz.) condensed cream of mushroom soup, undiluted
- 1 cup sour cream
- ½ cup dry white wine or chicken broth
- ½ lb. fresh mushrooms, sliced
- ¼ cup water
- 2 Tbsp. cornstarch
  Additional paprika, optional

1. In a small bowl, combine the first 4 ingredients; rub over chicken. Place in a 3-qt. slow cooker. In a large bowl, combine the soup, sour cream and wine; stir in mushrooms. Pour over chicken.

2. Cover and cook on low for 4 hours or until meat is tender. In a small bowl, mix water and cornstarch until smooth; stir into the chicken mixture. Return to a boil, stirring constantly; cook and stir until thickened. If desired, sprinkle with additional paprika.

1 CHICKEN BREAST HALF: 317 cal., 13g fat (7g sat. fat), 118mg chol., 1065mg sod., 7g carb. (2g sugars, 1g fiber), 36g pro.

PRESSURE-COOKER ITALIAN TURKEY BREAST

This recipe makes some of the most succulent turkey I've ever eaten. High in lean protein, it's a smart dish for a special occasion.
—*Jessica Kunz, Springfield, IL*

Prep: 25 min. + standing
Cook: 25 min. + releasing
Makes: 14 servings

- 1 lb. carrots, cut into 2-in. pieces
- 2 medium onions, cut into wedges
- 3 celery ribs, cut into 2-in. pieces
- 1 can (14½ oz.) chicken broth
- 1 bone-in turkey breast (6 to 7 lbs.), thawed and skin removed
- 2 Tbsp. olive oil
- 1½ tsp. seasoned salt
- 1 tsp. Italian seasoning
- ½ tsp. pepper

ARLENE ERLBACH
Morton Grove, IL

SAGE TURKEY THIGHS

I created this for my boys, who love dark meat. It is more convenient than cooking a whole turkey and reminds me of our traditional Thanksgiving turkey that's seasoned with sage.
—*Natalie Swanson, Baltimore, MD*

Prep: 15 min. • **Cook:** 6 hours
Makes: 4 servings

- 4 medium carrots, halved
- 1 medium onion, chopped
- ½ cup water
- 2 garlic cloves, minced
- 1½ tsp. rubbed sage, divided
- 2 turkey thighs or turkey drumsticks (2 lbs. total), skin removed
- 1 Tbsp. cornstarch
- ¼ cup cold water
- ¼ tsp. salt
- ⅛ tsp. pepper
- 1 tsp. browning sauce, optional

1. In a 3-qt. slow cooker, combine the carrots, onion, water, garlic and 1 tsp. sage. Top with turkey. Sprinkle with remaining sage. Cover and cook on low for 6-8 hours or until a thermometer reads 170°-175°.

2. Remove turkey to a serving platter; keep warm. Strain broth, reserving vegetables. Skim fat from cooking juices; transfer to a small saucepan.

3. Place vegetables in a food processor; cover and process until smooth. Add to the cooking juices. Bring to a boil. Combine the cornstarch and water until smooth. Gradually stir into the pan. Add salt, pepper and, if desired, browning sauce. Bring to a boil; cook and stir 2 minutes or until thickened. Serve with turkey.

4 OZ. COOKED TURKEY: 277 cal., 8g fat (3g sat. fat), 96mg chol., 280mg sod., 15g carb. (0 sugars, 3g fiber), 34g pro. **DIABETIC EXCHANGES:** 4 lean meat, 3 vegetable.

SUPER EASY COUNTRY-STYLE RIBS

I'm a die-hard rib fan. When we were growing up, our mom made these for us all the time, and we still can't get enough of them.
—*Stephanie Loaiza, Layton, UT*

Prep: 10 min. • **Cook:** 5 hours
Makes: 4 servings

- 1½ cups ketchup
- ½ cup packed brown sugar
- ½ cup white vinegar
- 2 tsp. seasoned salt
- ½ tsp. liquid smoke, optional
- 2 lbs. boneless country-style pork ribs

1. In a 3-qt. slow cooker, mix ketchup, brown sugar, vinegar, seasoned salt and, if desired, liquid smoke. Add the ribs; turn to coat. Cook, covered, on low 5-6 hours or until meat is tender.

2. Remove pork to a serving plate. Skim fat from cooking liquid. If desired, transfer to a small saucepan to thicken; bring to a boil and cook 12-15 minutes or until sauce is reduced to 1½ cups. Serve with ribs.

TO MAKE AHEAD: In a large airtight container, combine ketchup, brown sugar, vinegar, seasoned salt and, if desired, liquid smoke. Add pork; cover and freeze. To use, place container in refrigerator 48 hours or until ribs are completely thawed. Cook as directed.

6 OZ. COOKED PORK: 550 cal., 21g fat (8g sat. fat), 131mg chol., 2003mg sod., 51g carb. (51g sugars, 0 fiber), 40g pro.

SLOW-COOKED RUMP ROAST

I enjoy a good pot roast, but I was tired of the same old thing so I started experimenting. Cooking the beef in horseradish sauce gives it a tangy flavor. Even my young children love this roast with its tender veggies and gravy.
—Mimi Walker, Palmyra, PA

Prep: 20 min. • **Cook:** 8½ hours
Makes: 8 servings

- 1 beef rump roast or bottom round roast (3 to 3½ lbs.)
- 2 Tbsp. canola oil
- 4 medium carrots, halved lengthwise and cut into 2-in. pieces
- 3 medium potatoes, peeled and cut into chunks
- 2 small onions, sliced
- ½ cup water
- 6 to 8 Tbsp. horseradish sauce
- ¼ cup red wine vinegar
- ¼ cup Worcestershire sauce
- 2 garlic cloves, minced
- 1½ to 2 tsp. celery salt
- 3 Tbsp. cornstarch
- ⅓ cup cold water

1. In a large skillet, brown roast on all sides in oil over medium-high heat; drain. Place carrots and potatoes in a 5-qt. slow cooker. Top with the meat and onions. Combine the water, horseradish sauce, red wine vinegar, Worcestershire sauce, garlic and celery salt; pour over the meat. Cover and cook on low until the meat and vegetables are tender, about 8 hours.
2. Combine cornstarch and cold water until smooth; stir into the slow cooker. Cover and cook on high until gravy is thickened, about 30 minutes.
1 SERVING: 378 cal., 15g fat (3g sat. fat), 113mg chol., 507mg sod., 23g carb. (6g sugars, 2g fiber), 35g pro. **DIABETIC EXCHANGES:** 4 lean meat, 1½ starch, 1 fat.

SLOW-COOKED CHICKEN & STUFFING

This tasty, no-fuss main dish has a flavorful blend of seasonings and the irresistible duo of tender chicken and moist dressing. It's nice enough for the holidays but easy enough to fix year-round.
—Angela Marquart, New Washington, OH

Prep: 25 min. • **Cook:** 4½ hours
Makes: 14 servings

- 2½ cups chicken broth
- 1 cup butter, cubed
- ½ cup chopped onion
- ½ cup chopped celery
- 1 can (4 oz.) mushroom stems and pieces, drained
- ¼ cup dried parsley flakes
- 1½ tsp. rubbed sage
- 1 tsp. poultry seasoning
- 1 tsp. salt
- ½ tsp. pepper
- 12 cups day-old bread cubes (½-in. pieces)
- 2 large eggs
- 1 can (10¾ oz.) condensed cream of chicken soup, undiluted
- 5 to 6 cups cubed cooked chicken

1. In a large saucepan, combine the first 10 ingredients. Simmer for 10 minutes; remove from the heat. Place bread cubes in a large bowl. Combine eggs and soup; stir into broth mixture until smooth. Pour over bread and toss well.
2. In a 5-qt. slow cooker, layer half each of the stuffing and the chicken; repeat layers. Cover and cook on low for 4½-5 hours or until a thermometer inserted into stuffing reads 160°.
1 SERVING: 332 cal., 20g fat (10g sat. fat), 109mg chol., 835mg sod., 18g carb. (2g sugars, 2g fiber), 19g pro.

READER REVIEW

"I made this for a church potluck and it turned out perfect. I got quite a few compliments on it. It was so handy. I will definitely make it again!"

SPARKLINGSEAMSTRESS,
TASTEOFHOME.COM

ROOT VEGETABLE POT ROAST

During the hectic holiday season, I make this roast often. We've scarfed it down before and after shopping, and while wrapping presents. Root vegetables and roast beef make everyone feel cozy and calm.
—*Pat Dazis, Charlotte, NC*

Prep: 30 min. • **Cook:** 7 hours
Makes: 8 servings

- 1   can (14½ oz.) reduced-sodium beef broth
- 2   chai black tea bags
- 2   medium potatoes (about 1 lb.), cut into 1½-in. cubes
- 2   medium turnips (about 9 oz.), cut into 1½-in. pieces
- 4   medium carrots, cut into ½-in. pieces
- 2   medium parsnips, peeled and cut into ½-in. pieces
- 1   large onion, cut into 1-in. wedges
- 2   celery ribs, cut into ½-in. pieces
- 1   Tbsp. olive oil
- 1   boneless beef chuck roast (about 3 lbs.)
- 1   tsp. salt
- ½   tsp. pepper
- 1   medium lemon, thinly sliced
- 3   Tbsp. cornstarch
- 3   Tbsp. cold water

1. In a small saucepan, bring broth to a boil; remove from heat. Add the tea bags; steep, covered, 3-5 minutes according to taste. Discard tea bags. Meanwhile, combine the vegetables in a 6-qt. slow cooker.

2. In a large skillet, heat oil over medium-high heat; brown the roast on all sides. Place over vegetables; pour tea-steeped broth over top. Sprinkle roast with salt and pepper; top with lemon slices. Cook, covered, on low until beef and vegetables are tender, 7-9 hours.

3. Discard lemon slices. Remove roast and vegetables from slow cooker; keep warm.

4. Transfer cooking juices to a saucepan; skim fat. Bring juices to a boil. In a small bowl, mix cornstarch and water until smooth; stir into juices. Return to a boil, stirring constantly; cook and stir until thickened, 1-2 minutes. Serve with roast and vegetables.

1 SERVING: 421 cal., 18g fat (7g sat. fat), 112mg chol., 523mg sod., 27g carb. (7g sugars, 5g fiber), 36g pro.

PRESSURE-COOKER PINEAPPLE CHICKEN

We love Hawaiian-style chicken in a slow cooker, but sometimes I need something that comes together fast. I tweaked our favorite recipe to work in a pressure cooker for a quick and easy weeknight dinner. Add a side salad for a complete meal.
—*Courtney Stultz, Weir, KS*

Prep: 10 min. • **Cook:** 20 min. + releasing
Makes: 6 servings

1½ lbs. boneless skinless chicken breasts
1 can (20 oz.) unsweetened pineapple chunks, undrained
¼ cup barbecue sauce
1 cup chicken broth
1 cup uncooked long grain brown rice
½ tsp. salt
Optional: Minced fresh cilantro and sliced green onions

1. Combine all non-optional ingredients in a 6-qt. electric pressure cooker. Lock lid; close pressure-release valve. Adjust to pressure-cook on high for 20 minutes.
2. Let pressure release naturally. Remove chicken to a cutting board and shred with 2 forks. Add shredded chicken back to pot and stir until combined. If desired, sprinkle with cilantro and green onions.

1 CUP: 313 cal., 4g fat (1g sat. fat), 63mg chol., 536mg sod., 41g carb. (16g sugars, 3g fiber), 27g pro. **DIABETIC EXCHANGES:** 3 lean meat, 2½ starch.

TEST KITCHEN TIP
On nights when you need to get dinner on the table fast, save time with the quick-release method. Waiting for the pressure to release naturally can sometimes take up to 30 minutes. Unless you're cooking something that might expel out of the top (such as a full pot of stock), don't wait for the pressure to release naturally. Let the pot naturally cool down for 10 minutes, then manually release the pressure. Be aware that steam is extremely hot, so be very careful when handling the cooker and food.

TENDER BEEF OVER NOODLES

I dress up thrifty stew meat with noodles and sweet red sauce for this satisfying main dish. It goes terrific with a salad and garlic bread.
—*Olivia Gust, Salem, OR*

Prep: 15 min. • **Cook:** 5½ hours
Makes: 2 servings

- ½ lb. beef stew meat
- ⅓ cup chopped onion
- 1 tsp. canola oil
- 1 cup water, divided
- ⅓ cup ketchup
- 1 Tbsp. brown sugar
- 1 Tbsp. Worcestershire sauce
- ½ tsp. paprika
- ¼ tsp. ground mustard
- 3 Tbsp. all-purpose flour
- 1 cup uncooked egg noodles
  Minced fresh parsley, optional

1. In a small skillet, brown beef and onion in oil; drain. Transfer to a 1½-qt. slow cooker.
2. In a small bowl, combine ½ cup water, ketchup, brown sugar, Worcestershire sauce, paprika and mustard; pour over meat. Cover and cook on low until meat is tender, about 5 hours.
3. Combine flour and remaining water until smooth; stir into the meat mixture. Cover and cook until thickened, about 30 minutes longer.
4. Meanwhile, cook the noodles according to package directions; drain. Stir in parsley if desired. Serve with beef.

1½ CUPS: 385 cal., 11g fat (3g sat. fat), 89mg chol., 611mg sod., 44g carb. (13g sugars, 2g fiber), 27g pro.

JENN TIDWELL
Fair Oaks, CA

SLOW-COOKER MUSHROOM CHICKEN & PEAS

Some amazingly fresh mushrooms I found at our local farmers market inspired this recipe. When you start with the best ingredients, you can't go wrong.
—*Jenn Tidwell, Fair Oaks, CA*

Prep: 10 min. • **Cook:** 3 hours 10 min.
Makes: 4 servings

- 4 boneless skinless chicken breast halves (6 oz. each)
- 1 envelope onion mushroom soup mix
- 1 cup water
- ½ lb. sliced baby portobello mushrooms
- 1 medium onion, chopped
- 4 garlic cloves, minced
- 2 cups frozen peas, thawed

1. Place the chicken in a 3-qt. slow cooker. Sprinkle with the soup mix, pressing to help seasonings adhere. Add water, mushrooms, onion and garlic.
2. Cook, covered, on low 3-4 hours or until chicken is tender (a thermometer inserted in chicken should read at least 165°). Stir in peas; cook, covered, 10 minutes longer or until heated through.

1 CHICKEN BREAST HALF WITH ¾ CUP VEGETABLE MIXTURE: 292 cal., 5g fat (1g sat. fat), 94mg chol., 566mg sod., 20g carb. (7g sugars, 5g fiber), 41g pro. **DIABETIC EXCHANGES:** 5 lean meat, 1 starch, 1 vegetable.

PRESSURE-COOKER SPICY SAUSAGE & BLUE CHEESE PEPPERS

I inherited an old pressure cooker from my aunt many years ago, before I was married. I made this delicious recipe often back then, and I have since incorporated a few easy tweaks to adapt it to my modern pressure cooker.
—Joan Hallford, North Richland Hills, TX

Prep: 35 min. • **Cook:** 10 min.
Makes: 4 servings

- 4 large sweet bell peppers
- 1 lb. bulk spicy pork sausage
- 4 green onions, sliced
- 1 garlic clove, minced
- 1 cup cooked brown rice
- ⅓ cup pasta sauce
- 1 tsp. dried oregano
- ¼ tsp. salt
- ¼ tsp. pepper
- 1 cup crumbled blue cheese
- 1 cup beef broth

1. Cut tops from peppers and remove seeds. Finely chop enough tops to measure ¼ cup for filling.
2. Select saute or browning setting on a 6-qt. electric pressure cooker; adjust for medium heat. Cook sausage, green onions, chopped peppers and garlic until sausage is no longer pink and vegetables are tender, 6-8 minutes, breaking the sausage into crumbles; drain. Press cancel.
3. Return to pressure cooker. Stir in the rice, pasta sauce, oregano, salt and pepper. Gently stir in blue cheese. Fill peppers with sausage mixture. Wipe pressure cooker clean.
4. Place trivet insert and broth in pressure cooker; place peppers on trivet. Lock lid; close pressure-release valve. Adjust to pressure-cook on high for 7 minutes. Quick-release pressure.
1 STUFFED PEPPER: 509 cal., 35g fat (14g sat. fat), 87mg chol., 1336mg sod., 27g carb. (6g sugars, 5g fiber), 23g pro.

ROUND STEAK ITALIANO

My mom used to make this wonderful dish, and I've always enjoyed it. The gravy is especially dense and flavorful.
—Deanne Stephens, McMinnville, OR

Prep: 15 min. • **Cook:** 7 hours
Makes: 8 servings

- 2 lbs. beef top round steak
- 1 can (8 oz.) tomato sauce
- 2 Tbsp. onion soup mix
- 2 Tbsp. canola oil
- 2 Tbsp. red wine vinegar
- 1 tsp. ground oregano
- ½ tsp. garlic powder
- ¼ tsp. pepper
- 8 medium potatoes (7 to 8 oz. each)
- 1 Tbsp. cornstarch
- 1 Tbsp. cold water

1. Cut steak into serving-sized pieces; place in a 5-qt. slow cooker. In a large bowl, combine tomato sauce, soup mix, oil, vinegar, oregano, garlic powder and pepper; pour over meat. Scrub and pierce potatoes; place over meat. Cover and cook on low for 7-8 hours or until meat and potatoes are tender.
2. Remove meat and potatoes; keep warm. For gravy, pour cooking juices into a small saucepan; skim fat. Combine cornstarch and water until smooth; gradually stir into juices. Bring to a boil; cook and stir for 2 minutes or until thickened. Serve with meat and potatoes.
1 SERVING: 357 cal., 7g fat (2g sat. fat), 64mg chol., 329mg sod., 42g carb. (4g sugars, 4g fiber), 31g pro. **DIABETIC EXCHANGES:** 3 lean meat, 2½ starch, ½ fat.

GREEN CHILE BEEF BURRITOS

Recipes that are leaner in fat and calories—like this one for beef burritos—helped me lose 30 pounds! The meat is so tender and delicious.
—*Shirley Davidson, Thornton, CO*

Prep: 20 min. • **Cook:** 8 hours
Makes: 2 dozen

- 2 beef sirloin tip roasts (3 lbs. each)
- 4 cans (4 oz. each) chopped green chiles
- 1 medium onion, chopped
- 3 medium jalapeno peppers, seeded and chopped
- 3 garlic cloves, sliced
- 3 tsp. chili powder
- 1½ tsp. ground cumin
- 1 tsp. salt-free seasoning blend, optional
- 1 cup reduced-sodium beef broth
- 24 fat-free flour tortillas (8 in.), warmed
  Optional: Chopped tomatoes, shredded lettuce and shredded reduced-fat cheddar cheese

1. Trim fat from roasts; cut the meat into large chunks. Place in a 5- to 6-qt. slow cooker. Top with the chiles, onion, jalapenos, garlic, chili powder, cumin and, if desired, seasoning blend. Pour broth over all. Cover and cook on low for 8-9 hours or until meat is tender.
2. Remove the beef; cool slightly. Shred with 2 forks. Cool cooking liquid slightly; skim fat. In a blender, cover and process cooking liquid in small batches until smooth.
3. Return liquid and beef to slow cooker; heat through. Place ⅓ cup beef mixture on each tortilla. Top with the tomatoes, lettuce and cheese as desired. Fold in ends and sides.
1 BURRITO: 262 cal., 5g fat (2g sat. fat), 72mg chol., 376mg sod., 26g carb. (0 sugars, 2g fiber), 26g pro. **DIABETIC EXCHANGES:** 3 lean meat, 2 starch.

TERIYAKI PORK ROAST

With three kids and a husband who works full time and attends school, it's fair to say we have a busy household. I'm always looking for no-fuss recipes, so I was thrilled to find this one. The juicy teriyaki seasoned pork roast has become a family favorite.
—*Roxanne Hulsey, Gainesville, GA*

Prep: 10 min. • **Cook:** 7 hours
Makes: 8 servings

- ¾ cup unsweetened apple juice
- 2 Tbsp. sugar
- 2 Tbsp. reduced-sodium soy sauce
- 1 Tbsp. white vinegar
- 1 tsp. ground ginger
- ¼ tsp. garlic powder
- ⅛ tsp. pepper
- 1 boneless pork loin roast (about 3 lbs.), halved
- 7½ tsp. cornstarch
- 3 Tbsp. cold water

1. In a greased 3-qt. slow cooker, combine the first 7 ingredients. Add roast and turn to coat. Cover and cook on low for 7-8 hours or until meat is tender.
2. Remove pork to a serving platter; keep warm. Skim fat from cooking juices. Transfer the juices to a small saucepan; bring to a boil. Combine cornstarch and water until smooth. Gradually stir into the pan. Bring to a boil; cook and stir for 2 minutes or until thickened. Serve with meat.
4 OZ. COOKED PORK: 247 cal., 8g fat (3g sat. fat), 85mg chol., 194mg sod., 9g carb. (5g sugars, 0 fiber), 33g pro. **DIABETIC EXCHANGES:** 4 lean meat, ½ starch.

TENDER BARBECUED CHICKEN

When you work long days, the slow cooker helps maximize mealtime success. We love this moist, slow-simmered chicken. Pick your favorite barbecue sauce and have at it!
—*Jacqueline Blanton, Gaffney, SC*

Prep: 15 min. • **Cook:** 4 hours
Makes: 6 servings

- 1 broiler/fryer chicken (3 to 4 lbs.), cut up
- 1 Tbsp. canola oil
- 1 medium onion, thinly sliced
- 1 medium lemon, thinly sliced
- 1 bottle (18 oz.) barbecue sauce
- ¾ cup cola

1. In a large skillet, brown chicken in oil in batches. Transfer to a 3-qt. slow cooker. Top with onion and lemon slices. Combine barbecue sauce and cola; pour over chicken.
2. Cover and cook on low until chicken is tender, 4-5 hours. If desired, skim fat and thicken cooking juices; serve with chicken.
4 OZ. COOKED CHICKEN: 478 cal., 20g fat (5g sat. fat), 104mg chol., 965mg sod., 39g carb. (31g sugars, 1g fiber), 34g pro.

ZESTY CHICKEN MARINARA

A friend served this slow-cooker chicken pasta before a church social, and I fell in love with it. My husband says it's restaurant quality.
—*Linda Baumann, Richfield, WI*

Prep: 15 min. • **Cook:** 4 hours
Makes: 4 servings

- 4 bone-in chicken breast halves (12 to 14 oz. each), skin removed
- 2 cups marinara sauce
- 1 medium tomato, chopped
- ½ cup Italian salad dressing
- 1½ tsp. Italian seasoning
- 1 garlic clove, minced
- ½ lb. uncooked angel hair pasta
- ½ cup shredded part-skim mozzarella cheese

1. Place chicken in a 4-qt. slow cooker. In a small bowl, combine the marinara sauce, tomato, salad dressing, Italian seasoning and garlic; pour over chicken. Cover and cook on low for 4-5 hours or until chicken is tender.
2. Cook the pasta according to the package directions, drain. Serve chicken and sauce with pasta; sprinkle with cheese.
FREEZE OPTION: Do not cook pasta. Freeze cooled chicken mixture in freezer containers. To use, partially thaw in refrigerator overnight. Cook pasta according to package directions. Place chicken mixture in a large skillet. Heat until a thermometer inserted in chicken reads 165°, stirring occasionally; add a little water if necessary. Serve as directed.
1 SERVING: 730 cal., 21g fat (5g sat. fat), 160mg chol., 929mg sod., 61g carb. (14g sugars, 5g fiber), 69g pro.

Breads, Rolls & Muffins

A fresh, aromatic baked beauty is one of life's best comforts. From easy quick breads and mixes to more complex loaves, these foolproof recipes are perfect for beginner and seasoned bread-makers alike.

CHEDDAR SKILLET CORNBREAD

Here's a tasty spin on traditional cornbread. It may become your new favorite!
—*Terri Adrian, Lake City, FL*

- -

Takes: 30 min. • **Makes:** 1 loaf (12 wedges)

- 2 Tbsp. butter
- 2 pkg. (8½ oz. each) cornbread/muffin mix
- 2 large eggs, room temperature, lightly beaten
- ½ cup 2% milk
- ½ cup plain yogurt
- 1 can (14¾ oz.) cream-style corn
- ½ cup shredded cheddar cheese

HONEY BUTTER
- ½ cup butter, softened
- 2 Tbsp. honey

1. Place butter in a 10-in. cast-iron or other ovenproof skillet. Place in a 400° oven until melted, 4-6 minutes.

2. Meanwhile, in a large bowl, combine the cornbread mix, eggs, milk and yogurt until blended. Stir in corn and cheese. Pour into hot skillet.

3. Bake at 400° until a toothpick inserted in the center comes out clean, 20-25 minutes. Cut into wedges.

4. In a small bowl, cream butter and honey. Serve with warm cornbread.

1 PIECE: 332 cal., 18g fat (9g sat. fat), 64mg chol., 547mg sod., 38g carb. (13g sugars, 3g fiber), 6g pro.

TEST KITCHEN TIP
Add spice and flavor to cornbread by adding chopped cooked bacon or diced jalapenos to the batter; a sprinkling of red pepper flakes; or any of your favorite herbs, such as sage, thyme or rosemary. Serve it alongside chili, soups, salads or any comforting dinner.

WHOLE WHEAT BREAD

I'm a young teen, and I make this bread with my mother, who got the recipe from her mother. I usually make the dough, and my mom bakes it.
—*Freida Stutman, Fillmore, NY*

Prep: 20 min. + rising • **Bake:** 40 min.
Makes: 2 loaves (16 slices each)

- 1   pkg. (¼ oz.) active dry yeast
- 3   cups warm water (110° to 115°), divided
- ¾   cup canola oil
- ¼   cup sugar
- ¼   cup molasses
- 1   Tbsp. salt
- 7   to 7½ cups all-purpose flour
- 3   cups whole wheat flour

1. In a large bowl, dissolve yeast in ¾ cup warm water. Add the oil, sugar, molasses, salt and remaining water. Combine flours; add 4-5 cups flour to mixture. Beat until smooth. Add enough remaining flour to form a firm dough.
2. Turn onto a floured surface; knead until smooth and elastic, 6-8 minutes. Place in a greased bowl, turning once to grease top. Cover and let rise in a warm place until doubled, about 1 hour.
3. Punch dough down. Turn onto a lightly floured surface; divide in half. Shape each portion into a loaf. Place in 2 greased 9x5-in. loaf pans. Cover and let rise until doubled, about 30 minutes.
4. Bake at 350° until loaves are golden brown, 40-45 minutes. Remove from pans to cool on wire racks.
1 SLICE: 168 cal., 6g fat (1g sat. fat), 0 chol., 223mg sod., 26g carb. (4g sugars, 2g fiber), 4g pro.

READER REVIEW
"This is now the only basic wheat bread we will be making at our house. It is moist and flavorful, and it's easy to see why the recipe has been passed on!"

RASPBERRYPARADE, TASTEOFHOME.COM

POTECA NUT ROLL

My mother-in-law brought this recipe from Yugoslavia in the early 1900s. Serving it for holidays and special occasions is our tradition.
—*Anthony Setta, Saegertown, PA*

Prep: 30 min. + rising • **Bake:** 35 min.
Makes: 1 coffee cake

- 1   pkg. (¼ oz.) active dry yeast
- ¼   cup warm water (110° to 115°)
- ¾   cup warm 2% milk (110° to 115°)
- ¼   cup sugar
- 1   tsp. salt
- 1   large egg, room temperature, lightly beaten
- ¼   cup shortening
- 3   to 3½ cups all-purpose flour

FILLING
- ½   cup butter, softened
- 1   cup packed brown sugar
- 2   large eggs, lightly beaten
- 1   tsp. vanilla extract
- 1   tsp. lemon extract, optional
- 4   cups ground or finely chopped walnuts
- ⅓   to ½ cup 2% milk

GLAZE (OPTIONAL)
- 2   cups confectioners' sugar
- 2   to 3 Tbsp. 2% milk

1. In a large bowl, dissolve yeast in warm water. Add the milk, sugar, salt, beaten egg, shortening, and 1½ cups flour; beat until smooth. Add enough remaining flour to form a soft dough.
2. Turn onto a floured surface; knead until smooth and elastic, 6-8 minutes. Place in a greased bowl, turning once to grease top. Cover and let rise in a warm place until doubled, about 1 hour.
3. Punch down. Turn onto a lightly floured surface; roll into a 30x20-in. rectangle. In a bowl , combine the butter, brown sugar, eggs, vanilla, lemon extract if desired and nuts. Stir in enough of the milk to achieve spreading consistency. Spread over rectangle to within 1 in. of edges.
4. Roll up jelly-roll style, starting with a long side; pinch seams and ends to seal. Place on a greased baking sheet; shape into a tight spiral. Cover and let rise until nearly doubled, about 1 hour.
5. Bake at 350° until golden brown, about 35 minutes. Remove from pan to a wire rack to cool. If desired, combine confectioners' sugar and enough milk to make a thin glaze; brush over roll.
1 PIECE: 304 cal., 19g fat (5g sat. fat), 45mg chol., 183mg sod., 30g carb. (14g sugars, 2g fiber), 6g pro.

SWEET POTATO PAN ROLLS

These tender rolls are one of my brother's favorites, so I make them often. Spiced with cinnamon and nutmeg, they are heavenly served alongside a wide variety of dishes, from chicken and turkey to a bowl of chili.
—Carly Curtin, Ellicott City, MD

Prep: 30 min. + rising • **Bake:** 20 min.
Makes: 16 rolls

- 1 pkg. (¼ oz.) active dry yeast
- ½ cup warm water (110° to 115°)
- ½ cup mashed sweet potato
- ¼ cup butter, melted
- 3 Tbsp. honey
- 2 Tbsp. canola oil
- 1 large egg, room temperature
- 1 tsp. salt
- ½ tsp. sugar
- ¼ tsp. ground cinnamon
  Dash ground nutmeg
- 3½ to 4 cups bread flour

1. In a large bowl, dissolve yeast in warm water. Add the sweet potato, butter, honey, oil, egg, salt, sugar, cinnamon, nutmeg and 1 cup flour. Beat on medium speed until smooth. Stir in enough remaining flour to form a soft dough (dough will be sticky).

2. Turn onto a floured surface; knead until smooth and elastic, 6-8 minutes. Place in a greased bowl, turning once to grease the top. Cover and let rise in a warm place until doubled, about 1 hour.

3. Punch dough down. Turn onto a lightly floured surface; divide into 16 pieces. Shape each piece into a ball. Place in 2 greased 9-in. round baking pans. Cover and let rise until doubled, 30 minutes.

4. Bake at 375° until rolls are golden brown, 20-25 minutes.

1 ROLL: 154 cal., 5g fat (2g sat. fat), 21mg chol., 175mg sod., 25g carb. (4g sugars, 1g fiber), 4g pro. **DIABETIC EXCHANGES:** 1½ starch, 1 fat.

APPLE ZUCCHINI BREAD

Apples and zucchini are abundant in this area, so it seemed natural to pair them in delicious baked goods. I don't know the origin of this bread recipe, but I do know it's been one of my favorites for many years.
—Patti Dillingham, Scranton, AR

Prep: 15 min. • **Bake:** 50 min. + cooling
Makes: 3 loaves (16 slices each)

- 4 cups all-purpose flour
- 1 Tbsp. baking soda
- 1½ tsp. ground cinnamon
- ½ tsp. ground nutmeg
- ¼ tsp. salt
- 5 large eggs, room temperature
- 1½ cups vegetable oil
- 2 cups sugar
- 1 cup packed brown sugar
- 1 Tbsp. vanilla extract
- 2 cups shredded unpeeled zucchini
- 1 cup shredded peeled apples
- 1½ cups chopped pecans

In a large bowl, combine flour, baking soda, cinnamon, nutmeg and salt. In another bowl, beat eggs. Add oil, sugars and vanilla. Pour over dry ingredients; mix well. Stir in zucchini, apples and pecans (batter will be stiff). Spoon into 3 greased 8x4-in. loaf pans. Bake at 350° until a toothpick inserted in center comes out clean, 50-55 minutes. Cool loaves in pans for 10 minutes before removing to a wire rack to cool completely.

1 SLICE: 185 cal., 10g fat (1g sat. fat), 22mg chol., 100mg sod., 22g carb. (13g sugars, 1g fiber), 2g pro.

JOAN HALLFORD
North Richland Hills, TX

❄

DOUBLE CRANBERRY
BANANA BREAD

We love quick breads, and I've found that
they freeze nicely if properly wrapped. This
cranberry-studded beauty is a scrumptious
recipe to make before the holidays and freeze
for last-minute company or to give as gifts.
—Joan Hallford, North Richland Hills, TX

- -

Prep: 25 min. • **Bake:** 50 min. + cooling
Makes: 1 loaf (12 slices)

⅓ cup shortening
⅔ cup sugar
2 large eggs, room temperature
1 cup mashed ripe banana
1 tsp. vanilla extract
1¾ cups all-purpose flour
2 tsp. baking powder
½ tsp. salt
¼ tsp. baking soda
1 cup whole-berry cranberry sauce
¾ cup chopped pecans, divided
½ cup dried cranberries

1. Preheat oven to 350°. In a large bowl, cream
shortening and sugar until light and crumbly.
Beat in eggs, banana and vanilla. In another
bowl, whisk the flour, baking powder, salt and
baking soda; gradually beat into the creamed
mixture. Stir in cranberry sauce, ½ cup pecans
and dried cranberries.

2. Transfer to a greased 8x4-in. loaf pan.
Sprinkle with remaining pecans. Bake until a
toothpick inserted in center comes out clean,
50-60 minutes. Cool in pan 10 minutes before
removing to a wire rack to cool completely.
FREEZE OPTION: Securely wrap cooled loaf
in foil, then freeze. To use, thaw loaf at room
temperature.

1 SLICE: 289 cal., 11g fat (2g sat. fat), 31mg
chol., 229mg sod., 45g carb. (24g sugars, 2g
fiber), 4g pro.

RHUBARB STREUSEL MUFFINS

It's a pleasure it is to set out a basket of these rhubarb muffins...although the basket doesn't stay full for very long! I have six children and two grandsons, so I do a lot of baking. This favorite is based on a coffee cake recipe.
—*Sandra Moreside, Regina, SK*

Prep: 15 min. • **Bake:** 25 min.
Makes: about 1½ dozen

- ½ cup butter, softened
- 1 cup packed brown sugar
- ⅓ cup sugar
- 1 large egg, room temperature
- 2 cups all-purpose flour
- 1 tsp. baking powder
- ½ tsp. baking soda
- ⅛ tsp. salt
- 1 cup sour cream
- 3 cups chopped fresh or frozen rhubarb, thawed

TOPPING
- ½ cup chopped pecans
- ¼ cup packed brown sugar
- 1 tsp. ground cinnamon
- 1 Tbsp. cold butter

1. Preheat oven to 350°. In a large bowl, cream butter and sugars until light and fluffy, 5-7 minutes. Beat in egg. Combine the flour, baking powder, baking soda and salt; add to creamed mixture alternately with sour cream, beating well after each addition. Fold in the chopped rhubarb.

2. Fill paper-lined or greased muffin cups three-fourths full. For topping, combine the pecans, brown sugar and cinnamon in a small bowl; cut in cold butter until crumbly. Sprinkle over batter.

3. Bake until a toothpick inserted in the center comes out clean, 22-25 minutes. Cool muffins for 5 minutes before removing from pans to wire racks. Serve warm.

1 MUFFIN: 238 cal., 11g fat (5g sat. fat), 36mg chol., 149mg sod., 33g carb. (22g sugars, 1g fiber), 3g pro.

WILD BLUEBERRY MUFFINS

Nothing is better than a warm blueberry muffin in the morning. These particular muffins are the best I have ever made. The wild blueberries make them extra special.
—*Dewey Grindle, Blue Hill, ME*

- -

Prep: 15 min. • **Bake:** 20 min.
Makes: 1 dozen

- ¼ cup butter, softened
- ⅓ cup sugar
- 1 large egg, room temperature
- 2⅓ cups all-purpose flour
- 4 tsp. baking powder
- ½ tsp. salt
- 1 cup 2% milk
- 1 tsp. vanilla extract
- 1½ cups fresh or frozen wild blueberries or 1 can (15 oz.) water-packed wild blueberries, well drained

STREUSEL TOPPING
- ½ cup sugar
- ⅓ cup all-purpose flour
- ½ tsp. ground cinnamon
- ¼ cup cold butter, cubed

In a bowl, cream butter and sugar. Add egg; mix well. Combine dry ingredients; add to creamed mixture alternately with milk. Stir in vanilla. Gently fold in blueberries. Fill greased or paper-lined muffin cups two-thirds full. In a small bowl, combine the sugar, flour and cinnamon; cut in the butter until crumbly. Sprinkle topping over muffins. Bake at 375° for 20-25 minutes.

1 MUFFIN: 252 cal., 9g fat (5g sat. fat), 41mg chol., 325mg sod., 39g carb. (17g sugars, 1g fiber), 4g pro.

GINGERBREAD COFFEE CAKE

At our house, we love gingerbread that's not too sweet. To sweeten it, mix powdered sugar, milk and vanilla extract for drizzling on top.
—*Barbara Humiston, Tampa, FL*

- -

Prep: 20 min. • **Bake:** 20 min. + cooling
Makes: 8 servings

- 1 cup all-purpose flour
- ½ cup plus 1 Tbsp. sugar, divided
- 1¾ tsp. ground cinnamon, divided
- 1 tsp. ground ginger
- ¼ tsp. salt
- ¼ tsp. ground allspice
- ¼ cup cold butter
- ¾ tsp. baking powder
- ½ tsp. baking soda
- 1 large egg, room temperature
- ½ cup buttermilk
- 2 Tbsp. molasses

1. Preheat oven to 350°. In a large bowl, mix flour, ½ cup sugar, ¾ tsp. cinnamon, ginger, salt and allspice; cut in butter until crumbly. Reserve ⅓ cup for topping.
2. Stir baking powder and baking soda into remaining flour mixture. In a small bowl, whisk egg, buttermilk and molasses. Add to flour mixture; stir just until moistened. Transfer batter to a greased 8-in. round baking pan.
3. Add remaining sugar and cinnamon to reserved topping; sprinkle over batter. Bake 20-25 minutes or until a toothpick inserted in center comes out clean. Cool completely in pan on a wire rack.

1 PIECE: 195 cal., 7g fat (4g sat. fat), 39mg chol., 283mg sod., 31g carb. (19g sugars, 1g fiber), 3g pro. **DIABETIC EXCHANGES:** 2 starch, 1½ fat.

1 large egg, room temperature
1 cup lemon yogurt
⅓ cup canola oil
1 Tbsp. lemon juice

1. In a large bowl, combine the flour, sugar, salt, baking soda and baking powder. In another bowl, combine the egg, yogurt, oil and lemon juice. Stir into dry ingredients just until moistened.

2. Pour into an 8x4-in. loaf pan coated with cooking spray. Bake at 325° for 45-50 minutes or until a toothpick inserted in the center comes out clean. Cool for 10 minutes before removing from pan to a wire rack.

1 SLICE: 177 cal., 7g fat (1g sat. fat), 18mg chol., 176mg sod., 26g carb. (14g sugars, 1g fiber), 3g pro. **DIABETIC EXCHANGES:** 1½ starch, 1 fat.

BASIC PIZZA CRUST

I double this recipe and keep one baked crust in the freezer to pull out for a quick and easy meal in the future.
—*Beverly Anderson, Sinclairville, NY*

Prep: 10 min. + resting • **Bake:** 25 min.
Makes: 1 pizza crust (6 slices)

1 pkg. (¼ oz.) active dry yeast
1 cup warm water (110° to 115°)
2 Tbsp. canola oil
1 tsp. sugar
¼ tsp. salt
2½ to 2¾ cups all-purpose flour
Cornmeal
Pizza toppings of your choice

1. In a large bowl, dissolve yeast in warm water. Add the oil, sugar, salt and 1½ cups flour. Beat until smooth. Stir in enough remaining flour to form a firm dough. Turn onto a floured surface; cover and let rest for 10 minutes.

2. Roll into a 13-in. circle. Grease a 12-in. pizza pan and sprinkle with cornmeal. Transfer dough to prepared pan, building up edges slightly. Do not let rise. Bake at 425° until browned, 12-15 minutes. Add toppings; bake 10-15 minutes longer.

1 PIECE: 236 cal., 5g fat (1g sat. fat), 0 chol., 100mg sod., 41g carb. (2g sugars, 2g fiber), 6g pro.

DILL BATTER BREAD

Even those who don't consider themselves bakers can make this bread with success. And your guests will be delighted!
—*Donna Lindecamp, Morganton, NC*

Prep: 15 min. + rising • **Bake:** 45 min. + cooling
Makes: 16 servings

¼ cup sugar
2 pkg. (¼ oz. each) active dry yeast
2 tsp. dill weed
1½ tsp. salt
4½ cups all-purpose flour
1 cup water
1 cup 2% milk
¼ cup canola oil
1 large egg, room temperature
2 tsp. butter, melted
½ tsp. kosher salt

1. In a large bowl, mix sugar, yeast, dill weed, salt and 2 cups flour. In a small saucepan, heat water, milk and oil to 120°-130°. Add to dry ingredients; beat on medium speed 2 minutes. Add egg; beat on high for 2 minutes. Stir in remaining flour to form a stiff batter. Cover and let rise until doubled, about 1 hour.

2. Preheat oven to 375°. Stir down batter. Transfer batter to a greased 2½ qt. round baking dish. Bake until bread is deep golden brown and sounds hollow when tapped, 45-50 minutes.

3. Cool 5 minutes before removing to a wire rack. Brush with butter; sprinkle with salt. Cool completely.

1 PIECE: 191 cal., 5g fat (1g sat. fat), 14mg chol., 298mg sod., 31g carb. (4g sugars, 1g fiber), 5g pro.

LEMON YOGURT BREAD

This tender bread reminds me of pound cake. Its mild lemon flavor and cakelike texture makes it perfect for brunch, a snack or even as dessert topped with berries and cream.
—*Suzy Horvath, Milwaukie, OR*

Prep: 15 min. • **Bake:** 45 min. + cooling
Makes: 1 loaf (12 slices)

1½ cups all-purpose flour
¾ cup sugar
½ tsp. salt
½ tsp. baking soda
¼ tsp. baking powder

OLIVE FOCACCIA

After adding my own special touches to a basic focaccia recipe—including olives, sun-dried tomatoes and roasted sweet red peppers—the results were simply delectable. The flavorful, chewy loaf makes a wonderful accompaniment to any meal.

—*Dee Froemel, Hayward, WI*

Prep: 30 min. + rising • **Bake:** 15 min.
Makes: 1 loaf (8 wedges)

- 1⅛ tsp. active dry yeast
- ½ cup warm water (110° to 115°)
- 1 Tbsp. sugar
- 1 Tbsp. Italian seasoning
- ¼ tsp. salt
- ¼ tsp. pepper
- 1⅓ to 1⅔ cups all-purpose flour
- 2 Tbsp. oil-packed sun-dried tomatoes, chopped
- 2 Tbsp. roasted sweet red peppers, drained and chopped
- 2 Tbsp. sliced ripe olives, drained
- 5 Greek olives, sliced
- 5 sliced green olives with pimientos, drained
- 2 Tbsp. minced fresh parsley
- 1 Tbsp. olive oil
- 1 tsp. kosher salt
- 1 tsp. shredded Parmesan cheese
- 1 tsp. shredded Romano cheese

1. In a large bowl, dissolve yeast in warm water. Add the sugar, Italian seasoning, salt, pepper and 1 cup flour. Beat until smooth. Stir in enough remaining flour to form a firm dough. Stir in tomatoes, peppers, olives and minced parsley.

2. Turn onto a floured surface; knead until smooth and elastic, 6-8 minutes. Place in a greased bowl, turning once to grease the top. Cover; let rise in a warm place until doubled, about 50 minutes.

3. Punch dough down. Shape into a 9-in. circle on a greased baking sheet. Cover; let rise in a warm place until doubled, about 25 minutes. With fingertips, make several dimples over top of dough. Brush with oil. Sprinkle with kosher salt and cheeses.

4. Bake at 400° until focaccia is golden brown, 14-18 minutes. Remove to a wire rack.
1 PIECE: 118 cal., 3g fat (0 sat. fat), 0 chol., 418mg sod., 19g carb. (2g sugars, 1g fiber), 3g pro.

✳ CHERRY-CHIP OAT SCONES

My family loves scones and anything with oatmeal. I started with my basic scone recipe and added oat flour to increase the oat taste and texture, as well as ingredients that are harmonious with the mellow taste of oats. I have learned that everyone loves them most when I add special ingredients you can find in each bite.

—*Amy Brnger, Portsmouth, NH*

Prep: 15 min. • **Bake:** 20 min.
Makes: 10 servings

- 1½ cups all-purpose flour
- ½ cup oat flour
- ½ cup old-fashioned oats
- 3 Tbsp. brown sugar
- 1 tsp. baking soda
- 1 tsp. cream of tartar
- ½ tsp. salt
- 3 Tbsp. cold butter, cubed
- 1 cup buttermilk
- ⅓ cup dried cherries, chopped
- ⅓ cup miniature semisweet chocolate chips
- ¼ cup finely chopped pecans, toasted

TOPPING
- 1 Tbsp. coarse sugar
- 1 Tbsp. old-fashioned oats

1. Preheat oven to 400°. Whisk together the first 7 ingredients; cut in butter until mixture resembles coarse crumbs. Add buttermilk, stirring just until moistened. Stir in cherries, chocolate chips and pecans.

2. Transfer to a parchment-lined baking sheet; pat into a 6-in. circle. Cut into 10 wedges, but do not separate. Sprinkle with coarse sugar and oats.

3. Bake until golden brown, 20-25 minutes. Serve warm.
FREEZE OPTION: Freeze cooled scones in freezer containers. To use, thaw at room temperature or, if desired, microwave each scone on high until heated through, 20-30 seconds.
1 SCONE: 229 cal., 8g fat (4g sat. fat), 10mg chol., 321mg sod., 36g carb. (13g sugars, 2g fiber), 5g pro.

PEANUT BUTTER PUMPKIN BREAD

My husband brought this recipe home from the office more than 20 years ago. Each fall, I bake several of these lovely loaves to share with family and friends. Pumpkin and peanut butter are a unique, delicious combination.

—*Anita Chicke, Frisco, TX*

Prep: 10 min. • **Bake:** 1 hour + cooling
Makes: 2 loaves (16 slices each)

- 3½ cups all-purpose flour
- 3 cups sugar
- 2 tsp. baking soda
- 1½ tsp. salt
- 1 tsp. ground cinnamon
- 1 tsp. ground nutmeg
- 1 can (15 oz.) solid-pack pumpkin
- 4 large eggs, room temperature
- 1 cup vegetable oil
- ¾ cup water
- ⅔ cup peanut butter

1. In a large bowl, combine the flour, sugar, baking soda, salt, cinnamon and nutmeg. In another bowl, combine the pumpkin, eggs, oil, water and peanut butter. Stir into dry ingredients just until moistened.

2. Pour into 2 greased 9x5-in. loaf pans. Bake at 350° until a toothpick inserted in the center comes out clean, 60-70 minutes. Cool loaves for 10 minutes before removing from pans to wire racks.
1 SLICE: 228 cal., 10g fat (2g sat. fat), 27mg chol., 223mg sod., 31g carb. (19g sugars, 1g fiber), 4g pro.

BLUEBERRY CORNBREAD

My husband is a fourth-grade teacher, and he incorporates monthly baking projects into the curriculum. His recipe for blueberry cornbread is a class favorite.
—*Jennifer Martin, Martinez, CA*

Prep: 10 min. • **Bake:** 30 min.
Makes: 9 servings

- 1½ cups all-purpose flour
- ½ cup sugar
- ½ cup yellow cornmeal
- 1 Tbsp. baking powder
- ½ tsp. salt
- 2 large eggs, room temperature
- 1¼ cups soy or 2% milk
- ⅓ cup canola oil
- 1 cup fresh or frozen blueberries

1. Preheat oven to 350°. Grease an 8-in. square baking pan.
2. Whisk together first 5 ingredients. In another bowl, whisk together eggs, milk and oil; add to dry ingredients, stirring just until moistened. Fold in blueberries. Transfer to prepared pan.
3. Bake until a toothpick inserted in center comes out clean, 30-35 minutes. Cool on a wire rack. Serve cornbread warm or at room temperature.

1 PIECE: 264 cal., 10g fat (1g sat. fat), 41mg chol., 325mg sod., 38g carb. (14g sugars, 1g fiber), 5g pro.

CINNAMON ROLLS

My wife likes to tell people that after I retired, I went from being the breadwinner to the bread baker! It all started with a bread-making class at a nearby community college. Now my breads and rolls are favorites of friends and family.
—*Ben Middleton, Walla Walla, WA*

Prep: 20 min. + rising • **Bake:** 25 min.
Makes: 2 dozen

- 2 pkg. (¼ oz. each) active dry yeast
- ½ cup sugar, divided
- 1 cup warm water (110° to 115°)
- 1 cup 2% milk
- 6 Tbsp. butter
- 7 to 7½ cups all-purpose flour
- 3 large eggs, room temperature, lightly beaten
- 1 tsp. salt

FILLING
- ¼ cup butter, softened
- 5 tsp. ground cinnamon
- ¾ cup packed brown sugar
- ¾ cup raisins or dried currants
  Vanilla frosting, optional

1. In a large bowl, dissolve yeast and 1 Tbsp. sugar in water. In a saucepan, heat milk and butter to 110°-115°; add to yeast mixture. Stir in 3 cups flour, eggs, salt and remaining sugar. Stir in enough of the remaining flour to make a soft dough.
2. Turn out onto a lightly floured surface. Knead until smooth and elastic, 6-8 minutes. Place in a greased bowl, turning once to grease top. Cover and let rise in a warm place until doubled, about 1 hour.
3. Punch dough down and divide in half. Roll each half into a 15x12-in. rectangle. Brush dough with softened butter. Combine the cinnamon, brown sugar and raisins; sprinkle evenly over rectangle. Roll up tightly, jelly-roll style, starting with a long side. Slice each roll into 12 pieces. Place in 2 greased standard muffin pans or 2 greased 13x9-in. baking pans. Cover and let rise until dough doubles, about 30 minutes.
4. Bake at 350° until rolls are golden brown, 25-30 minutes. Cool in pans 5 minutes; invert onto a wire rack. Frost if desired. Serve warm.

1 ROLL: 248 cal., 6g fat (3g sat. fat), 41mg chol., 164mg sod., 43g carb. (15g sugars, 1g fiber), 5g pro.

PLUM STREUSEL KUCHEN

This recipe is actually called *platz* in German (translated as "flat") and has been in my family since before I was born. The fresh fruits of summer make it a favorite.
—Lisa Warkentin, Winnipeg, MB

Prep: 25 min. • **Bake:** 35 min.
Makes: 15 servings

- 2 cups all-purpose flour
- ¼ cup sugar
- 2 tsp. baking powder
- ¼ tsp. salt
- 2 Tbsp. shortening
- 1 large egg, room temperature
- 1 cup heavy whipping cream
- 6 fresh plums, sliced

TOPPING
- ⅔ cup all-purpose flour
- ⅔ cup sugar
- 2 Tbsp. cold butter
- 2 Tbsp. heavy whipping cream

1. Preheat oven to 350°. In a large bowl, combine flour, sugar, baking powder and salt; cut in shortening until mixture resembles fine crumbs. In another bowl, whisk the egg and cream; add to crumb mixture, tossing gently with a fork until mixture forms a ball.
2. Press dough into a greased 13x9-in. baking dish. Arrange plums over crust.
3. For topping, in a small bowl, combine flour and sugar; cut in butter until the mixture resembles fine crumbs. Add cream, mixing gently with a fork until moist crumbs form. Sprinkle over plums.
4. Bake until a toothpick inserted in center of kuchen comes out clean, 35-40 minutes. Cool on wire rack. Cut into squares.
1 PIECE: 235 cal., 10g fat (6g sat. fat), 37mg chol., 126mg sod., 33g carb. (15g sugars, 1g fiber), 3g pro.

GARLIC POTATO BISCUITS

The beauty of these biscuits is you can enjoy the aroma of oven-fresh bread with less work than yeast breads.
— Diane Hixon, Niceville, FL

Prep: 25 min. • **Bake:** 10 min.
Makes: 15 biscuits

- 1 large potato (½ lb.), peeled and diced
- 3 to 4 garlic cloves, peeled
- ⅓ cup butter, softened
- 1 tsp. salt
- ¼ tsp. pepper
- 2 cups all-purpose flour
- 3 tsp. baking powder
- ⅓ cup 2% milk

1. Place potato and garlic in a saucepan; cover with water. Bring to a boil. Reduce heat; cover and simmer until tender. Drain. Add butter, salt and pepper to potato and garlic; mash. In a large bowl, combine flour and baking powder; stir in potato mixture until mixture resembles coarse crumbs. Add the milk and stir well.
2. Turn dough onto a lightly floured surface. Roll out to ½-in. thickness. Cut with a floured 2-in. biscuit cutter. Place 1 in. apart on an ungreased baking sheet. Bake at 450° for 10-12 minutes or until golden brown. Serve biscuits warm.
1 BISCUIT: 120 cal., 4g fat (3g sat. fat), 12mg chol., 283mg sod., 18g carb. (1g sugars, 1g fiber), 2g pro.

MAPLE NUT COFFEE CAKE

This flower-shaped coffee cake is quite easy to make and always disappears in a hurry.
—*Rosadene Herold, Lakeville, IN*

Prep: 35 min. + rising • **Bake:** 20 min.
Makes: 16 servings

  1 pkg. (16 oz.) hot roll mix
  3 Tbsp. sugar
  ¾ cup warm water (120° to 130°)
  6 Tbsp. butter, melted
  1 large egg, room temperature
  1 tsp. maple flavoring

FILLING

  ½ cup sugar
  ⅓ cup chopped walnuts
  1 tsp. ground cinnamon
  ½ tsp. maple flavoring
  2 Tbsp. butter, melted

GLAZE

  1½ cups confectioners' sugar
  ¼ tsp. maple flavoring
  1 to 2 Tbsp. 2% milk

1. In a large bowl, combine the contents of the roll mix and yeast packets with the sugar. Stir in water, butter, egg and maple flavoring; mix well.

2. Turn onto a floured surface; knead until smooth and elastic, 2-3 minutes. Place in a greased bowl, turning once to grease top. Cover and let rise in a warm place until doubled, 45-60 minutes.

3. In a small bowl, combine sugar, walnuts, cinnamon and maple flavoring. Grease a 12-in. pizza pan. Punch dough down. Turn onto a lightly floured surface; divide into 3 portions. Roll each into a 12-in. circle. Place 1 circle on prepared pan. Brush with a third of the melted butter; sprinkle with a third of the filling. Repeat the layers twice. Pinch around edge to seal.

4. Place a small glass in center of circle. With kitchen scissors, cut from outside edge just to the glass, forming 16 wedges. Twist each wedge 5 or 6 times; tuck ends under. Remove glass. Cover with a kitchen towel; let rise in a warm place until doubled, 30-45 minutes.

5. Preheat oven to 375°. Bake until golden brown, 20-25 minutes. Remove from pan to a wire rack to cool. Combine glaze ingredients; drizzle over warm coffee cake.

1 PIECE: 255 cal., 8g fat (4g sat. fat), 29mg chol., 251mg sod., 40g carb. (21g sugars, 1g fiber), 4g pro.

SESAME FRENCH BREAD

Homemade bread isn't difficult to make, and it's perfect alongside hearty meals like pasta or beef stew. If you're not serving a large group, freeze one loaf to enjoy later.
—*Peggy Van Arsdale, Trenton, NJ*

Prep: 25 min. + rising
Bake: 25 min. + cooling
Makes: 2 loaves (16 slices each)

 2 pkg. (¼ oz. each) active dry yeast
 2½ cups water (110° to 115°)
 2 Tbsp. sugar
 2 Tbsp. canola oil
 2 tsp. salt
 6 to 6½ cups all-purpose flour
  Cornmeal
 1 large egg white
 1 Tbsp. water
 2 Tbsp. sesame seeds

1. In a large bowl, dissolve yeast in warm water. Add the sugar, oil, salt and 4 cups of flour; beat until smooth. Add enough remaining flour to form a soft dough.

2. Turn onto a floured surface; knead until smooth and elastic, 6-8 minutes. Place in a greased bowl, turning once to grease top. Cover; let rise in a warm place until doubled, about 1 hour.

3. Punch dough down. Divide in half. Roll each half into a 15x10-in. rectangle. Roll up from a long side; seal well. Place seam side down on a greased baking sheet sprinkled with cornmeal.

4. Beat egg white and water; brush over loaves. Sprinkle with sesame seeds. Cover with plastic wrap sprayed with cooking spray; let rise until nearly doubled, about 30 minutes.

5. With a sharp knife, make 4 shallow diagonal cuts across top. Bake at 400° until lightly browned, about 25 minutes. Remove from pan and cool on a wire rack.

1 SLICE: 99 cal., 1g fat (0 sat. fat), 0 chol., 150mg sod., 19g carb. (1g sugars, 1g fiber), 3g pro.

FLAKY BISCUITS WITH HERB BUTTER

Nothing says spring like fresh herbs...and these flaky, flavorful biscuits are the ideal way to showcase tarragon and chives. They can be on the table in 30 minutes, which makes them an ideal choice for last-minute entertaining.
—*Theresa Stanek, Evans City, PA*

Takes: 30 min. • **Makes:** 1 dozen

2 cups all-purpose flour
3 tsp. baking powder
1 Tbsp. sugar
1½ tsp. minced fresh chives
1½ tsp. minced fresh tarragon
1 tsp. salt
½ tsp. garlic powder
½ cup shortening
¾ cup 2% milk
HERB BUTTER
½ cup butter, softened
1½ tsp. minced fresh chives
1½ tsp. minced fresh tarragon
½ tsp. garlic powder

1. In a small bowl, combine first 7 ingredients. Cut in the shortening until mixture resembles coarse crumbs. Stir in the milk just until moistened. Turn onto a lightly floured surface; knead 8-10 times.
2. Pat or roll out to ½-in. thickness; cut with a floured 2½-in. biscuit cutter. Place 2 in. apart on an ungreased baking sheet.
3. Bake at 425° for 8-12 minutes or until golden brown.
4. Meanwhile, in a small bowl, beat the herb butter ingredients until blended; serve with warm biscuits.
1 BISCUIT WITH 2 TSP. BUTTER: 229 cal., 16g fat (7g sat. fat), 21mg chol., 359mg sod., 18g carb. (2g sugars, 1g fiber), 3g pro.

PARMESAN GARLIC BREADSTICKS

These tender breadsticks fill the kitchen with a tempting aroma when they are baking, and they're wonderful served warm. My family tells me I can't make them enough.
—*Gaylene Anderson, Sandy, UT*

Prep: 40 min. + rising • **Bake:** 10 min.
Makes: 3 dozen

2 pkg. (¼ oz. each) active dry yeast
1½ cups warm water (110° to 115°)
½ cup warm 2% milk (110° to 115°)
3 Tbsp. sugar
3 Tbsp. plus ¼ cup butter, softened, divided
1 tsp. salt
4½ to 5½ cups all-purpose flour
¼ cup grated Parmesan cheese
½ tsp. garlic salt

1. In a large bowl, dissolve yeast in warm water. Add the milk, sugar, 3 Tbsp. butter, salt and 2 cups flour. Beat until smooth. Stir in enough remaining flour to form a soft dough.
2. Turn onto a floured surface; knead until smooth and elastic, 6-8 minutes. Place in a greased bowl, turning once to grease top. Cover and let rise in a warm place until doubled, about 45 minutes.
3. Punch the dough down. Turn onto a floured surface; divide into 36 pieces. Shape each piece into a 6-in. rope. Place 2 in. apart on greased baking sheets. Cover and let rise until doubled, about 25 minutes.
4. Melt remaining butter; brush over dough. Sprinkle with Parmesan and garlic salt. Bake at 400° until golden brown, 8-10 minutes. Remove from pans to wire racks.
1 BREADSTICK: 86 cal., 3g fat (2g sat. fat), 7mg chol., 126mg sod., 13g carb. (1g sugars, 0 fiber), 2g pro.

GAYLENE ANDERSON
Sandy, UT

HERBED PEASANT BREAD

Our daughter-in-law, Karen, gave us the recipe for this beautiful, flavorful loaf. Everyone who enjoys a slice asks me for the recipe.
—*Ardath Effa, Villa Park, IL*

Prep: 30 min. + rising • **Bake:** 25 min.
Makes: 1 loaf (16 slices)

- ½ cup chopped onion
- 3 Tbsp. butter
- 1 cup warm 2% milk (110° to 115°) plus 2 Tbsp. warm 2% milk (110° to 115°)
- 1 Tbsp. sugar
- 1½ tsp. salt
- ½ tsp. dill weed
- ½ tsp. dried basil
- ½ tsp. dried rosemary, crushed
- 1 pkg. (¼ oz.) active dry yeast
- 3 to 3½ cups all-purpose flour
  Melted butter

1. In a large skillet, cook onion in butter over low heat until tender. Cool for 10 minutes.
2. Transfer to a large bowl. Add milk, sugar, salt, herbs, yeast and 3 cups flour; beat until smooth. Stir in enough remaining flour to form a soft dough.
3. Turn onto a floured board; knead until smooth and elastic, 6-8 minutes. Place in a greased bowl, turning once to grease top. Cover and let rise in a warm place until doubled, about 45 minutes.
4. Punch the dough down. Shape into a ball and place on a greased baking sheet. Cover and let rise until doubled, about 45 minutes.
5. Bake at 375° for 25-30 minutes. Remove to a wire rack; brush with melted butter. Cool.
1 PIECE: 121 cal., 3g fat (2g sat. fat), 8mg chol., 252mg sod., 20g carb. (2g sugars, 1g fiber), 3g pro.

READER REVIEW
"This bread is delicious, soft and moist. Makes great turkey or club sandwiches. Toasting it really enchances the flavor. And if there is ever any leftover stale bread, you can make croutons, bread crumbs or dressing."
SRSEXTON, TASTEOFHOME.COM

GLUTEN-FREE SANDWICH BREAD

In my search for a satisfying gluten-free bread, this recipe rose to the top. Unlike some other varieties, it's soft and has a tender texture.
—*Doris Kinney, Merrimack, NH*

Prep: 20 min. + rising
Bake: 30 min. + cooling
Makes: 1 loaf (16 slices)

- 1 Tbsp. active dry yeast
- 2 Tbsp. sugar
- 1 cup warm fat-free milk (110° to 115°)
- 2 large eggs, room temperature
- 3 Tbsp. canola oil
- 1 tsp. cider vinegar
- 2½ cups gluten-free all-purpose baking flour
- 2½ tsp. xanthan gum
- 1 tsp. unflavored gelatin
- ½ tsp. salt

1. Grease a 9x5-In. loaf pan and sprinkle with gluten-free flour; set aside.
2. In a small bowl, dissolve yeast and sugar in warm milk. In a stand mixer with a paddle attachment, combine the eggs, oil, vinegar and yeast mixture. Gradually beat in the flour, xanthan gum, gelatin and salt. Beat on low speed for 1 minute. Beat on medium for 2 minutes. (Dough will be softer than yeast bread dough with gluten.)
3. Transfer to prepared pan. Smooth the top with a wet spatula. Cover and let rise in a warm place until dough reaches the top of pan, about 25 minutes.
4. Bake at 375° for 20 minutes; cover loosely with foil. Bake until bread is golden brown, 10-15 minutes longer. Remove from pan to a wire rack to cool.
1 SLICE: 110 cal., 4g fat (0 sat. fat), 27mg chol., 95mg sod., 17g carb. (3g sugars, 2g fiber), 4g pro. **DIABETIC EXCHANGES:** 1 starch, ½ fat.

PUMPKIN SPICE BAGELS

Enjoy pumpkin pie flavor with these classic bagels. You can easily adjust the spices to suit your taste buds.
—*Kristy Reeves, LeRoy, KS*

- -

Prep: 30 min. + standing • **Bake:** 15 min.
Makes: 9 servings

- ⅔ cup plus 2 Tbsp. water (70° to 80°), divided
- ½ cup canned pumpkin
- ⅓ cup packed brown sugar
- 1 tsp. salt
- 1½ tsp. ground cinnamon
- ¾ tsp. ground nutmeg
- ½ tsp. ground allspice
- ½ tsp. ground cloves
- 3 cups bread flour
- 1 pkg. (¼ oz.) active dry yeast
- 1 large egg white
- 1 Tbsp. cornmeal
    Cream cheese, optional

1. In bread machine pan, place ⅔ cup water, pumpkin, brown sugar, salt, spices, flour and yeast in order suggested by manufacturer. Select dough setting (check the dough after 5 minutes of mixing; add 1 to 2 Tbsp. of water or flour if needed).
2. When cycle is completed, turn dough onto a lightly floured surface. Shape into 9 balls. Push thumb through centers to form a 1-in. hole. Stretch and shape dough to form an even ring. Cover and let rest for 10 minutes; flatten rings slightly.
3. Fill a Dutch oven two-thirds full with water; bring to a boil. Drop bagels, 2 at a time, into boiling water. Cook for 45 seconds; turn and cook 45 seconds longer. Remove with a slotted spoon; drain on paper towels.

4. Whisk egg white and remaining water; brush over bagels. Coat a baking sheet with cooking spray and sprinkle with cornmeal. Place bagels 2 in. apart on prepared pan. Bake at 400° for 15-20 minutes or until golden brown. Remove to wire racks to cool. If desired, serve with cream cheese.
1 BAGEL: 180 cal., 0 fat (0 sat. fat), 0 chol., 273mg sod., 40g carb. (8g sugars, 2g fiber), 6g pro.

🄵 CRUSTY FRENCH BREAD

I love to treat guests to these crusty loaves. Don't hesitate to try this recipe even if you are not an accomplished bread baker. It's so easy because there's no kneading required!
—*Christy Freeman, Central Point, OR*

- -

Prep: 30 min. + rising
Bake: 20 min. + cooling
Makes: 2 loaves (10 slices each)

- 1 pkg. (¼ oz.) active dry yeast
- 1½ cups warm water (110° to 115°), divided
- 1 Tbsp. sugar
- 2 tsp. salt
- 1 Tbsp. shortening, melted
- 4 to 5 cups all-purpose flour
    Cornmeal

1. In a large bowl, dissolve yeast in ½ cup water. Add the sugar, salt, shortening, the remaining water and 3½ cups flour. Beat until smooth. Stir in enough of the remaining flour to form a soft dough. Do not knead. Cover and let rise in a warm place until doubled, about 1 hour.
2. Turn dough onto a floured surface. Divide in half; let rest for 10 minutes. Roll each half into a 10x8-in. rectangle. Roll up from a long side; pinch to seal. Place seam side down on 2 greased baking sheets sprinkled with cornmeal. Sprinkle the tops with cornmeal. Cover dough and let rise until doubled, about 45 minutes.
3. With a very sharp knife, make 5 diagonal cuts across the top of each loaf. Bake at 400° until lightly browned, 20-30 minutes. Remove from pans to wire rack to cool.
1 SLICE: 100 cal., 1g fat (0 sat. fat), 0 chol., 233mg sod., 20g carb. (0 sugars, 0 fiber), 3g pro. **DIABETIC EXCHANGES:** 1½ starch.

BLUEBERRY SOUR CREAM COFFEE CAKE

At our house, special breakfasts would not be the same without this delicious coffee cake.
—*Susan Walschlager, Anderson, IN*

- -

Prep: 25 min. • **Bake:** 55 min. + cooling
Makes: 12 servings

- ¾ cup butter, softened
- 1½ cups sugar
- 4 large eggs, room temperature
- 1 tsp. vanilla extract
- 3 cups all-purpose flour
- 1½ tsp. baking powder
- ¾ tsp. baking soda
- ¼ tsp. salt
- 1 cup sour cream

FILLING
- ¼ cup packed brown sugar
- 1 Tbsp. all-purpose flour
- ½ tsp. ground cinnamon
- 2 cups fresh or frozen blueberries

GLAZE
- 1 cup confectioners' sugar
- 2 to 3 Tbsp. 2% milk

1. Preheat oven to 350°. In a large bowl, cream butter and sugar until light and fluffy, 5-7 minutes. Add eggs, 1 at a time, beating well after each addition. Beat in vanilla. Combine the flour, baking powder, baking soda and salt; add to creamed mixture alternately with sour cream, beating well after each addition.
2. Spoon a third of the batter into a greased and floured 10-in. fluted tube pan. Combine brown sugar, flour and cinnamon; sprinkle half over batter. Top with half of the blueberries. Repeat layers. Top with remaining batter.
3. Bake 55-65 minutes or until a toothpick inserted in the center comes out clean. Cool 10 minutes before removing from pan to a wire rack to cool completely. Combine glaze ingredients; drizzle over coffee cake.
1 PIECE: 448 cal., 17g fat (10g sat. fat), 114mg chol., 328mg sod., 68g carb. (42g sugars, 1g fiber), 6g pro.

TEST KITCHEN TIP
Unless a recipe states otherwise, a cake baked in fluted tube pan should cool for 10-15 minutes before moving it to a wire rack to cool completely. Removing a cake too soon can cause it to crack, break or stick to the pan.

Cakes, Pies & Desserts

Want a sweet crowd pleaser? Here are top requests for parties, potlucks, holidays or any occasion that calls for an extra-special treat.

CHOCOLATE RASPBERRY PIE

After tasting this at my sister-in-law's house, I had to get the recipe. A dreamy cream cheese filling separates the tangy raspberry layer from the chocolate topping.
—*Ruth Bartel, Morris, MB*

Prep: 30 min. + chilling
Bake: 15 min. + cooling
Makes: 8 servings

	Pastry for single-crust pie (see recipe on page 177)
3	Tbsp. sugar
1	Tbsp. cornstarch
2	cups fresh or frozen unsweetened raspberries, thawed

FILLING

1	pkg. (8 oz.) cream cheese, softened
⅓	cup sugar
½	tsp. vanilla extract
½	cup heavy whipping cream, whipped

TOPPING

2	oz. semisweet chocolate
3	Tbsp. butter

1. Line the unpricked pie shell with a double thickness of heavy-duty foil. Bake at 450° for 8 minutes. Remove foil; bake 5 minutes longer. Cool on a wire rack.

2. In a large saucepan, combine sugar and cornstarch. Stir in raspberries; bring to a boil over medium heat. Boil and stir for 2 minutes. Remove from the heat; cool for 15 minutes. Spread into shell, refrigerate.

3. In a large bowl, beat the cream cheese, sugar and vanilla until fluffy. Fold in whipped cream. Carefully spread over raspberry layer. Cover and refrigerate for at least 1 hour.

4. In a microwave, melt chocolate and butter; stir until smooth.

5. Cool for 4-5 minutes. Pour over the filling. Cover and chill for at least 2 hours. Store in the refrigerator.

1 SLICE: 395 cal., 28g fat (16g sat. fat), 68mg chol., 233mg sod., 34g carb. (18g sugars, 2g fiber), 4g pro.

DID YOU KNOW?
You can freeze any extra fresh raspberries. Set them in a single layer on a baking sheet and freeze. After about 90 minutes, the berries should be frozen, and you can transfer them to a freezer bag.

VANILLA CAKE WITH VANILLA BUTTERCREAM FROSTING

Indulge in this layer cake topped with rich buttercream—a vanilla lover's dream. I use pure vanilla extract for the best flavor.
—*Michelle Dorsey, Wilmington, DE*

Prep: 15 min. • **Bake:** 25 min. + cooling
Makes: 16 servings

- ¾ cup unsalted butter, softened
- 1½ cups sugar
- 3 large eggs, room temperature
- 1½ tsp. vanilla extract
- 2⅓ cups cake flour
- 2½ tsp. baking powder
- ½ tsp. salt
- ¾ cup 2% milk

FROSTING
- 1 cup unsalted butter, softened
- 3 tsp. clear vanilla extract
- 2½ cups confectioners' sugar
  Optional: Colored sprinkles or nonpareils

1. Preheat oven to 350°. Line the bottoms of 2 greased 9-in. round baking pans with parchment; grease parchment.
2. In a large bowl, cream the butter and sugar until light and fluffy, 5-7 minutes. Add eggs, 1 at a time, beating well after each addition. Beat in the vanilla. In another bowl, mix the flour, baking powder and salt; add to creamed mixture alternately with milk, beating well after each addition. Pour into prepared pans, dividing batter evenly.
3. Bake at 350° until a toothpick inserted in center comes out clean, 25-30 minutes. Cool in pans 10 minutes before removing to wire racks; remove the parchment. Cool completely.
4. For frosting, in a small bowl, beat butter and vanilla until blended. Gradually beat in the confectioners' sugar until smooth. Spread frosting between layers and over top and sides of cake. Decorate with sprinkles if desired.
1 SLICE: 420 cal., 22g fat (13g sat. fat), 89mg chol., 171mg sod., 54g carb. (38g sugars, 0 fiber), 3g pro.

5i

RIBBON PUDDING PIE

Cool and creamy, this light dessert is a little slice of heaven for diabetics or anyone looking to reduce fat and sugar. The yummy filling goes in a ready-made graham cracker crust.
—*Doris Morgan, Verona, MS*

Prep: 20 min. + chilling • **Makes:** 8 servings

- 4 cups cold fat-free milk, divided
- 1 pkg. (1 oz.) sugar-free instant vanilla pudding mix
- 1 reduced-fat graham cracker crust (9 in.)
- 1 pkg. (1 oz.) sugar-free instant butterscotch pudding mix
- 1 pkg. (1.4 oz.) sugar-free instant chocolate pudding mix
  Optional: Whipped topping and finely chopped pecans

1. Whisk 1⅓ cups milk and vanilla pudding mix 2 minutes. Spread into crust.
2. In another bowl, whisk 1⅓ cups milk and butterscotch pudding mix 2 minutes. Carefully spoon over vanilla layer, spreading evenly.
3. In a third bowl, whisk remaining 1⅓ cups milk and chocolate pudding mix 2 minutes. Carefully spread over top. Refrigerate until set, at least 30 minutes. If desired, serve with whipped topping and pecans.
1 PIECE: 184 cal., 3g fat (1g sat. fat), 2mg chol., 427mg sod., 32g carb. (13g sugars, 1g fiber), 6g pro. **DIABETIC EXCHANGES:** 2 starch, 1 fat.

MICHELLE DORSEY
Wilmington, DE

STRAWBERRY CRUNCH ICE CREAM CAKE

While growing up, I was always thrilled when the ice cream truck came through our neighborhood. This wonderful cake is inspired by one of those crunchy strawberry novelties.
—Lisa Kaminski, Wauwatosa, WI

Prep: 20 min. + freezing
Bake: 25 min. + cooling
Makes: 9 servings

- 36   Golden Oreo cookies, divided
- 4   Tbsp. butter, melted
- 3   cups vanilla ice cream, softened
- 5   cups strawberry ice cream, softened
- 1   carton (8 oz.) frozen whipped topping, thawed
- 1   pkg. (1 oz.) freeze-dried strawberries, coarsely crushed
      Fresh strawberries, optional

1. Line a 9x9-in. baking pan with parchment. Preheat oven to 350°. Finely crush 24 cookies. In a small bowl, mix cookie crumbs and butter. Press onto bottom of prepared pan. Bake until firm, 25-30 minutes. Cool on a wire rack.
2. Spread vanilla ice cream onto crust; freeze, covered, until firm. Spread with strawberry ice cream and then whipped topping; freeze, covered, until firm.
3. Coarsely crush remaining cookies. Combine cookie crumbs and freeze-dried strawberries; sprinkle on whipped topping. Freeze, covered, until firm, about 8 hours or overnight. Remove cake from freezer 10 minutes before serving. If desired, garnish with fresh strawberries.

1 PIECE: 584 cal., 30g fat (16g sat. fat), 54mg chol., 280mg sod., 72g carb. (33g sugars, 2g fiber), 6g pro.

PRESSURE-COOKER LIME CHEESECAKE

I love my pressure cooker and get a kick out of creating recipes for it. When I wanted to try a cheesecake, I did some research and put together my own version. Success! It was not only beautiful with no cracks but also tasted absolutely scrumptious.
—Joan Hallford, North Richland Hills, TX

Prep: 20 min. • **Cook:** 50 min. + cooling
Makes: 8 servings

- ¾   cup graham cracker crumbs
- 1   Tbsp. sugar
- 3   Tbsp. butter, melted

FILLING
- 2   pkg. (8 oz. each) cream cheese, softened
- ¾   cup sugar
- ¼   cup sour cream
- 2   to 3 tsp. grated lime zest
- 1   Tbsp. lime juice
- 1   tsp. vanilla extract
- 2   large eggs, room temperature, lightly beaten
      Optional: Lime slices and whipped cream

1. Place the trivet insert and 1 cup water in a 6-qt. electric pressure cooker. Grease a 6-in. springform pan; place on a double thickness of heavy-duty foil (about 12 in. square). Wrap securely around pan.
2. In a small bowl, combine graham cracker crumbs and sugar. Stir in melted butter. Press onto bottom and up the sides of prepared pan. Place in freezer. Meanwhile, in a large bowl, beat cream cheese and sugar until smooth. Beat in sour cream, lime zest, lime juice and vanilla. Add eggs; beat on low speed just until blended. Pour into prepared pan. Cover pan with foil. Fold an 18x12-in. piece of foil lengthwise into thirds, making a sling. Use the sling to lower pan onto trivet.
3. Lock the lid; close the pressure-release valve. Adjust to pressure-cook on high for 50 minutes. Let pressure release naturally for 10 minutes; quick-release any remaining pressure. Using foil sling, carefully remove the springform pan. Let stand 10 minutes. Remove foil from pan. Cool cheesecake on a wire rack 1 hour.
4. Loosen the sides from pan with a knife. Refrigerate overnight, covering when cooled. To serve, remove rim from pan. If desired, garnish with lime slices and whipped cream.

1 SLICE: 292 cal., 18g fat (10g sat. fat), 88mg chol., 187mg sod., 30g carb. (24g sugars, 0 fiber), 4g pro.

GRANDMA'S RED VELVET CAKE

It's just not Christmas at our house until this festive cake appears. This is different from other red velvets I've had; the icing is as light as snow.
—*Kathryn Davison, Charlotte, NC*

Prep: 30 min. • **Bake:** 20 min. + cooling
Makes: 14 servings

½ cup butter, softened
1½ cups sugar
2 large eggs, room temperature
2 bottles (1 oz. each) red food coloring
1 Tbsp. white vinegar
1 tsp. vanilla extract
2¼ cups cake flour
2 Tbsp. baking cocoa
1 tsp. baking soda
1 tsp. salt
1 cup buttermilk

FROSTING
½ cup cold water
1 Tbsp. cornstarch
2 cups butter, softened
2 tsp. vanilla extract
3½ cups confectioners' sugar

1. Preheat oven to 350°. Cream the butter and sugar until light and fluffy, 5-7 minutes. Add eggs, 1 at a time, beating well after each addition. Beat in food coloring, vinegar and vanilla. In another bowl, whisk together flour, cocoa, baking soda and salt; add to creamed mixture alternately with buttermilk, beating well after each addition.

2. Pour into 2 greased and floured 9-in. round baking pans. Bake until a toothpick inserted in the center comes out clean, 20-25 minutes. Cool the layers 10 minutes before removing from pans to wire racks to cool completely.

3. For frosting, combine water and cornstarch in a small saucepan over medium heat. Stir until thickened and opaque, 2-3 minutes. Cool to room temperature. Beat butter and vanilla until light and fluffy. Beat in the cornstarch mixture. Gradually add confectioners' sugar; beat until light and fluffy. Spread between layers and over top and sides of cake.

1 SLICE: 595 cal., 34g fat (21g sat. fat), 115mg chol., 564mg sod., 71g carb. (52g sugars, 1g fiber), 4g pro.

🎗 CONTEST-WINNING PEACH COBBLER

I use canned peaches instead of fresh for my cobbler. That way, I can reserve some of the syrup to make a warm butterscotch sauce.
—*Ellen Merick, North Pole, AK*

- -

Prep: 20 min. + standing
Bake: 50 min. + cooling
Makes: 12 servings

- 2 cans (29 oz. each) sliced peaches
- ½ cup packed brown sugar
- 6 Tbsp. quick-cooking tapioca
- 1 tsp. ground cinnamon, optional
- 1 tsp. lemon juice
- 1 tsp. vanilla extract

TOPPING
- 1 cup all-purpose flour
- 1 cup sugar
- 1 tsp. baking powder
- ½ tsp. salt
- ¼ cup cold butter, cubed
- 2 large eggs, room temperature, lightly beaten

BUTTERSCOTCH SAUCE
- ½ cup packed brown sugar
- 2 Tbsp. all-purpose flour
- ⅛ tsp. salt
- ¼ cup butter, melted
- 2 Tbsp. lemon juice
  Vanilla ice cream, optional

1. Drain peaches, reserving ½ cup syrup for butterscotch sauce. In a large bowl, combine peaches, brown sugar, tapioca, cinnamon if desired, lemon juice and vanilla. Transfer to an ungreased 11x7-in. baking dish. Let stand for 15 minutes.

2. In a large bowl, combine flour, sugar, baking powder and salt; cut in butter until mixture resembles coarse crumbs. Stir in eggs. Drop by spoonfuls onto peach mixture; spread evenly. Bake at 350° until filling is bubbly and a toothpick inserted in topping comes out clean, 50-55 minutes. Cool for 10 minutes.

3. For butterscotch sauce, in a small saucepan, combine brown sugar, flour, salt, butter and reserved peach syrup. Bring to a boil over medium heat; cook and stir until thickened, 1 minute. Remove from the heat; add lemon juice. If desired, serve cobbler with ice cream.

½ CUP: 352 cal., 9g fat (5g sat. fat), 51mg chol., 248mg sod., 67g carb. (51g sugars, 1g fiber), 2g pro.

CHERRY DREAM CAKE

I love serving this because it's impressive yet easy. No one will know your secret is adding a package of gelatin to a boxed mix!
—*Margaret McNeil, Germantown, TN*

Prep: 15 min. + chilling
Bake: 30 min. + cooling
Makes: 20 servings

1   pkg. white cake mix (regular size)
1   pkg. (3 oz.) cherry gelatin
1½ cups boiling water
1   pkg. (8 oz.) cream cheese, softened
2   cups whipped topping
1   can (21 oz.) cherry pie filling

1. Prepare cake mix according to package directions, using a greased 13x9-in. baking pan. Bake at 350° for 30-35 minutes or until a toothpick comes out clean.
2. Dissolve gelatin in boiling water. Cool cake on a wire rack for 3-5 minutes. Poke holes in cake with a meat fork or wooden skewer; gradually pour gelatin over cake. Cool for 15 minutes. Cover; refrigerate for 30 minutes.
3. In a large bowl, beat cream cheese until fluffy. Fold in whipped topping. Carefully spread over cake. Top with cherry pie filling. Cover and refrigerate for at least 2 hours before serving.
1 PIECE: 245 cal., 11g fat (5g sat. fat), 39mg chol., 242mg sod., 34g carb. (22 sugars, 1g fiber), 3g pro. **DIABETIC EXCHANGES:** 1½ starch, 1 fat, ½ fruit.

SALTED CARAMEL CAPPUCCINO CHEESECAKE

Living in Seattle turned me into a coffee junkie! When I had to relocate across the country for a time, I created a java-flavored cheesecake. Making it always lifted my spirits on days I felt blue about leaving one of the world's amazing coffee destinations.
—*Julie Merriman, Seattle, WA*

Prep: 30 min. • **Bake:** 55 min. + chilling
Makes: 12 servings

1   pkg. (9 oz.) chocolate wafers
1   cup semisweet chocolate chips
½   cup packed brown sugar
2   Tbsp. instant espresso powder
⅛   tsp. ground nutmeg
½   cup butter, melted
FILLING
3   pkg. (8 oz. each) cream cheese, softened
1   cup packed brown sugar
½   cup sour cream
¼   cup Kahlua (coffee liqueur)
2   Tbsp. all-purpose flour
2   Tbsp. instant espresso powder
4   large eggs, lightly beaten
TOPPING
½   cup hot caramel ice cream topping
½   tsp. coarse sea salt

1. Preheat oven to 350°. Place a greased 9-in. springform pan on a double thickness of heavy-duty foil (about 18 in. square). Securely wrap foil around pan.
2. Place the first 5 ingredients in a food processor; cover and pulse until fine crumbs form. Gradually add melted butter, pulsing until combined. Press mixture onto bottom and 2 in. up sides of prepared pan.
3. In a large bowl, beat cream cheese and brown sugar until smooth. Beat in sour cream, Kahlua, flour and espresso powder. Add eggs; beat on low speed just until blended. Pour into crust. Place springform pan in a larger baking pan; add 1 in. of hot water to larger pan.
4. Bake 55-65 minutes or until the center is just set and the top appears dull. Remove springform pan from water bath; remove foil. Cool cheesecake on a wire rack 10 minutes; loosen the sides from pan with a knife. Cool 1 hour longer. Refrigerate overnight, covering when completely cooled.
5. Pour hot caramel ice cream topping over cheesecake. Refrigerate at least 15 minutes. Remove rim from pan. Sprinkle with sea salt just before serving.
1 SLICE: 618 cal., 38g fat (22g sat. fat), 160mg chol., 530mg sod., 64g carb. (42g sugars, 2g fiber), 9g pro.

OATMEAL CAKE WITH CARAMEL ICING

Here's a lighter dessert that tastes anything but light. The icing sets up quickly, so be sure to frost the cake immediately after it cools.
—*Summer Marks, Louisville, KY*

Prep: 30 min. • **Bake:** 20 min. + cooling
Makes: 20 servings

- 1¼ cups boiling water
- 1 cup quick-cooking oats
- ¼ cup butter, softened
- 1 cup packed brown sugar
- ½ cup sugar
- 2 large eggs, room temperature
- ¼ cup unsweetened applesauce
- 1 tsp. vanilla extract
- 1½ cups all-purpose flour
- 2 tsp. baking powder
- ¾ tsp. ground cinnamon
- ½ tsp. baking soda
- ½ tsp. salt
- ¼ tsp. ground nutmeg

ICING

- ½ cup packed brown sugar
- ¼ cup butter, cubed
- ¼ cup fat-free milk
- ½ tsp. vanilla extract
- ⅛ tsp. salt
- 1½ cups confectioners' sugar

1. In a small bowl, pour the boiling water over oats; let stand 10 minutes.

2. Meanwhile, preheat oven to 350°. In a large bowl, beat butter and sugars until crumbly, about 2 minutes. Add the eggs, 1 at a time, beating well after each addition. Beat in the applesauce and vanilla. Combine the flour, baking powder, cinnamon, baking soda, salt and nutmeg. Gradually add to the creamed mixture. Stir in the oats. Pour into a greased 13x9-in. baking pan.

3. Bake until a toothpick inserted in the center comes out with moist crumbs, 18-22 minutes. Cool completely on a wire rack.

4. For the icing, in a small saucepan, combine the brown sugar and butter. Bring to a boil over medium heat, stirring constantly. Cook and stir for 1 minute. Gradually whisk in the milk. Return to a boil. Cook and stir 1 minute. Transfer to a small bowl. Stir in vanilla and salt. Gradually beat in confectioners' sugar until smooth. Immediately spread icing over cake. Let stand until set.

1 PIECE: 218 cal., 5g fat (3g sat. fat), 31mg chol., 203mg sod., 41g carb. (30g sugars, 1g fiber), 2g pro.

DUTCH OVEN APPLE COBBLER

This homey treat is always a hit with my family. I top each warm bowlful with a scoop of ice cream or a dollop of whipped cream.
—*Cindy Jajuga, Weed, CA*

Prep: 20 min. • **Bake:** 45 min.
Makes: 8 servings

- 8 large tart apples, peeled and sliced
- 1 cup sugar, divided
- ¾ tsp. ground cinnamon, divided
- 2 cups all-purpose flour
- ¾ cup packed brown sugar
- 1 tsp. baking powder
- ½ tsp. salt
- 2 large eggs, room temperature, lightly beaten
- ⅔ cup butter, melted
  Vanilla ice cream, optional

Preheat oven to 350°. In a 6-qt. Dutch oven, combine the apples, ¾ cup sugar and ½ tsp. cinnamon. In a bowl, whisk flour, brown sugar, remaining ¼ cup sugar, baking powder, salt and remaining ¼ tsp. cinnamon; stir in eggs (mixture will be lumpy). Spoon over apples. Drizzle butter over batter (do not stir). Cover and bake until lightly browned and apples are tender, 45-50 minutes. Serve warm with ice cream, if desired.

1 SERVING: 531 cal., 17g fat (10g sat. fat), 87mg chol., 354mg sod., 93g carb. (64g sugars, 3g fiber), 5g pro.

APRICOT-ALMOND TARTLETS

These delicate, buttery tarts absolutely melt in your mouth. With their bright apricot tops, they make an eye-catching choice for a holiday cookie tray.
—Julie Dunsworth, Oviedo, FL

Prep: 25 min. • **Bake:** 20 min. + cooling
Makes: 2 dozen

- 1 cup all-purpose flour
- 3 Tbsp. confectioners' sugar
- ⅓ cup cold butter
- 1 large egg yolk
- 1 to 2 Tbsp. water

FILLING

- ½ cup almond paste
- ¼ cup butter, softened
- 1 large egg white
- ¼ tsp. almond extract
- ½ cup apricot preserves

1. In a large bowl, combine the flour and confectioners' sugar; cut in the butter until mixture resembles coarse crumbs. Add egg yolk and water; stir until dough forms a ball. Roll into twenty-four 1-in. balls. Press onto the bottoms and up the sides of greased miniature muffin cups.
2. In a small bowl, beat almond paste and butter until blended; beat in egg white and almond extract. Spoon into tart shells, about 2 tsp. in each.
3. Bake at 350° 20-25 minutes or until golden brown. Cool for 5 minutes before removing from pans to wire racks. Top with preserves.
1 TARTLET: 103 cal., 6g fat (3g sat. fat), 20mg chol., 37mg sod., 12g carb. (5g sugars, 0 fiber), 1g pro.

BLUEBERRY BANANA CREAM PIE

Here's a recipe I found in a book years ago and have made countless times since. People love the unusual but delicious pairing of fresh blueberries and bananas.
—Loraine Meyer, Bend, OR

Prep: 15 min. + chilling • **Makes:** 8 servings

- 6 oz. cream cheese, softened
- 1 can (14 oz.) sweetened condensed milk
- ¾ cup cold water
- 1 pkg. (3.4 oz.) instant vanilla pudding mix
- 1 cup heavy whipping cream, whipped
- 2 medium bananas, cut into ¼-in. slices
- 2 tsp. lemon juice
- 35 vanilla wafers
- 1 cup fresh blueberries

1. In a large bowl, beat the cream cheese until smooth. Beat in the milk, water and pudding mix. Fold in whipped cream.
2. In a bowl or shallow dish, add the bananas and lemon juice; toss until bananas are coated. Drain and discard lemon juice.
3. Line an ungreased deep-dish 9-in. pie plate with the vanilla wafers. Spread with half the cream cheese mixture. Top with bananas and blueberries. Spread with remaining cream cheese mixture. Refrigerate for 3 hours or until set. Refrigerate leftovers.
1 PIECE: 490 cal., 26g fat (15g sat. fat), 84mg chol., 359mg sod., 61g carb. (48g sugars, 2g fiber), 7g pro.

⑤ⁱ LEMONADE ICEBOX PIE

You'll get the refreshing taste of lemonade in every bite of this simple but tongue-tingling pie. High and fluffy with a creamy-smooth consistency, it's a cool dessert I frequently put on my summer menus.
—Cheryl Wilt, Eglon, WV

Prep: 15 min. + chilling • **Makes:** 8 servings

- 1 pkg. (8 oz.) cream cheese, softened
- 1 can (14 oz.) sweetened condensed milk
- ¾ cup thawed lemonade concentrate
- 1 carton (8 oz.) frozen whipped topping, thawed Yellow food coloring, optional
- 1 graham cracker crust (9 in.)

In a large bowl, beat cream cheese and milk until smooth. Beat in lemonade concentrate. Fold in whipped topping and, if desired, food coloring. Pour into graham cracker crust. Cover and refrigerate until set.
1 PIECE: 491 cal., 24g fat (15g sat. fat), 48mg chol., 269mg sod., 61g carb. (52g sugars, 0 fiber), 7g pro.

GRAN'S APPLE CAKE

My grandmother would occasionally bring over this treasured treat warm from the oven. With nicely spiced flavor and a cream cheese frosting, her apple cake always disappeared quickly. I've lightened up the ingredients a bit, but it's still a family favorite.
—Lauris Conrad, Turlock, CA

Prep: 20 min. • **Bake:** 35 min. + cooling
Makes: 24 servings

- 1⅔ cups sugar
- 2 large eggs, room temperature
- ½ cup unsweetened applesauce
- 2 Tbsp. canola oil
- 2 tsp. vanilla extract
- 2 cups all-purpose flour
- 2 tsp. baking soda
- 2 tsp. ground cinnamon
- ¾ tsp. salt
- 6 cups chopped peeled tart apples
- ½ cup chopped pecans

FROSTING

- 4 oz. reduced-fat cream cheese
- 2 Tbsp. butter, softened
- 1 tsp. vanilla extract
- 1 cup confectioners' sugar

1. Preheat oven to 350°. Coat a 13x9-in. baking pan with cooking spray.
2. In a large bowl, beat the sugar, eggs, applesauce, oil and vanilla until well blended. In another bowl, whisk the flour, baking soda, cinnamon and salt; gradually beat into sugar mixture. Fold in apples and pecans.
3. Transfer to the prepared pan. Bake 35-40 minutes or until top is golden brown and a toothpick inserted in center comes out clean. Cool completely in pan on a wire rack.
4. In a small bowl, beat cream cheese, butter and vanilla until smooth. Gradually beat in confectioners' sugar (mixture will be soft). Spread over cake. Refrigerate leftovers.
1 PIECE: 181 cal., 5g fat (2g sat. fat), 21mg chol., 213mg sod., 32g carb. (22g sugars, 1g fiber), 2g pro. **DIABETIC EXCHANGES:** 2 starch, 1 fat.

MOM'S CUSTARD PIE

A bite of this takes me back to the days when Mom would fix it for Dad, Grandfather and me. She often prepared food for large parties as well, and this pie was always a top request.
—*Barbara Hyatt, Folsom, CA*

Prep: 25 min. + standing
Bake: 40 min. + cooling
Makes: 8 servings

    Pastry for single-crust pie (see recipe on page 177)
4 **large eggs**
½ **cup sugar**
¼ **tsp. salt**
1 **tsp. vanilla extract**
2½ **cups 2% milk**
¼ **tsp. ground nutmeg**

1. On a lightly floured surface, roll dough to a ⅛-in.-thick circle; transfer to a 9-in. pie plate. Trim to ½ in. beyond rim of plate; flute edge. Refrigerate 30 minutes. Preheat oven to 425°. Line unpricked crust with a double thickness of foil. Fill with pie weights, dried beans or uncooked rice. Bake on a lower oven rack until edges are light golden brown, 15-20 minutes. Remove foil and weights; bake until bottom is golden brown, 3-6 minutes longer. Cool on a wire rack. Reduce oven setting to 350°.
2. Separate 1 egg; set the white aside in a large bowl and let stand for 15 minutes. In a small bowl, beat the yolk and remaining eggs just until combined. Blend in the sugar, salt and vanilla. Stir in milk. Beat reserved egg white until stiff peaks form; fold into egg mixture.
3. Carefully pour into crust. Cover the edges of pie with foil. Bake for 25 minutes. Remove foil; bake until a knife inserted in the center comes out clean, 15-20 minutes longer. Cool on a wire rack. Sprinkle with nutmeg. Store in the refrigerator.
1 PIECE: 254 cal., 12g fat (5g sat. fat), 122mg chol., 243mg sod., 29g carb. (17g sugars, 0 fiber), 7g pro.

CONTEST-WINNING MOIST CHOCOLATE CAKE

Making a special cake from scratch doesn't have to be time-consuming—here's proof! You can quickly mix the batter in one bowl, then just bake and enjoy.
—*Christa Hageman, Telford, PA*

Prep: 15 min. • **Bake:** 45 min. + cooling
Makes: 12 servings

2 **cups sugar**
1¾ **cups all-purpose flour**
¾ **cup baking cocoa**
2 **tsp. baking soda**
1 **tsp. baking powder**
1 **tsp. salt**
2 **large eggs, room temperature**
1 **cup strong brewed coffee**
1 **cup buttermilk**
½ **cup canola oil**
1 **tsp. vanilla extract**
1 **Tbsp. confectioners' sugar**

1. In a large bowl, combine the first 6 ingredients. Add eggs, coffee, buttermilk, oil and vanilla; beat on medium speed for 2 minutes (batter will be thin). Pour into a greased and floured 10-in. fluted tube pan.
2. Bake at 350° for 45-50 minutes or until a toothpick inserted in the center comes out clean. Cool for 10 minutes before removing from pan to a wire rack to cool completely. Dust with confectioners' sugar.
1 SLICE: 315 cal., 11g fat (2g sat. fat), 36mg chol., 473mg sod., 52g carb. (34g sugars, 1g fiber), 5g pro.

GINGERSNAP PUMPKIN PIE

Butterscotch pudding and canned pumpkin make a yummy layer in this spiced dessert featuring a gingersnap crust.
—Taste of Home *Test Kitchen*

Prep: 30 min. + chilling • **Makes:** 8 servings

- 1½ cups finely crushed gingersnaps (about 32 cookies)
- ¼ cup butter, melted
- 4 oz. cream cheese, softened
- 1 Tbsp. sugar
- 1½ cups whipped topping
- 1 cup cold 2% milk
- 2 pkg. (3.4 oz. each) instant butterscotch pudding mix
- ½ cup canned pumpkin
- ½ tsp. pumpkin pie spice
- ½ tsp. vanilla extract
- ¼ tsp. ground cinnamon
  Additional whipped topping, optional

1. Preheat oven to 375°. In a small bowl, combine gingersnap cookie crumbs and butter. Press onto the bottom and up the sides of an ungreased 9-in. pie plate. Bake 8-10 minutes or until crust is lightly browned. Cool on a wire rack.
2. For the filling, in a small bowl, beat the cream cheese and sugar until smooth. Fold in whipped topping. Spread over crust.
3. In a small bowl, beat milk and pudding mixes 1 minute. Stir in pumpkin, pie spice, vanilla and cinnamon. Spread over cream cheese layer. Cover and refrigerate overnight. Garnish with additional whipped topping if desired.
1 PIECE: 429 cal., 18g fat (11g sat. fat), 34mg chol., 746mg sod., 62g carb. (31g sugars, 2g fiber), 5g pro.

FROSTED HARVEST CAKE

Craving brownies but want something a little bit different? Indulge in a fall-flavored version topped with a cream cheese frosting.
—*Iola Egle, Bella Vista, AR*

Prep: 15 min. • **Bake:** 20 min. + cooling
Makes: 3½ dozen

- 1 can (15 oz.) pumpkin
- 4 large eggs, room temperature
- ¾ cup canola oil
- 2 tsp. vanilla extract
- 2 cups all-purpose flour
- 2 cups sugar
- 1 Tbsp. pumpkin pie spice
- 2 tsp. ground cinnamon
- 2 tsp. baking powder
- 1 tsp. baking soda
- ½ tsp. salt

FROSTING

- 6 Tbsp. butter, softened
- 3 oz. cream cheese, softened
- 1 tsp. vanilla extract
- 1 tsp. milk
- ⅛ tsp. salt
- 1½ to 2 cups confectioners' sugar

1. In a large bowl, beat the pumpkin, eggs, oil and vanilla until blended. Combine the dry ingredients; gradually stir into the pumpkin mixture.
2. Pour into a greased 15x10x1-in. baking pan. Bake at 350° until a toothpick inserted in the center comes out clean, 20-25 minutes. Cool in pan on a wire rack.
3. In a small bowl, beat the butter, cream cheese, vanilla, milk and salt until smooth. Gradually add the confectioners' sugar until smooth. Frost the cake; cut into bars. Store in the refrigerator.
1 SERVING: 83 cal., 4g fat (1g sat. fat), 16mg chol., 66mg sod., 11g carb. (8g sugars, 0 fiber), 1g pro.

TEST KITCHEN TIP
To save time, skip making the cream cheese frosting and top this cake with your favorite canned variety.

PINK VELVET CUPCAKES

My daughter loves all things pink, so I surprised her with these for her birthday. My teenage son (not a fan of pink) ate his share, too!
—*Paulette Smith, Winston-Salem, NC*

- -

Prep: 30 min. + chilling
Bake: 25 min. + cooling
Makes: 2 dozen

- 1   cup butter, softened
- 1¼   cups sugar
- ⅛   tsp. pink paste food coloring
- 3   large eggs, room temperature
- 1   tsp. vanilla extract
- 2½   cups all-purpose flour
- 1½   tsp. baking powder
- ¼   tsp. baking soda
- ¼   tsp. salt
- 1   cup buttermilk

WHITE CHOCOLATE GANACHE

- 2   cups white baking chips
- ½   cup heavy whipping cream
- 1   Tbsp. butter
       Pink coarse sugar and sugar pearls

1. In a large bowl, cream the butter, sugar and pink paste food coloring until light and fluffy, 5-7 minutes. Add the eggs, 1 at a time, beating well after each addition. Beat in the vanilla. Combine the flour, baking powder, baking soda and salt; add to creamed mixture alternately with buttermilk, beating well after each addition.

2. Fill 24 paper-lined muffin cups two-thirds full. Bake at 350° for 23-27 minutes or until a toothpick inserted in the center comes out clean. Cool for 10 minutes before removing from pans to wire racks to cool completely.

3. Meanwhile, place white chips in a small bowl. In a small saucepan, bring cream just to a boil. Pour over chips; whisk until smooth. Stir in butter. Transfer to a large bowl. Chill for 30 minutes, stirring once.

4. Beat on high speed for 2-3 minutes or until soft peaks form and frosting is light and fluffy. Frost cupcakes. Top cupcakes with coarse sugar and sugar pearls. Store in refrigerator.

1 CUPCAKE: 266 cal., 15g fat (9g sat. fat), 57mg chol., 154mg sod., 29g carb. (20g sugars, 0 fiber), 3g pro.

PEANUT BUTTER SILK PIE

My son wanted homemade pies placed around his wedding cake. This decadent peanut butter pie was one of his requests.
—*Lee Steinmetz, Lansing, MI*

Prep: 10 min. + chilling • Makes: 8 servings

- ¾ cup peanut butter
- 4   oz. cream cheese, softened
- 1   cup confectioners' sugar
- 1   carton (8 oz.) frozen whipped topping, thawed
- 1   graham cracker crust (9 in.)
      Salted chopped peanuts
      Optional: Additional whipped topping, chocolate sauce and peanut butter sauce

In a large bowl, beat the peanut butter, cream cheese and confectioners' sugar until smooth. Fold in the whipped topping; pour into crust. Refrigerate at least 2 hours before serving. Sprinkle with peanuts and, if desired, top with additional whipped topping, chocolate sauce and peanut butter sauce.

1 PIECE: 434 cal., 27g fat (11g sat. fat), 16mg chol., 276mg sod., 40g carb. (29g sugars, 2g fiber), 8g pro.

PASTRY FOR SINGLE-CRUST PIE

Takes: 10 min.
Makes: 1 pie crust (8 servings)

- 1¼ cups all-purpose flour
- ½   tsp. salt
- ⅓   cup shortening
      4 to 5 Tbsp. cold water

1. In a large bowl, combine flour and salt; cut in shortening until crumbly. Gradually add water, tossing with a fork until a ball forms. Roll out the dough to fit a 9-in. or 10-in. pie plate.

2. Transfer crust to pie plate. Trim crust to ½ in. beyond edge of pie plate; flute edges. Fill or bake the crust according to recipe directions. Double the recipe for double-crust pies.

1 SERVING: 144 cal., 8g fat (2g sat. fat), 0 chol., 148mg sod., 15g carb. (0 sugars, 1g fiber), 2g pro.

BEST ANGEL FOOD CAKE

For our daughter's wedding, a friend made this from a recipe she's used for decades. I've never tasted a better angel food cake! Serve slices plain or dress them up with a garnish of fresh fruit and whipped topping.
—Marilyn Niemeyer, Doon, IA

- -

Prep: 15 min. • **Bake:** 35 min. + cooling
Makes: 16 servings

- 1¼ cups large egg whites (about 9)
- 1½ cups sugar, divided
- 1 cup cake flour
- 1¼ tsp. cream of tartar
- 1 tsp. vanilla extract
- ¼ tsp. almond extract
- ¼ tsp. salt

1. Place egg whites in a large bowl; let stand at room temperature 30 minutes. Sift ½ cup sugar and flour together twice; set aside.
2. Place oven rack in the lowest position. Preheat oven to 350°. Add cream of tartar, extracts and salt to the egg whites; beat on medium speed until soft peaks form. Gradually add the remaining sugar, about 2 Tbsp. at a time, beating on high until stiff peaks form. Gradually fold in flour mixture, about ½ cup at a time.
3. Gently spoon into an ungreased 10-in. tube pan. Cut through batter with a knife to remove air pockets. Bake until lightly browned andthe entire top appears dry, 35-40 minutes. Immediately invert the pan; cool completely, about 1 hour.
4. Run a knife around side and center tube of pan. Remove cake to a serving plate.
1 SLICE: 115 cal., 0 fat (0 sat. fat), 0 chol., 68mg sod., 26g carb. (19g sugars, 0 fiber), 3g pro. **DIABETIC EXCHANGES:** 1½ starch.

TEST KITCHEN TIP
When baking an angel food cake, it's important to bring the egg whites to room temperature. When at the right temperature, the egg whites will beat up to a full volume that ultimately results in a high, fluffy and light cake.

FROZEN CHOCOLATE CHEESECAKE TART

When expecting company for dinner, I decided to try a frozen cheesecake in a cookie crust. Our guests couldn't stop raving about the rich flavor. My husband took one bite and said it was the best dessert he'd ever eaten!
—Heather Bennett, Dunbar, WV

- -

Prep: 15 min. + freezing • **Makes:** 12 servings

- 2¼ cups crushed Oreo cookies (about 22 cookies)
- ⅓ cup butter, melted
FILLING
- 2 pkg. (8 oz. each) cream cheese, softened
- ⅓ cup confectioners' sugar
- 3 cups vanilla or white chips, melted and cooled
- ⅓ cup heavy whipping cream
- 1 tsp. vanilla extract
- ½ cup miniature semisweet chocolate chips
  Additional miniature semisweet chocolate chips, optional

1. In a small bowl, combine the cookie crumbs and butter. Press onto the bottom and up the sides of a greased 9-in. fluted tart pan with a removable bottom. Cover and freeze for at least 1 hour.
2. In a large bowl, beat the cream cheese and sugar until smooth. Beat in the vanilla chips, cream and vanilla until well combined. Stir in the chocolate chips; pour over the crust. Cover and freeze for 8 hours or overnight.
3. Uncover and refrigerate 3-4 hours before serving. If desired, sprinkle with chocolate chips. Refrigerate leftovers.
1 SLICE: 546 cal., 36g fat (20g sat. fat), 52mg chol., 291mg sod., 53g carb. (18g sugars, 2g fiber), 6g pro

TEXAS SHEET CAKE

When I was growing up, this chocolaty delight was one of the treats I loved most. It's really moist and bakes in a large pan. The yummy homemade icing is a must!
—Susan Ormond, Jamestown, NC

Prep: 20 min. • **Bake:** 20 min. + cooling
Makes: 15 servings

- 1 cup butter, cubed
- 1 cup water
- ¼ cup baking cocoa
- 2 cups all-purpose flour
- 2 cups sugar
- 1 tsp. baking soda
- ½ tsp. salt
- ½ cup sour cream

ICING

- ½ cup butter, cubed
- ¼ cup plus 2 Tbsp. 2% milk
- 3 Tbsp. baking cocoa
- 3¾ cups confectioners' sugar
- 1 tsp. vanilla extract

1. In a large saucepan, bring the butter, water and cocoa to a boil. Remove from the heat. Combine the flour, sugar, baking soda and salt; add to cocoa mixture. Stir in the sour cream until smooth.

2. Pour into a greased 15x10x1-in. baking pan. Bake at 350° for 20-25 minutes or until a toothpick inserted in the center comes out clean.

3. In a small saucepan, melt butter; add milk and cocoa. Bring to a boil. Remove from the heat. Whisk in confectioners' sugar and vanilla until smooth. Pour over warm cake. Cool completely on a wire rack.

1 PIECE: 418 cal., 14g fat (9g sat. fat), 35mg chol., 266mg sod., 72g carb. (57g sugars, 1g fiber), 3g pro.

EASY COCONUT CREAM PIE

I came up with my own coconut cream pie years ago, and it's been a favorite with family and friends ever since. I've even made enough to feed a threshing crew of 21 men.
—Vera Moffitt, Oskaloosa, KS

Prep: 20 min. + chilling • **Makes:** 8 servings

- ¾ cup sugar
- 3 Tbsp. all-purpose flour
- ⅛ tsp. salt
- 3 cups whole milk
- 3 large eggs, beaten
- 1½ cups sweetened shredded coconut, toasted, divided
- 1 Tbsp. butter
- 1½ tsp. vanilla extract
- 1 sheet refrigerated pie crust, baked

1. In a medium saucepan, combine the sugar, flour and salt. Stir in milk; cook and stir over medium-high heat until thickened and bubbly. Reduce heat; cook and stir 2 minutes longer.

2. Remove from the heat; gradually stir about 1 cup of hot mixture into beaten eggs. Return all to saucepan; cook and stir over medium heat until nearly boiling. Reduce heat; cook and stir about 2 minutes more (do not boil). Remove from the heat; stir in 1 cup coconut, butter and vanilla.

3. Pour into the pie crust; sprinkle with remaining coconut. Chill for several hours before serving.

1 PIECE: 376 cal., 18g fat (11g sat. fat), 84mg chol., 249mg sod., 47g carb. (32g sugars, 1g fiber), 7g pro.

NIKKI BARTON
Providence, UT

SPARKLING CIDER POUND CAKE

This tempting pound cake reminds me of fall with every bite. Sparkling apple cider goes into both the batter and the glaze.
—*Nikki Barton, Providence, UT*

Prep: 20 min. • **Bake:** 40 min. + cooling
Makes: 12 servings

¾ cup butter, softened
1½ cups sugar
3 large eggs, room temperature
1½ cups all-purpose flour
¼ tsp. baking powder
¼ tsp. salt
½ cup sparkling apple cider

GLAZE
¾ cup confectioners' sugar
3 to 4 tsp. sparkling apple cider

1. Preheat oven to 350°. Line the bottom of a greased 9x5-in. loaf pan with parchment; grease parchment.
2. In a large bowl, cream the butter and sugar until light and fluffy, 5-7 minutes. Add eggs, 1 at a time, beating well after each addition. In another bowl, whisk flour, baking powder and salt; add to creamed mixture alternately with cider, beating well after each addition.
3. Transfer to prepared pan. Bake until a toothpick inserted in the center comes out clean, 40-50 minutes. Cool in the pan 10 minutes before removing to a wire rack to cool completely.
4. In a small bowl, mix the glaze ingredients until smooth; spoon over top of cake, allowing it to flow over sides.
1 SLICE: 308 cal., 13g fat (8g sat. fat), 77mg chol., 169mg sod., 46g carb. (34g sugars, 0 fiber), 3g pro.

CONTEST-WINNING RHUBARB MERINGUE PIE

My husband's grandmother was an excellent cook, but she didn't always share her secrets. Luckily, we have her rhubarb pie recipe! I've only added one of my favorite crusts and a never-fail meringue.
—*Elaine Sampson, Colesburg, IA*

Prep: 50 min. + chilling
Bake: 65 min. + cooling
Makes: 8 servings

¾ cup all-purpose flour
¼ tsp. salt
¼ tsp. sugar
¼ cup shortening
1 Tbsp. beaten large egg, room temperature
¼ tsp. white vinegar
3 to 4½ tsp. cold water

FILLING
3 cups chopped fresh or frozen rhubarb
1 cup sugar
3 Tbsp. all-purpose flour
Dash salt
3 large egg yolks
1 cup heavy whipping cream

MERINGUE
4 tsp. plus ⅓ cup sugar, divided
2 tsp. cornstarch
⅓ cup water
3 large egg whites, room temperature
⅛ tsp. cream of tartar

1. In a small bowl, combine the flour, salt and sugar; cut in shortening until crumbly. Combine egg and vinegar; sprinkle over the crumb mixture. Gradually add water, tossing with a fork until a ball forms. Cover and chill for 1 hour or until easy to handle.
2. On a lightly floured surface, roll out dough to fit a 9-in. pie plate. Trim to ½ in. beyond edge of plate; flute edges.
3. Place rhubarb in crust. Whisk sugar, flour, salt, egg yolks and cream; pour over rhubarb. Bake at 350° until filling is set and pie jiggles when gently shaken, 50-60 minutes.
4. Meanwhile, in a small saucepan, combine 4 tsp. sugar and cornstarch. Gradually stir in water. Bring to a boil, stirring constantly; cook until thickened, 1-2 minutes. Cool to room temperature.
5. In a small bowl, beat egg whites and cream of tartar until frothy. Add cornstarch mixture; beat on high until soft peaks form. Gradually beat in remaining sugar, 1 Tbsp. at a time, on high until stiff glossy peaks form and the sugar is dissolved.
6. Spread evenly over hot filling, sealing the edges to crust. Bake until meringue is golden brown, about 15 minutes. Cool on a wire rack for 1 hour. Store in the refrigerator.
1 PIECE: 388 cal., 19g fat (9g sat. fat), 129mg chol., 131mg sod., 50g carb. (37g sugars, 1g fiber), 5g pro.

PEACH BLUEBERRY PIE

"What a flavor!" That's what I hear most often when guests taste this dessert. I invented it one day when I was short on peaches.
—*Sue Thumma, Shepherd, MI*

Prep: 15 min. • **Bake:** 40 min. + cooling
Makes: 8 servings

1 cup sugar
⅓ cup all-purpose flour
½ tsp. ground cinnamon
⅛ tsp. ground allspice
3 cups sliced peeled fresh peaches
1 cup fresh or frozen unsweetened blueberries
   Pastry for double-crust pie (see recipe on page 177)
1 Tbsp. butter
1 Tbsp. 2% milk
   Cinnamon sugar

1. In a large bowl, combine the sugar, flour, cinnamon and allspice. Add the peaches and blueberries; toss to coat.
2. Preheat oven to 400°. On a lightly floured surface, roll half the dough to a ⅛-in.-thick circle; transfer to a 9-in. pie plate. Trim crust to ½ in. beyond rim of plate. Add filling; dot with butter.
3. Roll remaining dough to a ⅛-in.-thick circle; cut into ½-in.-wide strips. Arrange over filling in a lattice pattern. Trim and seal strips to edge of bottom crust; flute edge. Brush lattice strips with milk; sprinkle with cinnamon sugar.
4. Bake until crust is golden brown and filling is bubbly, 40-45 minutes. Cool on a wire rack.
1 PIECE: 406 cal., 16g fat (7g sat. fat), 14mg chol., 215mg sod., 65g carb. (34g sugars, 2g fiber), 3g pro.

OLD-TIME CUSTARD ICE CREAM

I think my most memorable summer dessert for a crowd has always been homemade ice cream. This one is so rich and creamy—the perfect splurge on a hot afternoon.
—*Martha Self, Montgomery, TX*

- -

Prep: 55 min. + chilling
Process: 55 min./batch + freezing
Makes: 2¾ qt.

- 1½ cups sugar
- ¼ cup all-purpose flour
- ½ tsp. salt
- 4 cups whole milk
- 4 large eggs, lightly beaten
- 2 pints heavy whipping cream
- 3 Tbsp. vanilla extract

1. In a large heavy saucepan, combine the sugar, flour and salt. Gradually add the milk until smooth. Cook and stir over medium heat until thickened and bubbly. Reduce heat to low; cook and stir 2 minutes longer. Remove from heat.
2. In a small bowl, whisk a small amount of hot mixture into eggs; return all to pan, whisking constantly. Bring to a gentle boil; cook and stir 2 minutes. Remove from heat immediately.
3. Quickly transfer to a large bowl; place the bowl in a pan of ice water. Stir gently and occasionally for 2 minutes. Press plastic wrap onto the surface of custard. Refrigerate for several hours or overnight.
4. Stir the cream and vanilla into custard. Fill cylinder of ice cream freezer two-thirds full; freeze according to manufacturer's directions. (Refrigerate the remaining mixture until ready to freeze.) Transfer the ice cream to freezer containers, allowing headspace for expansion. Freeze 2-4 hours or until firm. Repeat with remaining ice cream mixture.
½ CUP: 252 cal., 18g fat (11g sat. fat), 88mg chol., 98mg sod., 18g carb. (17g sugars, 0 fiber), 4g pro.

**1 FAVORITE
9 WAYS**
*Ice Cream
Toppers*

1. VANILLA ICE CREAM WITH BACON & MAPLE SYRUP

Enjoy breakfast favorites for dessert by topping ice cream with syrup and crispy bacon.
—Taste of Home *Test Kitchen*

Takes: 5 min. • **Makes:** 1 serving

- 2 scoops vanilla ice cream
- 2 Tbsp. maple syrup
- 2 slices cooked bacon strips, crumbled

Top ice cream with maple syrup and bacon.
1 SERVING: 348 cal., 15g fat (7g sat. fat), 52mg chol., 445mg sod., 43g carb. (38g sugars, 0 fiber), 10g pro.

2. VANILLA ICE CREAM WITH BALSAMIC & FRUIT

Cinnamon-infused, pear, chocolate, even plain—whatever the flavor, balsamic vinegar on ice cream is amazing!
—Allison Ochoa, Hays, KS

Takes: 5 min. • **Makes:** 1 serving

- 2 scoops vanilla ice cream
- 2 Tbsp. balsamic vinegar
- ½ cup mixed fruit

Drizzle balsamic vinegar over ice cream. Top with mixed fruit.
1 SERVING: 227 cal., 7g fat (4g sat. fat), 29mg chol., 63mg sod., 39g carb. (36g sugars, 1g fiber), 2g pro.

3. VANILLA ICE CREAM WITH CORNFLAKES

The sweet crunch of this combination is so good that you'll crave another scoop!
—Taste of Home *Test Kitchen*

Takes: 5 min. • **Makes:** 1 serving

- 2 scoops vanilla ice cream
- ½ cup cornflakes

Top ice cream with cornflakes.
1 SERVING: 137 cal., 7g fat (4g sat. fat), 29mg chol., 53mg sod., 16g carb. (14g sugars, 0 fiber), 2g pro.

4. VANILLA ICE CREAM WITH ESPRESSO

Give your scoops a jolt of java for a dessert and pick-me-up all in one.
—Taste of Home *Test Kitchen*

Takes: 5 min. • **Makes:** 1 serving

 2 **scoops vanilla ice cream**
 ¼ **cup brewed espresso**

Pour espresso over ice cream.
1 SERVING: 142 cal., 7g fat (5g sat. fat), 29mg chol., 61mg sod., 17g carb. (14g sugars, 0 fiber), 2g pro.

5. VANILLA ICE CREAM WITH CRUSHED POTATO CHIPS

If you like the combination of sweet and salty, you're sure to love this!
—Taste of Home *Test Kitchen*

Takes: 5 min. • **Makes:** 1 serving

 2 **scoops vanilla ice cream**
 ½ **cup crushed potato chips**

Top ice cream with crushed potato chips.
1 SERVING: 287 cal., 17g fat (8g sat. fat), 29mg chol., 219mg sod., 30g carb. (14g sugars, 2g fiber), 4g pro.

6. VANILLA ICE CREAM WITH FRENCH FRIES

French fries and hot fudge ice cream topping, too? It's just plain...wow!
—Taste of Home *Test Kitchen*

Takes: 5 min. • **Makes:** 1 serving

 2 **scoops vanilla ice cream**
 ½ **cup cooked french fries**
 2 **Tbsp. hot fudge ice cream topping**

Top ice cream with french fries. Drizzle with hot fudge.
1 SERVING: 331 cal., 13g fat (6g sat. fat), 29mg chol., 326mg sod., 50g carb. (32g sugars, 3g fiber), 6g pro.

(7)

7. VANILLA ICE CREAM WITH NERDS

These tiny rainbow candies add bits of extra flavor and lots of festive color.
—*Rachel Bernhard Seis, Milwaukee, WI*

- -

Takes: 5 min. • **Makes:** 1 serving

  2   scoops vanilla ice cream
  1   Tbsp. rainbow Nerds candy

Sprinkle ice cream with rainbow candies.
1 SERVING: 153 cal., 7g fat (4g sat. fat), 29mg chol., 53mg sod., 20g carb. (18g sugars, 0 fiber), 2g pro.

8. VANILLA ICE CREAM WITH MELTED PEANUT BUTTER

Melted creamy peanut butter—what else do I need to say? Yum!
—*Rd Stendel-Freels, Albuquerque, NM*

- -

Takes: 5 min. • **Makes:** 1 serving

  2   scoops vanilla ice cream
  ¼   cup creamy peanut butter, melted

Top ice cream with melted peanut butter.
1 SERVING: 519 cal., 40g fat (11g sat. fat), 29mg chol., 325mg sod., 30g carb. (21g sugars, 4g fiber), 17g pro.

9. VANILLA ICE CREAM WITH RITZ CRACKERS

We drizzle on some chocolate sauce for extra appeal. It's oh, so good.
—*Taste of Home Test Kitchen*

- -

Takes: 5 min. • **Makes:** 1 serving

  2   scoops vanilla ice cream
  6   Ritz crackers, crushed
  2   Tbsp. chocolate sauce

Top ice cream with crushed Ritz crackers. Drizzle with chocolate sauce.
1 SERVING: 333 cal., 13g fat (6g sat. fat), 29mg chol., 236mg sod., 50g carb. (35g sugars, 2g fiber), 5g pro.

(8)

(9)

Cookies & Candies

It's time to fill the cookie jar with the best-of-the-best sweets *Taste of Home* has to offer. Grab a cold glass of milk, turn these pages, and settle in for the sort of cookies, bars, fudge and other bites you'll turn to time and again.

MOM'S CHOCOLATE CHIP COOKIES

My mom always brightened my lunch with these yummy, quick-to-fix cookies.
—*Tammy Orr, Wharton, NJ*

Takes: 30 min. • **Makes:** 4 dozen

- 1 **cup butter, softened**
- ¾ **cup packed brown sugar**
- ¼ **cup sugar**
- 1 **pkg. (3.4 oz.) instant vanilla pudding mix**
- 2 **large eggs, room temperature, lightly beaten**
- 1 **tsp. vanilla extract**
- 2¼ **cups all-purpose flour**
- 1 **tsp. baking soda**
- 2 **cups semisweet chocolate chips**

In a bowl, cream butter and sugars. Add pudding mix, eggs and vanilla. Combine flour and baking soda; add to creamed mixture and mix well. Fold in chocolate chips. Drop by teaspoonfuls onto ungreased baking sheets. Bake at 375° for 10-12 minutes or until lightly browned.

1 COOKIE: 117 cal., 5g fat (3g sat. fat), 8mg chol., 45mg sod., 20g carb. (14g sugars, 1g fiber), 1g pro.

READER REVIEW

"Wow! These cookies are out of this world! Of all the chocolate chip cookies I have made, these are definitely the best. Very easy to make, too!"

KRISTICOOKE, TASTEOFHOME.COM

5i
PEANUT BUTTER CHOCOLATE BARS

These chewy peanut butter chocolate bars are the perfect no-fuss contribution to a potluck or bake sale. Just be sure to get them into the refrigerator to set up before they disappear!
—*Lorri Speer, Centralia, WA*

- -

Prep: 30 min. + chilling • **Makes:** 2 dozen

- 1 **cup sugar**
- 1 **cup light corn syrup**
- 1 **cup peanut butter**
- 6 **cups crisp rice cereal**
- 2 **cups semisweet chocolate chips, melted**

In a large saucepan, combine sugar, corn syrup and peanut butter. Cook and stir over medium-low heat until sugar is dissolved. Remove from heat; stir in cereal. Spread into a greased 13x9-in. pan; press lightly. Spread melted chocolate over top; refrigerate until set. Cut into bars.

1 BAR: 302 cal., 14g fat (6g sat. fat), 0 chol., 96mg sod., 46g carb. (37g sugars, 2g fiber), 4g pro.

GLUTEN-FREE PEANUT BUTTER BLONDIES

I converted these blondies to be gluten-free so that my entire family could enjoy a comforting dessert, and the cakelike treat really hits the spot when we crave brownies. They are an enticing spin on gluten-free peanut butter chocolate chip cookies.
—*Becky Klope, Loudonville, NY*

- -

Prep: 15 min. • **Bake:** 20 min. + cooling
Makes: 16 servings

- ⅔ **cup creamy peanut butter**
- ½ **cup packed brown sugar**
- ¼ **cup sugar**
- ¼ **cup unsweetened applesauce**
- 2 **large eggs, room temperature**
- 1 **tsp. vanilla extract**
- 1 **cup gluten-free all-purpose baking flour**
- 1¼ **tsp. baking powder**
- 1 **tsp. xanthan gum**
- ¼ **tsp. salt**
- ½ **cup semisweet chocolate chips**
- ¼ **cup salted peanuts, chopped**

1. In a large bowl, combine the peanut butter, sugars and applesauce. Beat in eggs and vanilla until blended. Combine the flour, baking powder, xanthan gum and salt; gradually add to peanut butter mixture and mix well. Stir in chocolate chips and peanuts.
2. Transfer to a 9-in. square baking pan coated with cooking spray. Bake at 350° until a toothpick inserted in the center comes out clean, 20-25 minutes. Cool on a wire rack. Cut into squares.

1 BAR: 176 cal., 9g fat (2g sat. fat), 26mg chol., 142mg sod., 22g carb. (14g sugars, 2g fiber), 5g pro. **DIABETIC EXCHANGES:** 1½ starch, 1½ fat.

> **TEST KITCHEN TIP**
> Looking to cut back on sugar? You can decrease some of the sugar in these bars by making this recipe with natural peanut butter.

5T BIRTHDAY CAKE FUDGE

This decadent treat is the perfect thing to make a birthday special. Or prepare it ahead and package it as a surprise gift for a friend.
—Rashanda Cobbins, Milwaukee, WI

Prep: 10 min. + chilling • **Makes:** 64 pieces

- 1 can (14 oz.) sweetened condensed milk
- 1½ cups white baking chips
- 3 Tbsp. butter
- ⅛ tsp. salt
- 1¼ cups unprepared funfetti cake mix
- 3 Tbsp. sprinkles

1. Line an 8-in. square pan with foil or parchment; grease foil lightly. In a large heavy saucepan, cook and stir milk, baking chips, butter and salt over low heat until smooth. Remove from heat; stir in cake mix until dissolved. Spread into pan; top with sprinkles. Refrigerate, covered, until firm, about 2 hours.
2. Using foil, lift fudge out of pan. Remove foil; cut fudge into 1-in. squares. Store in an airtight container in the refrigerator.
1 PIECE: 59 cal., 2g fat (2g sat. fat), 4mg chol., 47mg sod., 9g carb. (7g sugars, 0 fiber), 1g pro.

DIPPED CHERRY COOKIES

Our children and grandchildren declared this flavorful cookie a keeper. We gave a batch to our mail carrier, and she requested the recipe.
Ruth Anne Dale, Titusville, PA

Prep: 30 min.
Bake: 10 min./batch + standing
Makes: about 4 dozen

- 2½ cups all-purpose flour
- ¾ cup sugar, divided
- 1 cup cold butter, cubed
- ½ cup finely chopped maraschino cherries, patted dry
- 12 oz. white baking chocolate, finely chopped, divided
- ½ tsp. almond extract
- 2 tsp. shortening
  Coarse sugar and red edible glitter

1. In a large bowl, combine flour and ½ cup sugar; cut in butter until crumbly. Knead in cherries, ⅔ cup white chocolate and the extract until dough forms a ball.
2. Shape into ¾-in. balls. Place 2 in. apart on ungreased baking sheets. Flatten slightly with a glass dipped in remaining sugar. Bake at 325° for 10-12 minutes or until edges are lightly browned. Remove to wire racks to cool completely.
3. In a microwave, melt shortening and remaining white chocolate; stir until smooth.
4. Dip half of each cookie into chocolate; allow excess to drip off. Place on waxed paper; sprinkle with coarse sugar and edible glitter. Let stand until set. Store in an airtight container.
1 COOKIE: 108 cal., 6g fat (4g sat. fat), 11mg chol., 34mg sod., 12g carb. (7g sugars, 0 fiber), 1g pro.

DELUXE SUGAR COOKIES

For variety, I sprinkle half of the cookies with colored sugar before baking and frost the remaining ones after they're cooled.
—*Dawn Fagerstrom, Warren, MN*

Prep: 20 min. + chilling • **Bake:** 10 min./batch
Makes: 5 dozen (2-in.) cookies

- 1 cup butter, softened
- 1½ cups confectioners' sugar
- 1 large egg, room temperature, beaten
- 1 tsp. vanilla extract
- ½ tsp. almond extract
- 2½ cups all-purpose flour
- 1 tsp. baking soda
- 1 tsp. cream of tartar

1. In a large bowl, cream butter and sugar until light and fluffy, 5-7 minutes. Beat in egg and extracts. Combine flour, baking soda and cream of tartar; gradually add to the creamed mixture and mix well. Chill for at least 1 hour or until easy to handle.

2. Divide dough into fourths. On a surface lightly sprinkled with confectioners' sugar, roll out 1 portion of dough to ⅛-in. thickness. Cut into desired shapes using 2-in. cookie cutters. Place on ungreased baking sheets. Repeat with remaining dough. Bake at 350° until the edges begin to brown, 7-8 minutes. Remove to wire racks to cool.

1 COOKIE: 59 cal., 3g fat (2g sat. fat), 11mg chol., 47mg sod., 7g carb. (3g sugars, 0 fiber), 1g pro.

READER REVIEW

"This is the only recipe I have used in almost 40 years of baking. I would give them six stars if I could!"

KENDALLSKABIN, TASTEOFHOME.COM

PECAN PIE BARS

These bars are decadently rich—just like pecan pie! They're sure to disappear from the dessert table at your next gathering, so you might want to save a piece or two for later.
—*Carolyn Custer, Clifton Park, NY*

- -

Prep: 10 min. • **Bake:** 35 min. + chilling
Makes: 4 dozen

- 2 cups all-purpose flour
- ½ cup confectioners' sugar
- 1 cup butter, softened
- 1 can (14 oz.) sweetened condensed milk
- 1 large egg, room temperature
- 1 tsp. vanilla extract
  Pinch salt
- 1 pkg. (8 oz.) milk chocolate English toffee bits
- 1 cup chopped pecans

1. In a large bowl, combine flour and sugar. Cut in butter until mixture resembles coarse meal. Press firmly onto the bottom of a greased 13x9-in. baking dish. Bake at 350° for 15 minutes.

2. Meanwhile, in a large bowl, beat milk, egg, vanilla and salt until smooth. Stir in toffee bits and pecans; spread evenly over baked crust.

3. Bake until lightly browned, 20-25 minutes longer. Cool. Cover and chill; cut into bars. Store in refrigerator.

1 BAR: 127 cal., 8g fat (4g sat. fat), 18mg chol., 100mg sod., 13g carb. (9g sugars, 0 fiber), 2g pro.

CHOCOLATE FUDGE PEANUT BUTTER COOKIES

These fudgy, tempting cookies need only five ingredients—what could be easier? The moist, delicious goodies go over big with kids and make a fantastic pick-me-up for adults.
—*Elaine Stephens, Carmel, IN*

Prep: 20 min. • **Bake:** 10 min./batch + cooling
Makes: 3½ dozen

- 2 cans (16 oz. each) chocolate fudge frosting, divided
- 1 large egg, room temperature
- 1 cup chunky peanut butter
- 1½ cups all-purpose flour
  Sugar

1. Preheat oven to 375°. Reserve 1 can plus ⅓ cup frosting for topping cookies. In a large bowl, mix egg, peanut butter and remaining frosting until blended. Stir in flour just until moistened.
2. Drop dough by rounded tablespoonfuls 2 in. apart onto greased baking sheets. Flatten with a fork dipped in sugar.
3. Bake until set, 7-9 minutes. Remove from pans to wire racks to cool completely. Spread with reserved frosting.
1 COOKIE: 143 cal., 7g fat (1g sat. fat), 5mg chol., 79mg sod., 18g carb. (12g sugars, 1g fiber), 2g pro. **DIABETIC EXCHANGES:** 1 starch, 1 fat.

COURTNEY STULTZ
Weir, KS

NUT BUTTER CUPS

This indulgent nutty treat is simple to make and looks fabulous. At my house, we love using all-natural ingredients because it's important to know what we're putting in our bodies.
—*Courtney Stultz, Weir, KS*

Prep: 20 min. + chilling • **Makes:** 1 dozen

- 1 cup unblanched almonds
- 1 cup pitted dates
- 1 cup creamy cashew butter or peanut butter
- ½ cup baking cocoa
- ¼ cup coconut oil, melted
- 2 tsp. honey
  Chopped almonds, optional

Pulse almonds and dates in a food processor until mixture starts to hold together when pressed. Spoon nut mixture into 12 paper-lined muffin cups; press into bottom. Gently spread cashew butter over nut mixture. In a small bowl, whisk together cocoa, coconut oil and honey; pour over nut butter. If desired, top with chopped almonds. Refrigerate, covered, until chocolate is set, about 1 hour.
1 DATE NUT BITE: 293 cal., 23g fat (7g sat. fat), 0 chol., 73mg sod., 21g carb. (11g sugars, 4g fiber), 6g pro.

CHIPPY BLOND BROWNIES

If you love chocolate and butterscotch, you won't be able to resist these chewy brownies. I often include this recipe inside a baking dish as a wedding present. Everyone, young and old, enjoys these delectable treats.
—*Anna Allen, Owings Mills, MD*

Prep: 15 min. • **Bake:** 25 min.
Makes: 2 dozen

- 6 Tbsp. butter, softened
- 1 cup packed brown sugar
- 2 large eggs, room temperature
- 1 tsp. vanilla extract
- 1¼ cups all-purpose flour
- 1 tsp. baking powder
- ½ tsp. salt
- 1 cup semisweet chocolate chips
- ½ cup chopped pecans

1. In a large bowl, cream butter and brown sugar until light and fluffy, 5-7 minutes. Add the eggs, 1 at a time, beating well after each addition. Beat in vanilla. Combine the flour, baking powder and salt; gradually add to creamed mixture. Stir in the chocolate chips and chopped pecans.

2. Spread into a greased 11x7-in. baking pan. Bake at 350° for 25-30 minutes or until a toothpick inserted in the center comes out clean. Cool on a wire rack; cut into bars.

1 BAR: 141 cal., 7g fat (3g sat. fat), 25mg chol., 104mg sod., 19g carb. (13g sugars, 1g fiber), 2g pro.

SCOTTISH SHORTBREAD

My mother, who is of Scottish heritage, passed this recipe, as with most of my favorite recipes, on to me. When I entered Scottish Shortbread at our local fair, it won a red ribbon.
—*Rose Mabee, Selkirk, MB*

Prep: 15 min. • **Bake:** 20 min./batch + cooling
Makes: about 4 dozen

- 2 cups butter, softened
- 1 cup packed brown sugar
- 4 to 4½ cups all-purpose flour

1. Preheat oven to 325°. Cream butter and brown sugar until light and fluffy, 5-7 minutes. Add 3¾ cups flour; mix well. Turn dough onto a floured surface; knead for 5 minutes, adding enough remaining flour to form a soft dough.

2. Roll to ½-in. thickness. Cut into 3x1-in. strips. Place 1 in. apart on ungreased baking sheets. Prick with fork. Bake until cookies are lightly browned, 20-25 minutes. Cool.

1 COOKIE: 123 cal., 8g fat (5g sat. fat), 20mg chol., 62mg sod., 12g carb. (5g sugars, 0 fiber), 1g pro.

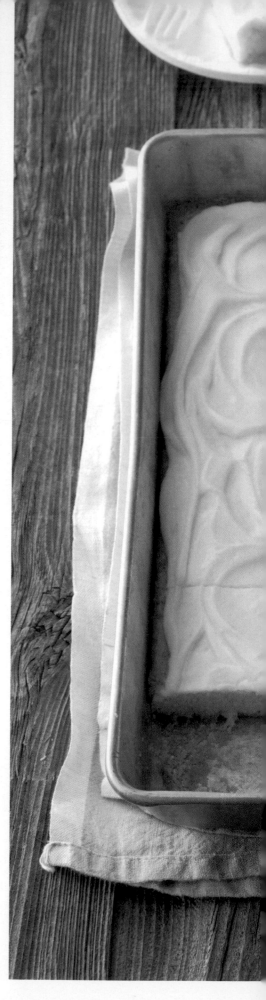

DATE-NUT PINWHEELS

Pinwheel cookies with dates and walnuts are a family treasure at our house. There are a few steps when prepping, so I sometimes freeze the dough and bake the cookies later.
—*Frieda Whiteley, Lisbon, CT*

- -

Prep: 30 min. + chilling • **Bake:** 10 min./batch
Makes: about 9 dozen

1 cup butter, softened
1 cup sugar
1 cup packed brown sugar
2 large eggs, room temperature
4 cups all-purpose flour
½ tsp. baking soda
FILLING
2 pkg. (8 oz. each) pitted dates
1 cup water
½ cup sugar
½ cup chopped walnuts

1. In a large bowl, cream butter and sugars until light and fluffy, 5-7 minutes. Beat in eggs. In another bowl, whisk flour and baking soda; gradually beat into creamed mixture. Divide dough into 3 portions. Shape each into a disk. Cover and refrigerate 1 hour or until firm enough to roll.

2. Place dates, water and sugar in a saucepan; bring to a boil. Reduce the heat; simmer, uncovered, until dates are tender and liquid is almost evaporated. Stir in walnuts; cool.

3. Roll each dough portion between 2 sheets of waxed paper into a 12x10-in. rectangle. Refrigerate 30 minutes. Remove waxed paper. Spread a third of the cooled filling over each rectangle. Roll up tightly jelly-roll style, starting with a long side. Wrap securely. Refrigerate until firm.

4. Preheat oven to 350°. Unwrap and cut dough crosswise into ⅓-in. slices. Place 2 in. apart on greased baking sheets. Bake 10-12 minutes or until set. Remove from pans to wire racks to cool.

1 COOKIE: 67 cal., 2g fat (1g sat. fat), 8mg chol., 21mg sod., 12g carb. (7g sugars, 1g fiber), 1g pro.

LEMON BARS WITH CREAM CHEESE FROSTING

I won a baking contest at Purdue University with this recipe for lemon bars with cream cheese frosting. I hope you'll love the dreamy topping as much as we do.
—*Michael Hunter, Fort Wayne, IN*

Prep: 20 min. • **Bake:** 20 min. + cooling
Makes: 2 dozen

- 1   **cup butter, softened**
- 2   **cups sugar**
- 4   **large eggs, room temperature**
- 2   **tsp. lemon extract**
- 1¾ **cups all-purpose flour**
- ½   **tsp. salt**
- 1   **tsp. grated lemon zest**

LEMON CREAM CHEESE FROSTING
- 4   **oz. cream cheese, softened**
- 2   **Tbsp. butter, softened**
- 2   **cups confectioners' sugar**
- 2   **tsp. lemon juice**
- 1½ **tsp. grated lemon zest**

1. In a large bowl, cream butter and sugar until light and fluffy, about 5 minutes. Beat in eggs and extract. Combine flour and salt; gradually add to creamed mixture and mix well. Stir in lemon zest.

2. Spread into a greased 13x9-in. baking pan. Bake at 350° for 18-22 minutes or until center is set and edges are golden brown. Cool completely.

3. For frosting, in a large bowl, beat cream cheese and butter until fluffy. Beat in confectioners' sugar, lemon juice and zest. Frost and cut into bars. Store in refrigerator.

1 BAR: 243 cal., 11g fat (7g sat. fat), 59mg chol., 145mg sod., 34g carb. (27g sugars, 0 fiber), 2g pro.

TEST KITCHEN TIP
These bars don't use baking soda or baking powder, and it's important to beat the butter and sugar together really well. During this time, you're incorporating all the air into the batter that will cause the bars to rise in the oven, so make sure you don't skimp on this step.

FUDGY OAT BROWNIES

These cakelike brownies have a rich, crunchy oat crust and a smooth homemade frosting. A packaged brownie mix keeps prep simple. Make it even easier by using canned frosting.
—*Diana Otterson, Canandaigua, NY*

Prep: 30 min. • **Bake:** 35 min. + cooling
Makes: 3 dozen

- 1½ cups quick-cooking oats
- ¾ cup all-purpose flour
- ¾ cup packed brown sugar
- ¼ tsp. baking soda
- ¼ tsp. salt
- ¾ cup butter, melted
- 1 pkg. fudge brownie mix (13x9-in. pan size)

FROSTING

- 3 Tbsp. butter
- 1½ oz. unsweetened chocolate
- 2¼ cups confectioners' sugar
- 3 to 4 Tbsp. hot water
- 1½ tsp. vanilla extract

1. In a large bowl, combine the oats, flour, brown sugar, baking soda and salt. Stir in the butter until combined. Gently press into an ungreased 13x9-in. baking pan. Bake at 350° for 10-11 minutes or until puffed and edges are lightly browned.

2. Meanwhile, prepare brownie mix according to package directions for cakelike brownies. Spread batter over crust. Bake 25-30 minutes longer or until a toothpick inserted in the center comes out clean.

3. For frosting, in a microwave-safe bowl, melt the butter and chocolate; stir until smooth. Immediately stir in the confectioners' sugar, 2 Tbsp. water and vanilla until smooth. Add remaining water as desired; stir until smooth. Immediately spread over brownies. Cool on a wire rack until firm. Cut into 36 bars.

1 BROWNIE: 217 cal., 11g fat (4g sat. fat), 29mg chol., 131mg sod., 29g carb. (20g sugars, 1g fiber), 2g pro.

DID YOU KNOW?
Because this recipe makes a lot of servings when the bars are cut as suggested above, the brownies are an ideal contribution to potlucks, church suppers and bake sales.

CARDAMOM SPRITZ

I've always loved cardamom. My grandmother often added the spice to her baked goods. I usually make these cookies in a camel design using a spritz press and camel disk I found at a thrift shop. It reminds me of a time when I rode a camel in the desert while deployed with the Navy. Of course, any design will do!
—*Crystal Schlueter, Northglenn, CO*

Prep: 20 min. • **Bake:** 10 min./batch
Makes: about 6 dozen

- 1 cup butter, softened
- 1 cup plus 2 Tbsp. sugar, divided
- 1 large egg, room temperature
- 1½ tsp. vanilla extract
- 1 tsp. lemon extract
- 2½ cups all-purpose flour
- 2 tsp. ground cardamom, divided
- ¼ tsp. salt

1. Preheat oven to 350°. Cream butter and 1 cup sugar until light and fluffy, 5-7 minutes. Beat in egg and extracts. In another bowl, whisk flour, ½ tsp. cardamom and salt; gradually beat into creamed mixture.

2. Using a cookie press fitted with a disk of your choice, press dough 1 in. apart onto ungreased baking sheets. Mix remaining sugar and remaining cardamom; sprinkle over cookies. Bake until set, 8-10 minutes (do not brown). Remove from pans to wire racks to cool.

1 COOKIE: 52 cal., 3g fat (2g sat. fat), 9mg chol., 30mg sod., 7g carb. (3g sugars, 0 fiber), 1g pro.

CRYSTAL SCHLUETER
Northglenn, CO

CHERRY NO-BAKE COOKIES

I've always loved my no-bake cookie recipe, but I was never able to place at the fair with it. So I mixed in some maraschino cherries, added a few drops of almond extract, and voila! We won a blue ribbon in 2010.
—*Denise Wheeler, Newaygo, MI*

Prep: 30 min. + chilling
Makes: about 5½ dozen

2	cups sugar
½	cup butter, cubed
6	Tbsp. 2% milk
3	Tbsp. baking cocoa
1	cup peanut butter
½	tsp. vanilla extract
¼	tsp. almond extract
3	cups quick-cooking oats
1	jar (10 oz.) maraschino cherries, well drained and finely chopped

1. In a large saucepan, combine sugar, butter, milk and cocoa. Bring to a boil, stirring constantly. Cook and stir 3 minutes.
2. Remove from heat; stir in the peanut butter and extracts until blended. Stir in the oats and cherries. Drop mixture by tablespoonfuls onto waxed paper-lined baking sheets. Refrigerate until set. Store in airtight containers.
1 COOKIE: 81 cal., 4g fat (1g sat. fat), 4mg chol., 29mg sod., 11g carb. (8g sugars, 1g fiber), 2g pro.

CHOCOLATE MINT BROWNIES

One of the best things about this recipe is that the brownies get moister if you leave them in the refrigerator for a day or two. The problem at our house is that no one can leave them alone for that long!
—*Helen Baines, Elkton, MD*

Prep: 20 min. • **Bake:** 30 min. + chilling
Makes: 6 dozen

½	cup butter, softened
1	cup sugar
4	large eggs, room temperature
1	can (16 oz.) chocolate syrup
1	tsp. vanilla extract
1	cup all-purpose flour
½	tsp. salt

FILLING

½	cup butter, softened
2	cups confectioners' sugar
1	Tbsp. water
½	tsp. mint extract
3	drops green food coloring

TOPPING

1	pkg. (10 oz.) mint chocolate chips
½	cup plus 1 Tbsp. butter, cubed

1. Preheat oven to 350°. In a large bowl, cream butter and sugar until light and fluffy, 5-7 minutes. Add eggs, 1 at a time, beating well after each addition. Beat in syrup and vanilla. Add flour and salt; mix well.
2. Pour into a greased 13x9-in. baking pan. Bake 30 minutes (top of brownies will still appear wet). Cool on a wire rack.
3. For filling, in a small bowl, cream butter and confectioners' sugar; add water, extract and food coloring until blended. Spread over cooled brownies. Refrigerate until set.
4. For topping, melt chocolate chips and butter. Cool 30 minutes, stirring occasionally. Spread over filling. Chill; cut into 72 bars. Store in refrigerator.
1 BROWNIE: 105 cal., 5g fat (3g sat. fat), 22mg chol., 63mg sod., 14g carb. (11g sugars, 0 fiber), 1g pro.

ICE CREAM KOLACHKES

These sweet pastries have Polish and Czech roots and can also be spelled "kolaches." They are usually filled with poppy seeds, nuts, jam or a mashed fruit mixture. The ice cream is a unique twist on traditional kolachkes, and it's simplest to use a square cookie cutter to cut the dough.

—*Diane Turner, Brunswick, OH*

Prep: 1 hour + chilling • **Bake:** 15 min./batch
Makes: 10 dozen

- 2 cups butter, softened
- 1 pint vanilla ice cream, softened
- 4 cups all-purpose flour
- 2 Tbsp. sugar
- 2 cans (12 oz. each) apricot and/or raspberry cake and pastry filling
- 1 to 2 Tbsp. confectioners' sugar, optional

1. In the bowl of a heavy-duty stand mixer, beat butter and ice cream until blended (mixture will appear curdled). Add flour and sugar; mix well. Divide dough into 4 portions; cover and refrigerate until easy to handle, about 2 hours.
2. Preheat oven to 350°. On a lightly floured surface, roll 1 portion of dough into a 12x10-in. rectangle; cut into 2-in. squares. Place 1 tsp. filling in the center of each square. Overlap 2 opposite corners of dough over filling; pinch tightly to seal. Place 2 in. apart on ungreased baking sheets. Repeat with remaining dough and filling.
3. Bake until bottoms are lightly browned, 11-14 minutes. Cool 1 minute before removing from pans to wire racks. Sprinkle with confectioners' sugar if desired.

1 PASTRY: 60 cal., 3g fat (2g sat. fat), 9mg chol., 27mg sod., 7g carb. (2g sugars, 0 fiber), 1g pro.

READER REVIEW
"I used pineapple preserves, raspberry preserves and orange marmalade, which made the cookies perfect with a hot cup of java!"
MAMAMIRUS, TASTEOFHOME.COM

WHITE CANDY BARK

I use walnuts from our tree to make this quick and easy recipe, but you can use whatever fruits and nuts are on hand. Pecans always work well, and dried cherries are an easy swap in place of the cranberries.

—*Marcia Snyder, Grand Junction, CO*

Prep: 20 min. + chilling
Makes: 2 lbs. (64 pieces)

- 1 Tbsp. butter, melted
- 2 pkg. (10 to 12 oz. each) white baking chips
- 1½ cups walnut halves
- 1 cup dried cranberries
- ¼ tsp. ground nutmeg

Line a 15x10x1-in. baking pan with foil. Brush with butter. Microwave white chips on high until melted; stir until smooth. Stir in walnuts, cranberries and nutmeg. Spread into prepared pan. Chill until firm. Break into pieces.

½ OZ.: 46 cal., 3g fat (1g sat. fat), 1mg chol., 6mg sod., 5g carb. (1g sugars, 0 fiber), 1g pro.

HAYSTACK COOKIES WITH PEANUT BUTTER

Peanut butter haystacks are one of my favorite desserts. I love to serve them to guests because my friends always marvel at how something so simple tastes so good!

—*Starrlette Howard, Ogden, UT*

Takes: 25 min. • **Makes:** 2 dozen

- ¾ cup butterscotch chips
- ½ cup peanut butter
- 1 can (3 oz.) chow mein noodles
- 1 cup miniature marshmallows

1. In a microwave or in a large bowl over simmering water, melt butterscotch chips and peanut butter; stir until smooth. Gently stir in noodles and marshmallows.
2. Drop by rounded tablespoonfuls onto waxed paper-lined baking sheets. Refrigerate until set, 10-15 minutes.

1 COOKIE: 95 cal., 5g fat (2g sat. fat), 0 chol., 71mg sod., 10g carb. (6g sugars, 0 fiber), 2g pro.

10-CUP COOKIES

My mother used to make this easy 10-cup cookie recipe for my sisters and me. You could find one of our favorite ingredients in every bite, whether it was chocolate, coconut, raisins or nuts.

—*Tracy Powers, Byron Center, MI*

Prep: 15 min. • **Bake:** 15 min./batch + cooling
Makes: 7 dozen

- 1 cup butter, softened
- 1 cup creamy peanut butter
- 1 cup sugar
- 1 cup packed brown sugar
- 2 large eggs, room temperature
- 1 cup all-purpose flour
- 1 tsp. baking soda
- ½ tsp. baking powder
- 1 cup semisweet chocolate chips
- 1 cup quick-cooking oats
- 1 cup sweetened shredded coconut
- 1 cup chopped pecans or walnuts
- 1 cup raisins

1. Preheat oven to 350°. In a large bowl, cream the butter, peanut butter and sugars until blended. Beat in the eggs. In another bowl, whisk flour, baking soda and baking powder; gradually beat into creamed mixture. Stir in the chocolate chips, oats, coconut, pecans and raisins.
2. Drop dough by tablespoonfuls 3 in. apart onto greased baking sheets. Bake until golden brown, 12-15 minutes. Cool on pans for 5 minutes. Remove to wire racks to cool completely.

1 COOKIE: 97 cal., 6g fat (3g sat. fat), 10mg chol., 54mg sod., 11g carb. (8g sugars, 1g fiber), 1g pro.

CHOCOLATE MINT CANDY

I had never made candy before I tried this recipe. Now I make it every year.
—*Kendra Pedersen, Battle Ground, WA*

Prep: 20 min. + chilling • **Makes:** about 2 lbs.

- 2 cups semisweet chocolate chips
- 1 can (14 oz.) sweetened condensed milk, divided
- 2 tsp. vanilla extract
- 6 oz. white candy coating, coarsely chopped
- 2 to 3 tsp. peppermint extract
- 3 drops green food coloring

1. In a heavy saucepan, melt the chocolate chips with 1 cup milk. Remove from the heat; stir in the vanilla. Spread half into a waxed paper-lined 8-in. square pan; chill for at least 10 minutes or until firm.

2. Meanwhile, in a heavy saucepan over low heat, cook and stir candy coating with the remaining milk until coating is melted and mixture is smooth. Stir in peppermint extract and food coloring. Spread over bottom layer; chill for 10 minutes or until firm.

3. Warm remaining chocolate mixture if necessary; spread over mint layer. Chill for 2 hours or until firm. Remove from pan; cut into 1-in. squares.

1 SQUARE: 60 cal., 3g fat (2g sat. fat), 2mg chol., 8mg sod., 9g carb. (8g sugars, 0 fiber), 1g pro.

LISA SPEER
Palm Beach, FL

NO-BAKE CHOCOLATE HAZELNUT THUMBPRINTS

This recipe is so easy! Years ago, a friend gave me a recipe for chocolate peanut treats that didn't require baking. I thought it was a quick and clever way to whip up a batch of sweet snacks without heating up the kitchen, and started making different variations. This variation includes luscious chocolate-hazelnut spread and crunchy hazelnuts. Yum! To melt the chocolate chips easily, place them in a microwave-safe glass bowl and microwave on 50% power at 30-second intervals until soft, then stir in the extras.
—*Lisa Speer, Palm Beach, FL*

Prep: 30 min. + chilling
Makes: about 3½ dozen

- 1 carton (8 oz.) spreadable cream cheese
- 1 cup semisweet chocolate chips, melted
- ½ cup Nutella
- 2¼ cups graham cracker crumbs
- 1 cup finely chopped hazelnuts, toasted
- 1 cup whole hazelnuts, toasted

1. Beat the cream cheese, melted chocolate chips and Nutella until blended. Stir in cracker crumbs. Refrigerate until firm enough to roll, about 30 minutes.

2. Shape mixture into 1-in. balls; roll in chopped hazelnuts. Make an indentation in the center of each with the end of a wooden spoon handle. Fill with a hazelnut. Store between layers of waxed paper in an airtight container in the refrigerator.

1 COOKIE: 111 cal., 8g fat (2g sat. fat), 3mg chol., 46mg sod., 10g carb. (6g sugars, 1g fiber), 2g pro.

CHOCOLATE-DIPPED PRETZEL RODS

Kids of all ages enjoy making and eating these fun treats. The decorated pretzels are a pretty gift in a cellophane bag or a glass jar.
—*Kay Waters, Benld, Il*

Prep: 25 min. + standing • **Cook:** 10 min.
Makes: about 4½ dozen

- 3   cups chopped toasted almonds
- 2   pkg. (14 oz. each) caramels, unwrapped
- 2   Tbsp. water
- 2   pkg. (10 oz. each) pretzel rods
- 2   pkg. (10 to 12 oz. each) white baking chips
- 2   pkg. (10 to 12 oz. each) dark chocolate chips
     Assorted sprinkles, optional

1. Place almonds in a shallow dish. In a large glass measuring cup, microwave caramels and water on high until caramels are melted, stirring every minute.
2. Dip three-fourths of each pretzel into caramel, allowing excess to drip off. (Reheat caramel in microwave if mixture becomes too thick for dipping.) Roll in almonds. Place on waxed paper until set.
3. In a microwave, melt white baking chips; stir until smooth. Dip half of the caramel-coated pretzels in white baking chips, allowing excess to drip off. Add sprinkles if desired; return to waxed paper to set. Repeat with chocolate chips and remaining pretzels.
4. Store in airtight containers or wrap in cellophane gift bags and tie with ribbon.
1 PRETZEL: 245 cal., 12g fat (5g sat. fat), 3mg chol., 278mg sod., 34g carb. (22g sugars, 2g fiber), 5g pro.

PECAN MELTAWAYS

These sweet, nutty treats are a tradition in our house at Christmastime, but they are delightful any time of the year.
—*Alberta McKay, Bartlesville, OK*

Prep: 15 min. + chilling
Bake: 10 min./batch + cooling
Makes: 4 dozen

- 1   cup butter, softened
- ½   cup confectioners' sugar
- 1   tsp. vanilla extract
- 2¼ cups all-purpose flour
- ¼   tsp. salt
- ¾   cup chopped pecans
     Additional confectioners' sugar

1. In a large bowl, cream the butter and confectioners' sugar until light and fluffy, 5-7 minutes. Beat in vanilla. Combine flour and salt; gradually add to creamed mixture and mix well. Stir in pecans. Refrigerate until chilled.
2. Preheat oven to 350°. Roll into 1-in. balls and place on ungreased baking sheets. Bake 10-12 minutes or until set. Roll warm cookies in additional confectioners' sugar; cool completely on wire racks. Roll cooled cookies again in confectioners' sugar.
1 COOKIE: 73 cal., 5g fat (3g sat. fat), 10mg chol., 39mg sod., 6g carb. (1g sugars, 0 fiber), 1g pro.

Seasonal Specialties

When planning a memorable get-together, make this chapter a priority. Here you'll find menus for 14 impressive holiday lineups as well as a bonus section on sweet Christmas treats!

51

CREAM CHEESE CANDIES

These homemade mints make an ideal last-minute addition to holiday treat trays. Pretty much everyone in my neighborhood has the recipe now!
—*Katie Koziolek, Hartland, MN*

Prep: 15 min. + standing
Makes: about 6 dozen

- 3 oz. cream cheese, softened
- ¼ tsp. peppermint or almond extract
- 3 cups confectioners' sugar, divided
   Sugar or colored sugar, optional

1. Mix cream cheese and extract until blended. Beat in 1½ cups confectioners' sugar. Knead in remaining confectioners' sugar.
2. Shape into ½-in. balls. If desired, roll in sugar. Place on waxed paper. Flatten with a fork. Let stand until firm, 1-2 hours. Store between layers of waxed paper in an airtight container in the refrigerator.
1 PIECE: 24 cal., 0 fat (0 sat. fat), 1mg chol., 4mg sod., 5g carb. (5g sugars, 0 fiber), 0 pro.

READER REVIEW

"These are the best! They are easy to make, and everyone who tries them asks me for the recipe."

LJHORE, TASTEOFHOME.COM

VALENTINE'S DAY

4 slices white bread
¼ cup butter, melted
⅛ tsp. salt
⅛ tsp. pepper
3 oz. tasso ham or fully cooked chorizo, finely chopped (about ½ cup)
2 Tbsp. chopped sweet onion
1 garlic clove, minced
2 cups heavy whipping cream
1 to 2 dashes Louisiana-style hot sauce
  Salt and pepper to taste
1 dozen fresh oysters in the shell, scrubbed

1. Preheat oven to 300°. Place bread on an ungreased baking sheet; bake 8-10 minutes on each side or until lightly browned. Break bread into smaller pieces; place in a food processor. Pulse until coarse crumbs form. Transfer to a small bowl. Add melted butter, salt and pepper; toss to combine.
2. In a skillet, cook ham over medium heat until lightly browned, stirring occasionally. Add onion and garlic; cook and stir until tender, 1-2 minutes. Stir in cream. Bring to a boil; cook until liquid is reduced by half, stirring occasionally. Add hot sauce; season with salt and pepper to taste. Keep warm.
3. Increase oven setting to 350°. Shuck oysters, leaving oysters in the half-shell. Arrange on a rack in a shallow baking pan; sprinkle with bread crumbs. Bake 8-10 minutes or until topping is golden brown and oysters are plump. Top with sauce just before serving.
1 OYSTER WITH 2 TBSP. SAUCE: 236 cal., 22g fat (13g sat. fat), 79mg chol., 229mg sod., 6g carb. (0 sugars, 0 fiber), 5g pro.

TENDERLOIN STEAK DIANE

We all love mushrooms, so I'll often toss some extras into this recipe. The mushroom sauce is fantastic with the steak.
—*Carolyn Turner, Reno, NV*

- -

Takes: 30 min. • **Makes:** 4 servings

4 beef tenderloin steaks (6 oz. each)
1 tsp. steak seasoning
2 Tbsp. butter
1 cup sliced fresh mushrooms
½ cup reduced-sodium beef broth
¼ cup heavy whipping cream
1 Tbsp. steak sauce
1 tsp. garlic salt with parsley
1 tsp. minced chives

1. Sprinkle steaks with steak seasoning. In a large skillet, heat butter over medium heat. Add steaks; cook until meat reaches desired doneness, 4-5 minutes on each side. Remove steaks from pan.

2. Add mushrooms to skillet; cook and stir over medium-high heat until tender. Add broth, stirring to loosen browned bits from pan. Stir in cream, steak sauce and garlic salt. Bring to a boil; cook and stir until sauce is slightly thickened, 1-2 minutes.
3. Return steaks to pan and turn to coat; heat through. Stir in chives.
1 STEAK WITH 2 TBSP. SAUCE: 358 cal., 21g fat (11g sat. fat), 111mg chol., 567mg sod., 2g carb. (1g sugars, 0 fiber), 37g pro.

BAKED OYSTERS WITH TASSO CREAM

I love nothing more than a cold beer and a shucked oyster, so when my partners and I opened Saw's Juke Joint in Birmingham, Alabama, we wanted to add them to the menu. We love making them, we love serving them and our guests love eating them.
—*Taylor Hicks, Las Vegas, NV*

- -

Prep: 1 hour
Bake: 10 min.
Makes: 1 dozen (1½ cups sauce)

DOUBLE CHOCOLATE MARTINI

Is it a beverage or a dessert? Don't let its looks fool you: This impressive chocolate martini is potent but good!
—*Deborah Williams, Peoria, AZ*

Takes: 5 min. • **Makes:** 1 serving

Grated chocolate
1 maraschino cherry
Chocolate syrup, optional
Ice cubes
2½ oz. half-and-half cream
1½ oz. vodka
1½ oz. chocolate liqueur
1¼ oz. creme de cacao

1. Sprinkle grated chocolate onto a plate. Moisten the rim of a martini glass with water; hold glass upside down and dip rim into chocolate. Place cherry in glass. If desired, garnish glass with chocolate syrup.
2. Fill a tumbler or mixing glass three-fourths full with ice. Add the cream, vodka, chocolate liqueur and creme de cacao; stir until condensation forms on outside of tumbler. Strain into glass; serve immediately.

1 MARTINI: 569 cal., 8g fat (5g sat. fat), 38mg chol., 45mg sod., 51g carb. (46g sugars, 0 fiber), 3g pro.

RASPBERRY MERINGUE HEARTS

Here's a lovely dessert your guests will think is almost too pretty to eat! I love the way the meringue easily drapes into a heart shape, and the filling makes a dramatic statement in red.
—*Mary Lou Wayman, Salt Lake City, UT*

Prep: 30 min. + standing
Bake: 35 min. + cooling
Makes: 6 servings

3 large egg whites
¼ tsp. cream of tartar
Dash salt
1 cup sugar
⅓ cup finely chopped almonds, toasted
1 tsp. vanilla extract
FILLING
3 cups fresh or frozen unsweetened raspberries, thawed
1 tsp. cornstarch
½ cup seedless raspberry jam
3 cups raspberry or lemon sorbet
⅓ cup sliced almonds, toasted
Additional fresh raspberries, optional

1. Place egg whites in a small mixing bowl; let stand at room temperature for 30 minutes. Beat egg whites, cream of tartar and salt on medium speed until soft peaks form. Add sugar, 1 Tbsp. at a time, beating on high until stiff peaks form and sugar is dissolved. Fold in chopped almonds and vanilla.
2. Drop meringue into 6 mounds on a parchment-lined baking sheet. Shape into 4-in. hearts with the back of a spoon, building up the edges slightly. Bake at 300° for 35 minutes. Turn oven off; leave meringues in the oven 1-1½ hours.
3. For filling, place raspberries in a food processor. Cover and process until blended; strain and discard seeds. In a small saucepan, combine the cornstarch, pureed raspberries and jam until smooth. Bring to a boil over medium heat, stirring constantly. Cook and stir for 1 minute or until thickened. Cool.
4. To serve, spoon sauce into meringue hearts. Place scoop of sorbet on top. Sprinkle with sliced almonds. Garnish with fresh raspberries if desired.
1 MERINGUE WITH ½ CUP SORBET AND ¼ CUP SAUCE: 423 cal., 7g fat (0 sat. fat), 0 chol., 53mg sod., 89g carb. (78g sugars, 6g fiber), 5g pro.

MARDI GRAS

MUFFULETTA

The muffuletta sandwich, which originated in New Orleans, is named after the round, crusty Sicilian loaf of bread it's traditionally served on. While I favor my own olive salad, several very good commercially produced versions are available in most supermarkets.
—Lou Sansevero, Ferron, UT

- -

Prep: 30 min. + chilling • **Makes:** 8 servings

- 1 cup pimiento-stuffed olives, chopped
- ¾ cup olive oil
- 1 celery rib, finely chopped
- ½ cup sliced pepperoncini, chopped
- ½ cup pitted Greek olives, chopped
- ¼ cup cocktail onions, drained and chopped
- ¼ cup red wine vinegar
- 2 Tbsp. capers, drained
- 3 garlic cloves, minced
- 1 tsp. dried oregano
- 1 tsp. dried basil
- ¾ tsp. pepper
- ½ tsp. kosher salt
- ½ tsp. celery seed
- 1 round loaf (1 lb.) unsliced Italian bread
- ½ lb. thinly sliced Genoa salami
- ½ lb. thinly sliced deli ham
- ½ lb. sliced mortadella
- ½ lb. sliced Swiss cheese
- ½ lb. sliced provolone cheese

1. In a large bowl, combine the first 14 ingredients. Cover and refrigerate at least 8 hours.

2. Cut bread in half horizontally; carefully hollow out top and bottom, leaving a 1-in. shell (discard removed bread or save for another use). Spoon half of olive mixture over bottom half of bread. Layer with salami, ham, mortadella, Swiss and provolone cheeses; top with remaining olive mixture. Replace bread top. Wrap tightly. Refrigerate at least 3 hours or overnight. Cut into 8 wedges.

1 SLICE: 762 cal., 59g fat (18g sat. fat), 103mg chol., 2326mg sod., 25g carb. (2g sugars, 2g fiber), 35g pro.

5i OKRA ROASTED WITH SMOKED PAPRIKA

When you want to cook okra without frying it, roast it with lemon juice for a lighter version. The smoked paprika gives it even more oomph.
—Lee Evans, Queen Creek, AZ

- -

Prep: 5 min. • **Cook:** 30 min.
Makes: 12 servings

- 3 lbs. fresh okra pods
- 3 Tbsp. olive oil
- 3 Tbsp. lemon juice
- 1½ tsp. smoked paprika
- ¼ tsp. garlic powder
- ¾ tsp. salt
- ½ tsp. pepper

Preheat oven to 400°. Toss together all ingredients. Arrange in a 15x10x1-in. baking pan; roast until okra is tender and lightly browned, 30-35 minutes.

⅔ CUP: 57 cal., 4g fat (1g sat. fat), 0 chol., 155mg sod., 6g carb. (3g sugars, 3g fiber), 2g pro. **DIABETIC EXCHANGES:** 1 vegetable, ½ fat.

BIG-BATCH JAMBALAYA

You can't have a Mardi Gras bash without jambalaya! I make this dish for our get-togethers because it feeds so many people. It's just right for football-watching parties, too.
—*Kecia McCaffrey, South Dennis, MA*

Prep: 25 min. • **Cook:** 55 min.
Makes: 13 servings

- 1 boneless skinless chicken breast, cubed
- 3 Tbsp. olive oil, divided
- ½ lb. cubed fully cooked ham
- ½ lb. smoked kielbasa or Polish sausage, cubed
- 2 medium green peppers, coarsely chopped
- 2 medium onions, coarsely chopped
- 6 garlic cloves, minced
- 2 cans (14½ oz. each) beef broth
- 1 can (28 oz.) crushed tomatoes
- 1½ cups water
- ¾ cup Dijon mustard
- ¼ cup minced fresh parsley
- 2 Tbsp. Worcestershire sauce
- 1½ to 2 tsp. cayenne pepper
- ½ tsp. dried thyme
- 1½ cups uncooked long grain rice
- 1 lb. uncooked medium shrimp, peeled and deveined

1. In a Dutch oven, cook chicken in 1 Tbsp. oil until no longer pink; remove and set aside. In the same pan, cook and stir the ham, kielbasa, peppers and onions in remaining oil until onions are tender. Add the garlic; cook 1 minute longer.

2. Stir in the broth, tomatoes, water, mustard, parsley, Worcestershire, cayenne and thyme. Bring to a boil. Reduce heat; cover and simmer for 10 minutes.

3. Add rice and return to a boil. Reduce heat; cover and simmer for 25-30 minutes or until rice is tender. Stir in shrimp and chicken; cook 2-4 minutes longer or until shrimp turn pink.

1 CUP: 288 cal., 11g fat (3g sat. fat), 71mg chol., 1185mg sod., 30g carb. (2g sugars, 2g fiber), 18g pro.

BRUNCH BEIGNETS

Enjoy breakfast the New Orleans way with these warm, crispy bites. Topped with powdered sugar, they are a delight!
—*Lois Rutherford, Elkton, FL*

Prep: 20 min. + standing
Cook: 5 min./batch
Makes: about 2 dozen

- 2 large eggs, separated
- 1¼ cups all-purpose flour
- 1 tsp. baking powder
- ⅛ tsp. salt
- ½ cup sugar
- ¼ cup water
- 1 Tbsp. butter, melted
- 2 tsp. grated lemon zest
- 1 tsp. vanilla extract
- 1 tsp. brandy, optional
    Oil for deep-fat frying
    Confectioners' sugar

1. Place egg whites in a small bowl; let stand at room temperature for 30 minutes.

2. Meanwhile, in a large bowl, combine the flour, baking powder and salt. Combine the egg yolks, sugar, water, butter, lemon zest, vanilla and, if desired, brandy; stir into dry ingredients just until combined. Beat egg whites on medium speed until soft peaks form; fold into batter.

3. In a cast-iron or electric skillet, heat oil to 375°. Drop batter by teaspoonfuls, a few at a time, into hot oil. Fry until golden brown, about 1½ minutes on each side. Drain on paper towels. Dust with confectioners' sugar. Serve warm.

1 PIECE: 66 cal., 3g fat (1g sat. fat), 17mg chol., 42mg sod., 9g carb. (4g sugars, 0 fiber), 1g pro.

MARDI GRAS CUPCAKES

Take these simple Mardi Gras cupcakes to a celebration and watch them disappear. Kids will love to help decorate them with the colorful sprinkles.
—Taste of Home *Test Kitchen*

Prep: 25 min. • **Bake:** 20 min. + cooling
Makes: 2 dozen

- 1 pkg. white cake mix (regular size)
- 1 cup sour cream
- ⅔ cup canola oil
- ⅓ cup sugar
- 4 large eggs, room temperature
- 3 Tbsp. each lemon, lime and grape gelatin powder
- 1 can (16 oz.) cream cheese frosting
    Purple, green and yellow sprinkles

1. Preheat oven to 350°. In a large bowl, combine the cake mix, sour cream, oil, sugar and eggs; beat on low speed for 30 seconds. Beat on medium for 2 minutes. Divide evenly among 3 bowls.

2. Stir 1 flavor of gelatin powder into each bowl until well blended. Carefully fill 24 paper-lined muffin cups with a scant 2 Tbsp. of each flavored batter.

3. Bake until a toothpick inserted in the center comes out clean, 18-22 minutes. Cool for 10 minutes before removing from pans to wire racks to cool completely. Spread frosting over cupcakes. Decorate with sprinkles.

1 CUPCAKE: 276 cal., 13g fat (4g sat. fat), 33mg chol., 217mg sod., 38g carb. (28g sugars, 0 fiber), 3g pro.

ST. PATRICK'S DAY

FAVORITE IRISH BREAD

Serve this classic from the Emerald Isle with butter, jam and a hot cup of tea.
—*Sadie Rotondo, Rockland, MA*

Prep: 10 min. • **Bake:** 40 min.
Makes: 16 servings

- 3 cups all-purpose flour
- 1 cup sugar
- 3 tsp. baking powder
- ¼ tsp. salt
- 1 large egg, room temperature
- 2 cups 2% milk, room temperature
- ½ cup butter, melted
- 1½ cups raisins
- 2 Tbsp. caraway seeds, optional

1. Preheat oven to 350°. In a large bowl, whisk flour, sugar, baking powder and salt. In a small bowl, whisk egg, milk and butter. Stir into dry ingredients just until moistened. Fold in raisins and, if desired, caraway seeds.
2. Transfer to a greased 9-in. square baking pan. Bake until a toothpick inserted in the center comes out clean, 40-45 minutes. Remove from the pan onto a wire rack. Serve warm.
1 PIECE: 245 cal., 7g fat (4g sat. fat), 29mg chol., 193mg sod., 43g carb. (22g sugars, 1g fiber), 4g pro.

CHUNKY POTATO LEEK SOUP

My family and I love a steaming bowl of potato soup on a cold winter evening, but we don't want the butter and fat content of regular soup recipes. So I created this lighter version. I have shared it with many folks, and everyone who has tried it comments on the satisfying, robust flavor, not just the lighter ingredients.
—*Christine Frye, Odessa, MO*

Prep: 20 min. • **Cook:** 25 min.
Makes: 8 servings

- 2 medium leeks, coarsely chopped
- 1 medium onion, chopped
- 3 Tbsp. all-purpose flour
- ½ tsp. garlic powder
- 2 Tbsp. olive oil
- 4 cups reduced-sodium chicken broth or vegetable broth
- 2 bay leaves
- ¾ tsp. salt
- ½ tsp. pepper
- ⅛ tsp. hot pepper sauce
- ⅛ tsp. Worcestershire sauce
  Dash ground nutmeg
- 5 cups diced potatoes
- 1½ cups fat-free milk
- 1 can (12 oz.) fat-free evaporated milk

1. In a lightly greased nonstick skillet, cook leeks and onion for 5 minutes or until tender and just beginning to brown; set aside.
2. In a large saucepan, cook flour and garlic powder in oil for about 2 minutes or until lightly browned. Gradually whisk in broth. Stir in the bay leaves, salt, pepper, pepper sauce, Worcestershire sauce and nutmeg. Bring to a boil; cook for 1-2 minutes or until thickened.
3. Stir in potatoes and leek mixture; return to a boil. Reduce heat; cover and simmer for 15-20 minutes or until potatoes are tender. Stir in milk and evaporated milk; heat through. Discard bay leaves.
1 CUP: 193 cal., 4g fat (1g sat. fat), 3mg chol., 593mg sod., 32g carb. (10g sugars, 3g fiber), 9g pro. **DIABETIC EXCHANGES:** 2 starch, ½ fat.

5. In a large heavy saucepan, bring sugar and liqueur to a gentle boil over medium heat; cook until sugar is dissolved. Remove from heat. Add a small amount of hot mixture to egg yolks; return all to pan, stirring constantly. Cook until mixture thickens, about 2 minutes longer, stirring constantly. Remove from heat; stir in vanilla. Cool to room temperature.

6. In a large bowl with a whisk attachment, cream butter until fluffy, about 5 minutes. Gradually beat in sugar mixture. Add milk powder; beat until fluffy, about 5 minutes. If necessary, refrigerate until frosting reaches spreading consistency.

7. Place bottom cake layer on a serving plate; spread with ⅔ cup frosting. Repeat layers. Top with remaining cake layer. Spread remaining frosting over top and sides of cake. Refrigerate at least 1 hour before serving. If desired, top with chopped malted milk balls.

1 SLICE: 821 cal., 48g fat (29g sat. fat), 220mg chol., 760mg sod., 90g carb. (64g sugars, 2g fiber), 7g pro.

ST. PATRICK'S DAY POPCORN

Everyone's eyes will be smilin' when they see this candied corn with an Irish twist. The color gives the snack instant holiday appeal.
—*Karen Weber, Salem, MO*

Prep: 15 min. + cooling • **Makes:** 6 qt.

- 4 qt. popped popcorn
- 1 cup sugar
- ½ cup packed brown sugar
- ½ cup water
- ½ cup light corn syrup
- 1 tsp. white vinegar
- ¼ tsp. salt
- ½ cup butter
- 8 to 10 drops green food coloring

1. Place popcorn in a large roasting pan; keep warm in a 250° oven. Meanwhile, in a large heavy saucepan, combine the sugars, water, corn syrup, vinegar and salt. Cook and stir over medium heat until mixture comes to a boil. Cook, stirring occasionally, until a candy thermometer reads 260° (hard-ball stage).

2. Remove from the heat; stir in butter until melted. Stir in food coloring. Drizzle over warm popcorn and toss to coat. Cool. Break into pieces. Store in an airtight container.

1 CUP: 139 cal., 6g fat (3g sat. fat), 10mg chol., 138mg sod., 22g carb. (16g sugars, 1g fiber), 1g pro.

MALTED CHOCOLATE & STOUT LAYER CAKE

If you want a dessert that will take the cake at your St. Patrick's Day celebration, look no further! The rich chocolate cake is incredibly moist and has a nice malt flavor that's perfectly complemented by the Irish cream frosting.
—*Jennifer Wayland, Morris Plains, NJ*

Prep: 45 min. + chilling
Bake: 35 min. + cooling
Makes: 16 servings

- 2 cups stout beer
- 1¾ cups butter, cubed
- 3 oz. bittersweet chocolate, chopped
- 1 cup malted milk powder
- 1 cup baking cocoa
- 1½ cups sour cream
- 4 large eggs, room temperature
- 3½ cups sugar
- 3½ cups cake flour
- 2½ tsp. baking soda
- 1 tsp. salt

FROSTING
- 1 cup sugar
- ½ cup Irish cream liqueur
- 6 large egg yolks, beaten
- 1½ tsp. vanilla extract
- 1½ cups butter, softened
- ½ cup malted milk powder
  Chopped malted milk balls, optional

1. Grease and flour three 9-in. round baking pans; set aside.

2. In a large saucepan, combine beer, butter and chocolate. Cook and stir over medium-low heat until butter and chocolate are melted. Remove from heat; whisk in milk powder and cocoa. Transfer to a large bowl. Let stand 15 minutes.

3. Preheat oven to 350°. Add sour cream and eggs to the chocolate mixture; beat until well blended. Combine sugar, flour, baking soda and salt; gradually beat into chocolate mixture until blended. Pour batter into prepared pans.

4. Bake until a toothpick inserted in the center comes out clean, 32-36 minutes. Cool for 10 minutes before removing from pans to wire racks to cool completely.

EASTER

MARMALADE CANDIED CARROTS

My crisp-tender carrots have a citrusy sweet flavor that's perfect for special occasions. This is my favorite carrot recipe.
—*Heather Clemmons, Supply, NC*

- -

Takes: 30 min. • **Makes:** 8 servings

    2   lbs. fresh baby carrots
    ⅔   cup orange marmalade
    3   Tbsp. brown sugar
    2   Tbsp. butter
    ½   cup chopped pecans, toasted
    1   tsp. rum extract

1. In a large saucepan, place steamer basket over 1 in. water. Place carrots in basket. Bring water to a boil. Reduce heat to maintain a low boil; steam, covered, 12-15 minutes or until carrots are crisp-tender.
2. Meanwhile, in a small saucepan, combine marmalade, brown sugar and butter; cook and stir over medium heat until mixture is thickened and reduced to about ½ cup. Stir in pecans and extract.
3. Place carrots in a large bowl. Add the marmalade mixture and toss gently to coat.
1 SERVING: 211 cal., 8g fat (2g sat. fat), 8mg chol., 115mg sod., 35g carb. (27g sugars, 4g fiber), 2g pro.

PLUM-GLAZED LAMB

Fruity and flavorful, this wonderful glaze is simple to prepare. The recipe makes enough glaze to baste the lamb during roasting and still leaves plenty to pass at serving time.
—*Ann Eastman, Santa Monica, CA*

- -

Prep: 5 min. • **Bake:** 1¾ hours
Makes: 6 servings

    1   bone-in leg of lamb (4 to 5 lbs.)
        Salt and pepper to taste
    2   cans (15 oz. each) plums, pitted
    2   garlic cloves
    ¼   cup lemon juice
    2   Tbsp. reduced-sodium soy sauce
    2   tsp. Worcestershire sauce
    1   tsp. dried basil

1. Preheat oven to 325°. Place lamb on a rack in a shallow baking pan, fat side up. Season with salt and pepper. Bake, uncovered, for 1¾-2¼ hours or until meat reaches desired doneness (for medium-rare, a thermometer should read 135°; medium, 140°; medium-well, 145°).
2. Meanwhile, drain plums, reserving ½ cup syrup. In a food processor, place the plums, reserved syrup, garlic, lemon juice, soy sauce, Worcestershire sauce and basil. Cover and process until smooth; set aside half of the plum sauce.
3. Baste lamb every 15 minutes during the last hour of roasting. In a small saucepan, simmer reserved sauce 5 minutes; serve with meat.
5 OZ. COOKED LAMB: 338 cal., 10g fat (4g sat. fat), 137mg chol., 283mg sod., 23g carb. (18g sugars, 2g fiber), 39g pro.

3. Punch dough down; place on a lightly floured surface. Divide into 4 portions. Roll each portion into a 14x6-in. rectangle. Combine softened butter and the Italian seasoning; spread over dough.

4. Score each rectangle widthwise at 2-in. intervals. Using marks as a guide, fold dough accordion-style back and forth along score lines. Cut folded dough into six 1-in. pieces. Place pieces cut side down in greased muffin cups. Cover and let rise until doubled, about 30 minutes.

5. Preheat oven to 375°. Uncover pans and let dough stand another 10 minutes before baking. Brush with egg white. Bake until golden brown, 18-22 minutes. Remove from pans to wire racks.

1 ROLL: 186 cal., 6g fat (4g sat. fat), 32mg chol., 200mg sod., 28g carb. (4g sugars, 1g fiber), 5g pro.

BUNNY TAILS

My granddaughters and I came up with this clever and easy idea for Easter.
—*Kelly Ciepluch, Kenosha, WI*

- -

Takes: 20 min. • **Makes:** about 4 dozen

- 1 **cup white baking chips, melted**
- 1 **cup sweetened shredded coconut**

Drop melted chocolate by teaspoonfuls onto waxed paper or parchment. Sprinkle each generously with sweetened flaked coconut and let stand until dry.

1 PIECE: 29 cal., 2g fat (1g sat. fat), 1mg chol., 8mg sod., 3g carb. (3g sugars, 0 fiber), 0 pro.

CHIVE SMASHED POTATOES

No need to peel the potatoes—in fact, this is the only way we make mashed potatoes anymore. Mixing in the flavored cream cheese is a delightful twist.
—*Beverly Norris, Evanston, WY*

- -

Takes: 30 min. • **Makes:** 12 servings

- 4 **lbs. red potatoes, quartered**
- 2 **tsp. chicken bouillon granules**
- 1 **carton (8 oz.) spreadable chive and onion cream cheese**
- ½ **cup half-and-half cream**
- ¼ **cup butter, cubed**
- 1 **tsp. salt**
- ¼ **tsp. pepper**
  Chopped chives, optional

1. Place potatoes and bouillon in a Dutch oven and cover with 8 cups water. Bring to a boil. Reduce heat; cover and cook until tender, 15-20 minutes.

2. Drain and return to pan. Mash potatoes with cream cheese, cream, butter, salt and pepper. Garnish with chives if desired.

⅔ CUP: 219 cal., 11g fat (7g sat. fat), 31mg chol., 428mg sod., 26g carb. (3g sugars, 3g fiber), 5g pro.

HERBED ACCORDION DINNER ROLLS

To dress up everyday dinner rolls, brush herbed butter over the dough and form accordion rolls. The aroma during baking is incredible!
—*Taste of Home Test Kitchen*

- -

Prep: 40 min. + rising • **Bake:** 20 min.
Makes: 2 dozen

- 2 **pkg. (¼ oz. each) active dry yeast**
- ½ **cup warm water (110° to 115°)**
- 1 **tsp. plus ⅓ cup sugar, divided**
- 1¼ **cups warm 2% milk (110° to 115°)**
- ½ **cup butter, melted**
- 2 **large eggs, room temperature**
- 1½ **tsp. salt**
- 6 **to 6½ cups all-purpose flour**
- 3 **Tbsp. butter, softened**
- 1 **tsp. Italian seasoning**
- 1 **large egg white, beaten**

1. In a large bowl, dissolve yeast in warm water with 1 tsp. sugar. Add milk, melted butter, eggs, salt, 3 cups flour and remaining sugar; beat until smooth. Stir in enough remaining flour to form a soft dough.

2. Turn onto a floured surface; knead until smooth and elastic, 6-8 minutes. Place in a greased bowl, turning once to grease the top. Cover and let rise in a warm place until doubled, about 1 hour.

CINCO DE MAYO

FRESH LIME MARGARITAS

This basic margarita recipe is easy to modify to your tastes. Try it frozen or with strawberries.
—Taste of Home *Test Kitchen*

Takes: 15 min. • **Makes:** 4 servings

- ½ cup tequila
- ¼ cup Triple Sec
- ¼ cup lime juice
- ¼ cup lemon juice
- 2 Tbsp. superfine sugar
- 4 lime wedges
- 1 Tbsp. kosher salt
- 1⅓ cups crushed ice

In a pitcher, combine the first 5 ingredients; stir until the sugar is dissolved. Moisten rims of 4 margarita or cocktail glasses with lime wedges. Sprinkle the salt on a plate; dip rims into the salt. Serve over crushed ice in prepared glasses.
⅓ CUP: 149 cal., 0 fat (0 sat. fat), 0 chol., 2mg sod., 15g carb. (13g sugars, 0 fiber), 0 pro.

GRILLED GUACAMOLE

If you're a guacamole lover, try this fun grilled version that gives it a smoky spin. The veggies tend to darken a bit when heated, so stir it gently to prevent further discoloration.
—Lindsay Sprunk, Noblesville, IN

Prep: 10 min. **Grill:** 10 min. + cooling
Makes: 12 servings

- 1 medium red onion, cut into ½-in. slices
- 2 plum tomatoes, halved and seeded
- 1 jalapeno pepper, halved and seeded
- 2 Tbsp. canola oil, divided
- 3 medium ripe avocados, halved and pitted
- ¼ cup fresh cilantro leaves, chopped
- 2 Tbsp. lime juice
- 2 tsp. ground cumin
- ¾ tsp. salt
  Tortilla chips

1. In a large bowl, combine onion, tomatoes, pepper and 1 Tbsp. oil; gently toss to coat. Grill, covered, over medium-high heat or broil 4 in. from the heat until tender and charred, turning occasionally, 6-8 minutes. Brush avocados with remaining oil. Grill or broil avocados, cut side facing heat, until charred, 4-6 minutes. Cool vegetables completely.
2. Chop onion, tomatoes and pepper; set aside. Peel avocados; transfer to a large bowl and mash with a fork. Stir in vegetables, cilantro, lime juice, cumin and salt. Serve immediately with chips.
¼ CUP: 85 cal., 8g fat (1g sat. fat), 0 chol., 152mg sod., 5g carb. (1g sugars, 3g fiber), 1g pro. **DIABETIC EXCHANGES:** 1½ fat.

SPINACH BURRITOS

I made up this recipe a couple of years ago after trying a similar dish in a restaurant. Our oldest son tells me these burritos are awesome! Plus, they're easy and inexpensive.
—Dolores Zornow, Poynette, WI

Prep: 20 min. • **Bake:** 20 min.
Makes: 6 servings

- ½ cup chopped onion
- 2 garlic cloves, minced
- 2 tsp. butter
- 1 pkg. (10 oz.) frozen chopped spinach, thawed and squeezed dry
- ⅛ tsp. pepper
- 6 flour tortillas (10 in.), warmed
- ¾ cup picante sauce, divided
- 2 cups shredded reduced-fat cheddar cheese, divided

1. In a large skillet, saute onion and garlic in butter until tender. Add spinach and pepper; cook for 2-3 minutes or until heated through.
2. Place about 3 Tbsp. spinach mixture off center on each tortilla; top with 1 Tbsp. picante sauce and 2 Tbsp. cheese. Fold sides and ends over filling and roll up.
3. Place seam side down in a 13x9-in. baking dish coated with cooking spray. Top with remaining picante sauce and cheese. Bake, uncovered, at 350° for 20-25 minutes or until sauce is bubbly and cheese is melted.
1 BURRITO: 382 cal., 15g fat (8g sat. fat), 30mg chol., 1049mg sod., 42g carb. (5g sugars, 4g fiber), 19g pro.

> **TEST KITCHEN TIP**
> It's very easy to customize these burritos to your liking. Try spreading a tablespoon or two of refried beans onto each tortilla before adding the spinach mixture. You can also use fresh spinach instead of the frozen if you'd like.

HOMEMADE CHURROS

Churros are the perfect way to top off a Cinco de Mayo bash—or any party for that matter!
—Taste of Home *Test Kitchen*

Prep: 15 min. + cooling • **Cook:** 20 min.
Makes: about 1 dozen

- ½ cup water
- ½ cup 2% milk
- 1 Tbsp. canola oil
- ¼ tsp. salt
- 1 cup all-purpose flour
- 1 large egg, room temperature
- ¼ tsp. grated lemon zest
  Additional oil for frying
- ½ cup sugar
- ¼ tsp. ground cinnamon

1. In a large saucepan, bring the water, milk, oil and salt to a boil. Add flour all at once and stir until a smooth ball forms. Transfer to a large bowl; let stand for 5 minutes.
2. Beat on medium-high speed for 1 minute or until the dough softens. Add egg and lemon zest; beat for 1-2 minutes. Set aside to cool.
3. In a deep cast-iron or heavy skillet, heat 1 in. oil to 375°. Insert a large star tip in a pastry bag; fill with dough. On a baking sheet, pipe dough into 4-in. strips.
4. Transfer strips to skillet and fry until golden brown on both sides. Drain on paper towels. Combine the sugar and cinnamon; sprinkle over churros. Serve warm.
1 FRITTER: 122 cal., 5g fat (1g sat. fat), 17mg chol., 60mg sod., 17g carb. (9g sugars, 0 fiber), 2g pro.

TACO-FILLED PASTA SHELLS

I've been stuffing pasta shells with different fillings for years, but my family enjoys this version with taco-seasoned meat the most. The frozen shells are so convenient, because you can take out only the number you need for a single-serving lunch or family dinner. Just add zippy taco sauce and bake.
—Marge Hodel, Roanoke, IL

Prep: 20 min. + chilling • **Bake:** 45 min.
Makes: 2 casseroles (6 servings each)

- 2 lbs. ground beef
- 2 envelopes taco seasoning
- 1½ cups water
- 1 pkg. (8 oz.) cream cheese, cubed
- 24 uncooked jumbo pasta shells
- ¼ cup butter, melted

ADDITIONAL INGREDIENTS
(FOR EACH CASSEROLE)

- 1 cup salsa
- 1 cup taco sauce
- 1 cup shredded cheddar cheese
- 1 cup shredded Monterey Jack cheese
- 1½ cups crushed tortilla chips
- 1 cup sour cream
- 3 green onions, chopped

1. In a Dutch oven, cook beef over medium heat until no longer pink; drain. Stir in taco seasoning and water. Bring to a boil. Reduce heat; simmer, uncovered, for 5 minutes. Stir in cream cheese until melted. Transfer to a bowl; cool. Chill for 1 hour.
2. Cook pasta according to the package directions; drain. Gently toss with butter. Fill each shell with about 3 Tbsp. meat mixture. Place 12 stuffed shells in a freezer container; cover and freeze for up to 3 months.
3. To prepare remaining shells, spoon 1 cup salsa into a greased 9-in. square baking dish. Top with remaining stuffed shells and 1 cup taco sauce. Cover and bake at 350° for 30 minutes. Uncover; sprinkle with 1 cup of each of the cheeses and 1½ cups chips. Bake 15 minutes longer or until heated through. Serve with sour cream and onions.
FREEZE OPTION: To use frozen shells, thaw in the refrigerator for 24 hours (shells will be partially frozen). Spoon 1 cup salsa into a greased 9-in. square baking dish; top with shells and 1 cup taco sauce. Cover and bake at 350° for 40 minutes. Uncover. Sprinkle with 1 cup of each of the cheeses and 1½ cups chips; proceed as directed.
2 SHELLS: 492 cal., 31g fat (16g sat. fat), 98mg chol., 982mg sod., 29g carb. (4g sugars, 1g fiber), 23g pro.

MOTHER'S DAY

SONYA LABBE
West Hollywood, CA

CHEESE &
FRESH HERB QUICHE

With herbs from the garden to use up, I created a quiche with basil, parsley and dill along with feta, Swiss, Gruyere and mozzarella. You can also try it with goat cheese.
—*Sonya Labbe, West Hollywood, CA*

- -

Prep: 15 min. • **Bake:** 25 min. + standing
Makes: 6 servings

- 1 sheet refrigerated pie crust
- ½ cup shredded part-skim mozzarella cheese
- ½ cup shredded Swiss cheese
- ½ cup shredded Gruyere or additional Swiss cheese
- ½ cup crumbled feta cheese
- 5 large eggs
- 1 cup half-and-half cream
- 1 Tbsp. minced fresh basil
- 1 Tbsp. minced fresh parsley
- 2 tsp. minced fresh dill

1. Preheat oven to 400°. Unroll crust into a 9-in. pie plate; flute edge. Sprinkle cheeses into crust. In a large bowl, whisk eggs and cream until blended. Stir in herbs; pour over the top.
2. Bake on a lower oven rack 25-30 minutes or until a knife inserted in the center comes out clean. Let stand 10 minutes before cutting.
1 PIECE: 394 cal., 26g fat (13g sat. fat), 209mg chol., 380mg sod., 21g carb. (3g sugars, 0 fiber), 17g pro.

⑤ⓘ AIR-FRYER MINI NUTELLA DOUGHNUT HOLES

You can make these air-fryer donuts in advance and refrigerate them before frying. Just be sure to bring the dough to room temperature before frying.
—*Renee Murphy, Smithtown, NY*

- -

Prep: 30 min. • **Cook:** 5 min./batch
Makes: 32 doughnuts

- 1 large egg
- 1 Tbsp. water
- 1 tube (16.3 oz.) large refrigerated flaky biscuits (8 count)
- ⅔ cup Nutella
  Oil for deep-fat frying
  Confectioners' sugar

1. Preheat air fryer to 300°. Whisk egg with water. On a lightly floured surface, roll each biscuit into a 6-in. circle; cut each circle into 4 wedges. Brush lightly with egg mixture; top each wedge with 1 tsp. Nutella. Bring up corners over filling; pinch edges firmly to seal.
2. In batches, arrange biscuits in a single layer on ungreased tray in air-fryer basket. Cook until golden brown, 8-10 minutes, turning once. Dust with the confectioners' sugar; serve warm.
1 DOUGHNUT: 94 cal., 6g fat (1g sat. fat), 6mg chol., 119mg sod., 10g carb. (4g sugars, 0 fiber), 1g pro.

ORANGE DREAM MIMOSAS

Toast Mom with this grown-up Creamsicle-style beverage. Make a nonalcoholic version for the kids with sparkling grape juice, cider or ginger ale.
—*Deirdre Cox, Kansas City, MO*

Prep: 15 min. + freezing
Makes: 16 servings (4 cups frozen mix)

- 4 tsp. grated orange zest
- 2½ cups orange juice
- 1 cup half-and-half cream
- ¾ cup superfine sugar
- 2 bottles (750 ml each) champagne or other sparkling wine
  Optional: Fresh strawberries or orange slices

1. Place the first 4 ingredients in a blender; cover and process until sugar is dissolved. Transfer to an 8-in. square dish; freeze, covered, 6 hours or overnight.
2. To serve, place ¼ cup orange mixture in each champagne glass. Top with champagne. Garnish with strawberries or oranges; serve mimosa immediately.
1 SERVING: 138 cal., 2g fat (1g sat. fat), 8mg chol., 8mg sod., 15g carb. (13g sugars, 0 fiber), 1g pro.

LAYERED FRESH FRUIT SALAD

Fresh fruit flavor shines through in this medley, always welcome at potlucks. It has a little zing from citrus zest and cinnamon—and is just sweet enough to feel like dessert.
—*Page Alexander, Baldwin City, KS*

Prep: 20 min. + chilling
Cook: 10 min. + cooling
Makes: 12 servings

- ½ tsp. grated orange zest
- ⅔ cup orange juice
- ½ tsp. grated lemon zest
- ⅓ cup lemon juice
- ⅓ cup packed light brown sugar
- 1 cinnamon stick

FRUIT SALAD
- 2 cups cubed fresh pineapple
- 2 cups sliced fresh strawberries
- 2 medium kiwifruit, peeled and sliced
- 3 medium bananas, sliced
- 2 medium oranges, peeled and sectioned
- 1 medium red grapefruit, peeled and sectioned
- 1 cup seedless red grapes

1. Place the first 6 ingredients in a saucepan; bring to a boil. Reduce heat; simmer, uncovered, 5 minutes. Cool completely. Remove cinnamon stick.
2. Layer the fruit in a large glass bowl. Pour juice mixture over top. Refrigerate, covered, several hours.
1 SERVING: 110 cal., 0 fat (0 sat. fat), 0 chol., 5mg sod., 28g carb. (21g sugars, 2g fiber), 1g pro. **DIABETIC EXCHANGES:** 1 starch, 1 fruit.

JUNETEENTH

SPICY SHRIMP & WATERMELON KABOBS

My three sons can polish off a watermelon in one sitting. Before they dig in, I set aside a few slices to make these zesty kabobs.
—*Jennifer Fisher, Austin, TX*

Takes: 30 min. • **Makes:** 4 servings

- 1 Tbsp. reduced-sodium soy sauce
- 1 Tbsp. Sriracha chili sauce
- 1 Tbsp. honey
- 1 garlic clove, minced
- 4 cups cubed seedless watermelon (1 in.), divided
- 1 lb. uncooked shrimp (16-20 per lb.), peeled and deveined
- 1 medium red onion, cut into 1-in. pieces
- ½ tsp. sea salt
- ¼ tsp. coarsely ground pepper
  Minced fresh cilantro, optional

1. For glaze, place soy sauce, chili sauce, honey, garlic and 2 cups watermelon in a blender; cover and process until pureed. Transfer to a small saucepan; bring to a boil. Cook, uncovered, over medium-high heat until the mixture is reduced by half, about 10 minutes. Reserve ¼ cup glaze for serving.
2. On 4 metal or soaked wooden skewers, alternately thread shrimp, onion and the remaining watermelon cubes. Sprinkle with salt and pepper.
3. Place kabobs on an oiled grill rack over medium heat. Grill, covered, 3-4 minutes on each side or until shrimp turn pink, brushing with remaining glaze during the last 2 minutes. If desired, sprinkle with cilantro. Serve with reserved glaze.

1 KABOB WITH 1 TBSP. GLAZE: 172 cal., 2g fat (0 sat. fat), 138mg chol., 644mg sod., 23g carb. (19g sugars, 2g fiber), 20g pro.
DIABETIC EXCHANGES: 3 lean meat, 1 fruit, ½ starch.

READER REVIEW

"Oh my goodness! A dream come true for using up watermelon. I absolutely love shrimp and spice, so with this sauce, it's a total win! Yum!"

SUMMY, TASTEOFHOME.COM

SWEET GINGER RIBS

People ask what's in the marinade of my glazed ribs with ginger, garlic and peach preserves. Now you know! By the way, it works on steaks and chicken, too.
—*Grace McKeone, Schenectady, NY*

Prep: 15 min. + marinating
Grill: 1½ hours
Makes: 8 servings

- ½ cup soy sauce
- ½ cup red wine vinegar
- ½ cup ketchup
- ½ cup peach preserves
- ⅓ cup minced fresh gingerroot
- 2 Tbsp. stone-ground mustard
- 2 Tbsp. brown sugar
- 6 garlic cloves, minced
- ½ tsp. crushed red pepper flakes
- ½ tsp. coarsely ground pepper
- 4 lbs. pork baby back ribs

1. In a small bowl, whisk first 10 ingredients until blended. In a small container, reserve 1 cup marinade for basting. Divide ribs and remaining marinade between 2 large resealable plastic bags; seal bags and turn to coat. Refrigerate ribs and the reserved marinade overnight.
2. Remove the ribs, discarding remaining marinade from bags. Grill the ribs, covered, over indirect medium heat 1½-2 hours or until tender, basting the ribs occasionally with reserved marinade during the last half hour.

1 SERVING: 338 cal., 21g fat (8g sat. fat), 81mg chol., 721mg sod., 13g carb. (10g sugars, 0 fiber), 24g pro.

STRAWBERRY RHUBARB CHEESECAKE BARS

These bars layer a buttery pecan shortbread crust with a rich and creamy cheesecake filling and sweet-tart strawberry rhubarb jam. For larger squares, cut into nine bars instead of 16.
—Amanda Scarlati, Sandy, UT

Prep: 30 min. + chilling
Bake: 15 min. + cooling
Makes: 16 servings

- 1 cup all-purpose flour
- ⅓ cup packed brown sugar
  Dash kosher salt
- ½ cup cold butter, cubed
- ⅓ cup finely chopped pecans

FILLING
- 1 pkg. (8 oz.) cream cheese, softened
- ¼ cup sugar
- 2 Tbsp. 2% milk
- 1 Tbsp. lemon juice
- ½ tsp. vanilla extract
  Dash kosher salt
- 1 large egg, room temperature, lightly beaten

JAM
- ½ cup sugar
- 2 Tbsp. cornstarch
- 1⅓ cups chopped fresh strawberries
- 1⅓ cups sliced fresh or frozen rhubarb
- 1 Tbsp. lemon juice

1. Preheat oven to 350°. Line an 8-in. square baking pan with parchment, letting the ends extend up the sides. In a small bowl, mix the flour, brown sugar and salt; cut in butter until crumbly. Stir in pecans.

2. Press into bottom of prepared pan. Bake until edges just begin to brown, 12-15 minutes. Cool completely on a wire rack.

3. In a large bowl, beat cream cheese and sugar until smooth. Beat in milk, lemon juice, vanilla and salt. Add egg; beat on low speed just until blended. Pour over crust.

4. Bake until filling is set, 15-20 minutes. Cool on a wire rack for 1 hour.

5. For jam, in a small saucepan, mix sugar and cornstarch. Add the strawberries, rhubarb and lemon juice. Bring to a boil. Reduce heat; simmer, uncovered, until the mixture begins to thicken, 6-8 minutes. Cool completely. Spread over filling. Refrigerate until set, 8 hours or overnight.

6. Using parchment, carefully remove cheesecake from baking pan. Cut into bars for serving.

1 BAR: 215 cal., 13g fat (7g sat. fat), 41mg chol., 113mg sod., 24g carb. (15g sugars, 1g fiber), 3g pro.

CAJUN PECAN CATFISH

Instead of dredging the catfish to bread it, I sprinkle the seasonings over the top. It's just as crunchy, but without the mess. Serve with biscuits and mixed fruit.
—Jan Wilkins, Blytheville, AR

Takes: 25 min. • **Makes:** 4 servings

- 2 Tbsp. olive oil
- 2 tsp. lemon juice
- 1 tsp. Cajun seasoning
- ½ tsp. dried thyme
- ⅓ cup finely chopped pecans
- 2 Tbsp. grated Parmesan cheese
- 1 Tbsp. dry bread crumbs
- 1 Tbsp. dried parsley flakes
- 4 catfish fillets (6 oz. each)

1. Preheat oven to 425°. In a small bowl, combine oil, lemon juice, Cajun seasoning and thyme. In another bowl, combine pecans, cheese, bread crumbs, parsley and 1 Tbsp. of the oil mixture.

2. Place catfish in a greased 15x10x1-in. baking pan. Brush with remaining oil mixture. Spread pecan mixture over fillets. Bake until fish flakes easily with a fork, 10-15 minutes.

1 FILLET: 377 cal., 28g fat (5g sat. fat), 82mg chol., 277mg sod., 3g carb. (1g sugars, 1g fiber), 29g pro.

STRAWBERRY WATERMELON LEMONADE

The nutrition department at my local hospital inspired me to create this refreshing summer sipper. I tweaked their recipe slightly to create this drink full of sweet-tart flavor.
—Dawn Lowenstein, Huntingdon Valley, PA

Takes: 20 min.
Makes: 12 servings (3 qt.)

- ¼ cup sugar
- 2 cups boiling water
- ½ lb. fresh strawberries, hulled and quartered (about 2 cups)
- 12 cups cubed watermelon (about 1 medium)
- 1 can (12 oz.) frozen lemonade concentrate, thawed
- 3 Tbsp. lemon juice
  Ice cubes

Dissolve sugar in boiling water. Place strawberries and watermelon in batches in a blender; cover and process until blended. Pour blended fruit though a fine mesh strainer; transfer to a large pitcher. Stir in lemonade concentrate, lemon juice and sugar water. Serve over ice.

1 CUP: 119 cal., 0 fat (0 sat. fat), 0 chol., 7mg sod., 34g carb. (30g sugars, 1g fiber), 1g pro.

FATHER'S DAY

SPICED GRILLED CORN

The wonderful spice mixture doesn't add heat...only incredible flavor. This just may be the best corn you've ever had!
—Taste of Home *Test Kitchen*

Takes: 20 min. • **Makes:** 8 servings

- 2 tsp. ground cumin
- 2 tsp. ground coriander
- 1 tsp. salt
- 1 tsp. dried oregano
- ½ tsp. ground ginger
- ¼ tsp. ground cinnamon
- ¼ tsp. pepper
- ⅛ tsp. ground cloves
- 2 Tbsp. olive oil
- 8 medium ears sweet corn, husked

1. In a small bowl, combine first 8 ingredients. Brush oil over corn; sprinkle with the spice mixture. Place each ear on a rectangle of heavy-duty foil (about 14x12 in.). Fold foil over corn, sealing tightly.
2. Grill corn, covered, over medium heat until tender, 10-12 minutes, turning occasionally. Open foil carefully to allow steam to escape.
1 EAR OF CORN: 113 cal., 5g fat (1g sat. fat), 0 chol., 310mg sod., 18g carb. (3g sugars, 3g fiber), 3g pro. **DIABETIC EXCHANGES:** 1 starch, ½ fat.

GRILLED RIBEYES WITH GREEK RELISH

The classic Grecian flavors of olives, feta cheese and tomatoes are a surefire hit. Combine them to complement a perfectly grilled steak, and it's magic.
—*Mary Lou Cook, Welches, OR*

Takes: 30 min. • **Makes:** 4 servings

- 4 plum tomatoes, seeded and chopped
- 1 cup chopped red onion
- ⅔ cup pitted Greek olives
- ¼ cup minced fresh cilantro
- ¼ cup lemon juice, divided
- 2 Tbsp. olive oil
- 2 garlic cloves, minced
- 2 beef ribeye steaks (¾ lb. each)
- 1 cup crumbled feta cheese

1. For relish, combine tomatoes, onion, olives, cilantro, 2 Tbsp. lemon juice, oil and garlic.
2. Drizzle remaining lemon juice over steaks. Grill steaks, covered, over medium heat or broil 4 in. from heat 5-7 minutes on each side or until meat reaches desired doneness (for medium-rare, a thermometer should read 135°; medium, 140°; medium-well, 145°). Let stand 5 minutes before cutting steaks in half. Serve with relish and cheese.
4 OZ. COOKED BEEF WITH ⅔ CUP RELISH AND ¼ CUP CHEESE: 597 cal., 44g fat (16g sat. fat), 115mg chol., 723mg sod., 11g carb. (4g sugars, 3g fiber), 37g pro.

CLASSIC CHOCOLATE CAKE

This recipe appeared on a can of Hershey's cocoa back in 1943. I tried it, my boys liked it and I've been making it ever since. I make all my cakes from scratch, and this is one of the best!
—*Betty Follas, Morgan Hill, CA*

Prep: 15 min. • **Bake:** 35 min.
Makes: 15 servings

2/3 cup butter, softened
1 2/3 cups sugar
3 large eggs, room temperature
2 cups all-purpose flour
2/3 cup baking cocoa
1 1/4 tsp. baking soda
1 tsp. salt
1 1/2 cups whole milk
Confectioners' sugar or frosting of your choice

1. In a bowl, cream butter and sugar until light and fluffy, 5-7 minutes. Add eggs, 1 at a time, beating well after each addition. Combine flour, cocoa, baking soda and salt; add to creamed mixture alternately with milk, beating until smooth after each addition. Pour batter into a greased and floured 13x9-in. baking pan.
2. Bake at 350° until a toothpick inserted in center comes out clean, 35-40 minutes. Cool on a wire rack. When cake is cool, dust with confectioners' sugar or top with frosting of your choice.
1 PIECE: 257 cal., 10g fat (6g sat. fat), 67mg chol., 368mg sod., 38g carb. (23g sugars, 1g fiber), 4g pro.

🄖 FRENCH FRIES

You can't beat the taste of homemade fries. And this recipe is so much better than any fast food or frozen variety.
—*Taste of Home Test Kitchen*

Prep: 20 min. + soaking • **Cook:** 5 min./batch
Makes: 4 servings

1 lb. russet potatoes
Oil for deep-fat frying
3/4 tsp. salt

1. Cut potatoes into 1/4-in. julienned strips; soak in cold water for 30 minutes.
2. Drain potatoes; pat dry with paper towels. In an electric skillet or deep-fat fryer, heat oil to 340°. Fry potatoes in batches 3-4 minutes or until lightly browned. Remove with a slotted spoon; drain on paper towels.
3. Increase temperature of oil to 375°. Fry potatoes again in batches for 1-2 minutes or until crisp and golden brown, turning frequently. Drain on paper towels; sprinkle with salt. Serve immediately.
3/4 CUP: 190 cal., 11g fat (1g sat. fat), 0 chol., 449mg sod., 20g carb. (2g sugars, 2g fiber), 2g pro.

DID YOU KNOW?
Soaking the julienned potato strips in water before frying helps to draw out some of the starch from the spuds. This leads to crispy fries that don't stick together. Just be sure to blot the strips dry before frying; water on the fries can actually lower the temperature of the oil, causing longer cooking times and additional fat absorption.

FOURTH OF JULY

GRILLED FIRECRACKER POTATO SALAD

I can eat potato salad all the time. A little spice is nice, so I use cayenne and paprika in this grilled salad that comes with its own fireworks.
—*Ashley Armstrong, Kingsland, GA*

Prep: 20 min. • **Grill:** 20 min. + chilling
Makes: 16 servings

- 3 lbs. small red potatoes (about 30), quartered
- 2 Tbsp. olive oil
- 1 tsp. salt
- ½ tsp. pepper

DRESSING
- 1½ cups mayonnaise
- ½ cup finely chopped onion
- ¼ cup Dijon mustard
- 2 Tbsp. sweet pickle relish
- ½ tsp. paprika
- ¼ tsp. cayenne pepper

SALAD
- 6 hard-boiled large eggs, chopped
- 2 celery ribs, finely chopped
  Minced fresh chives, optional

1. Toss potatoes with oil, salt and pepper; place in a grill wok or basket. Grill, covered, over medium heat 20-25 minutes or until potatoes are tender, stirring occasionally. Transfer potatoes to a large bowl; cool slightly.
2. In a small bowl, mix dressing ingredients. Add dressing, eggs and celery to potatoes; toss to combine. Refrigerate, covered, for 1-2 hours or until cold. If desired, sprinkle with chives.
1 CUP: 265 cal., 20g fat (3g sat. fat), 77mg chol., 398mg sod., 16g carb. (2g sugars, 2g fiber), 4g pro.

CONTEST-WINNING BARBECUED CHICKEN

When our neighborhood has a cookout, I always take along this chicken and watch it quickly disappear! My family loves this recipe because of the zesty seasoning blend and barbecue sauce.
—*Linda Scott, Hahira, GA*

Prep: 10 min. • **Grill:** 40 min.
Makes: 8 servings

- 2 broiler/fryer chickens (3 to 4 lbs. each), cut up

SPICE RUB
- 2 Tbsp. onion powder
- 4 tsp. salt or salt substitute
- 1 Tbsp. paprika
- 2 tsp. garlic powder
- 1½ tsp. chili powder
- 1½ tsp. pepper
- ¼ tsp. ground turmeric
  Pinch cayenne pepper

SAUCE
- 2 cups ketchup
- 3 Tbsp. brown sugar
- 2 Tbsp. dried minced onion
- 2 Tbsp. thawed orange juice concentrate
- ½ tsp. liquid smoke, optional

1. Pat chicken pieces dry. In a small bowl, mix spice rub ingredients; reserve 1 Tbsp. spice rub for sauce. Rub remaining spice rub on all sides of chicken pieces.
2. Grill chicken, uncovered, over medium heat for 20 minutes, skin side down. Meanwhile, combine all sauce ingredients; stir in reserved spice rub. Turn chicken; grill 20-30 minutes longer or until juices run clear, basting frequently with sauce.
7 OZ. COOKED CHICKEN: 471 cal., 21g fat (6g sat. fat), 131mg chol., 2062mg sod., 26g carb. (24g sugars, 1g fiber), 42g pro.

RED, WHITE & BLUE SALAD

Our striking flag salad drew plenty of attention at our Independence Day party. I use gelatin to help create the shimmering stripes.
—Laurie Neverman, Denmark, WI

Prep: 30 min. + chilling • **Makes:** 16 servings

- 1 pkg. (3 oz.) berry blue gelatin
- 2 cups boiling water, divided
- 2½ cups cold water, divided
- 1 cup fresh blueberries
- 1 envelope unflavored gelatin
- 1 cup heavy whipping cream
- 6 Tbsp. sugar
- 2 cups sour cream
- 1 tsp. vanilla extract
- 1 pkg. (3 oz.) raspberry gelatin
- 1 cup fresh raspberries
  Optional: Whipped topping and additional berries

1. Dissolve berry blue gelatin in 1 cup boiling water; stir in 1 cup cold water. Add the blueberries. Pour into a 3-qt. serving bowl. Refrigerate until firm, about 1 hour.
2. In a saucepan, sprinkle unflavored gelatin over ½ cup cold water; let stand for 1 minute. Add whipping cream and sugar; cook and stir over low heat until dissolved. Cool to room temperature. Whisk in sour cream and vanilla. Spoon over blue layer. Refrigerate until firm.
3. Dissolve raspberry gelatin in remaining hot water; stir in remaining cold water. Add raspberries. Spoon over cream layer. Chill until set. If desired, top with whipped topping and berries.

1 SERVING: 179 cal., 11g fat (7g sat. fat), 40mg chol., 46mg sod., 18g carb. (16g sugars, 1g fiber), 3g pro.

CHILI CORNBREAD SALAD

A co-worker brought this wonderful dish to a potluck several years ago. She had copies of the recipe next to the pan. Now I make it for get-togethers and also supply copies of the recipe. I never have any leftover salad—or recipes for that matter!
—Kelly Newsom, Jenks, OK

Prep: 20 min. + chilling
Bake: 20 min. + cooling
Makes: 15 servings

- 1 pkg. (8½ oz.) cornbread/muffin mix
- 1 can (4 oz.) chopped green chiles, undrained
- ⅛ tsp. ground cumin
- ⅛ tsp. dried oregano
  Pinch rubbed sage
- 1 cup mayonnaise
- 1 cup sour cream
- 1 envelope ranch salad dressing mix
- 2 cans (15 oz. each) pinto beans, rinsed and drained
- 2 cans (15¼ oz. each) whole kernel corn, drained
- 3 medium tomatoes, chopped
- 1 cup chopped green pepper
- 1 cup chopped green onions
- 10 bacon strips, cooked and crumbled
- 2 cups shredded cheddar cheese

1. Prepare cornbread batter according to package directions. Stir in chiles, cumin, oregano and sage. Spread in a greased 8-in. square baking pan. Bake at 400° until a toothpick inserted in the center comes out clean, 20-25 minutes. Cool.
2. In a small bowl, combine mayonnaise, sour cream and dressing mix; set aside. Crumble half of the cornbread into a 13x9-in. dish. Layer with half of the beans, mayonnaise mixture, corn, tomatoes, green pepper, onions, bacon and cheese. Repeat layers (dish will be very full). Cover and refrigerate for 2 hours.

1 SERVING: 383 cal., 24g fat (8g sat. fat), 39mg chol., 839mg sod., 30g carb. (9g sugars, 5g fiber), 12g pro.

OKTOBERFEST

🎗 COUNTRY PORK
& SAUERKRAUT

The fact that my mother and grandmother once ran a beanery for a train crew has inspired so much of my cooking and baking. I even adapted this recipe from one of theirs. Luckily for me, my husband likes to eat what I serve as much as I like to cook. The secret ingredient in this particular recipe is the applesauce. When everything is cooked up, you wouldn't know it's in there, yet the flavor is just a bit sweet.
—Donna Hellendrung, Minneapolis, MN

Prep: 15 min. • **Bake:** 1½ hours
Makes: 4 servings

- 2 lbs. bone-in country-style pork ribs
- 1 medium onion, chopped
- 1 Tbsp. canola oil
- 1 can (14 oz.) sauerkraut, undrained
- 1 cup unsweetened applesauce
- 2 Tbsp. brown sugar
- 2 tsp. caraway seeds
- 1 tsp. garlic powder
- ½ tsp. pepper

1. In a Dutch oven, cook ribs and onion in oil until ribs are browned and onion is tender. Remove from the heat. Combine remaining ingredients and pour over ribs.
2. Cover and bake at 350° until ribs are tender, 1½-2 hours.
1 SERVING: 477 cal., 24g fat (8g sat. fat), 130mg chol., 757mg sod., 23g carb. (15g sugars, 5g fiber), 41g pro.

🎗 KIELBASA CABBAGE STEW

If you like German potato salad, you'll love this sweet-and-sour stew. Caraway seeds, smoky kielbasa, tender potatoes and shredded cabbage make it a delicious, surprisingly light change of pace.
—Valrie Burrows, Shelby, MI

Prep: 10 min. • **Cook:** 35 min.
Makes: 4 servings

- ½ lb. smoked turkey kielbasa or Polish sausage, sliced
- 1 lb. potatoes, peeled and cubed
- 2 cups shredded cabbage
- 1 large onion, chopped
- 1 can (14½ oz.) reduced-sodium chicken broth
- ¾ cup water, divided
- 2 Tbsp. sugar
- 1 tsp. caraway seeds
- ¼ tsp. pepper
- 1 can (16 oz.) kidney beans, rinsed and drained
- 3 Tbsp. cider vinegar
- 2 Tbsp. all-purpose flour

1. In a large saucepan or nonstick skillet, brown the sausage over medium heat. Add the potatoes, cabbage, onion, broth, ½ cup water, sugar, caraway and pepper. Bring to a boil. Reduce heat; cover and simmer for 15-18 minutes or until the potatoes are tender, stirring occasionally.
2. Add beans and vinegar; cover and simmer 5-10 minutes longer. Combine flour and remaining water until smooth; stir into stew. Bring to a boil; cook and stir for 2 minutes or until thickened.
1¾ CUPS: 322 cal., 3g fat (1g sat. fat), 25mg chol., 1143mg sod., 57g carb. (0 sugars, 7g fiber), 17g pro. **DIABETIC EXCHANGES:** 3 starch, 2 lean meat, 1 vegetable.

OLD-WORLD RYE BREAD

Rye and caraway contribute to this bread's wonderful flavor, while the surprise of baking cocoa gives it a rich, dark color. For a variation, stir in a cup each of raisins and walnuts.
—*Perlene Hoekema, Lynden, WA*

Prep: 25 min. + rising
Bake: 35 min. + cooling
Makes: 2 loaves (12 slices each)

2 pkg. (¼ oz. each) active dry yeast
1½ cups warm water (110° to 115°)
½ cup molasses
6 Tbsp. butter, softened
2 cups rye flour
¼ cup baking cocoa
2 Tbsp. caraway seeds
2 tsp. salt
3½ to 4 cups all-purpose flour
   Cornmeal

1. In a large bowl, dissolve yeast in warm water. Beat in the molasses, butter, rye flour, cocoa, caraway seeds, salt and 2 cups all-purpose flour until smooth. Stir in enough of the remaining all-purpose flour to form a stiff dough.
2. Turn onto a floured surface; knead until smooth and elastic, 6-8 minutes. Place in a greased bowl, turning once to grease top.

Cover and let rise in a warm place until doubled, about 1½ hours.
3. Punch dough down. Turn onto a lightly floured surface; divide in half. Shape each piece into a loaf about 10 in. long. Grease 2 baking sheets and sprinkle with cornmeal. Place loaves on prepared pans. Cover and let rise until doubled, about 1 hour.
4. Bake at 350° for 35-40 minutes or until bread sounds hollow when tapped. Remove from pans to wire racks to cool.
1 SLICE: 146 cal., 3g fat (2g sat. fat), 8mg chol., 229mg sod., 26g carb. (5g sugars, 2g fiber), 3g pro.

GERMAN BEER CHEESE SPREAD

We love the bold flavors of our German heritage. Cheddar and beer make a tangy spread to serve with pretzels, pumpernickel, crackers and sausage. Choose your favorite beer because the flavor really comes through in the finished recipe.
—*Angela Spengler, Niceville, FL*

Takes: 15 min. • **Makes:** 2½ cups

1 lb. sharp cheddar cheese, cut into ½-in. cubes
1 Tbsp. Worcestershire sauce
1½ tsp. prepared mustard
1 small garlic clove, minced
¼ tsp. salt
⅛ tsp. pepper
⅔ cup German beer or nonalcoholic beer
   Assorted crackers or vegetables

1. Place cheese in a food processor; pulse until finely chopped, about 1 minute. Add Worcestershire sauce, mustard, garlic, salt and pepper. Gradually add the beer while continuing to process until mixture is smooth and spreadable, about 1½ minutes.
2. Transfer to a serving bowl or gift jars. Refrigerate, covered, up to 1 week. Serve with crackers or vegetables.
2 TBSP.: 95 cal., 8g fat (5g sat. fat), 24mg chol., 187mg sod., 1g carb. (0 sugars, 0 fiber), 6g pro.

RASPBERRY CUSTARD KUCHEN

Back where I grew up in Wisconsin, people have been baking this German treat for generations. We love it for breakfast or as a special dessert. It's no fuss to fix and impressive to serve.
—*Virginia Arndt, Sequim, WA*

Prep: 20 min. • **Bake:** 40 min.
Makes: 12 servings

1½ cups all-purpose flour, divided
½ tsp. salt
½ cup cold butter
2 Tbsp. heavy whipping cream
½ cup sugar
FILLING
3 cups fresh raspberries
1 cup sugar
1 Tbsp. all-purpose flour
2 large eggs, beaten
1 cup heavy whipping cream
1 tsp. vanilla extract

1. In a bowl, combine 1 cup flour and salt; cut in butter until the mixture resembles coarse crumbs. Stir in cream; pat onto the bottom of a greased 13x9-in. baking dish. Combine the sugar and remaining flour; sprinkle over crust.
2. Arrange raspberries over crust. In a large bowl, combine sugar and flour. Stir in eggs, cream and vanilla; pour over berries.
3. Bake at 375° for 40-45 minutes or until lightly browned. Serve warm or cold. Store in refrigerator.
1 PIECE: 328 cal., 17g fat (10g sat. fat), 86mg chol., 195mg sod., 42g carb. (27g sugars, 3g fiber), 4g pro.

HALLOWEEN

PUMPKIN SLOPPY JOES

When my granddaughter gave me eight pumpkins from her garden, I thought I'd tire of cooking with them. Thankfully, I recalled this recipe from a friend. Best of all, it works with canned pumpkin, too!

—Eleanor McReynolds, Scott City, KS

Takes: 30 min. • **Makes:** 8 servings

- 1 lb. ground beef
- ½ cup chopped onion
- 1 garlic clove, minced
- 1 cup canned pumpkin
- 1 can (8 oz.) tomato sauce
- 2 Tbsp. brown sugar
- 2 Tbsp. prepared mustard
- 2 tsp. chili powder
- ½ tsp. salt
  American and mozzarella cheese slices
- 8 hamburger buns, split

1. In a large skillet, cook the beef, onion and garlic over medium heat until meat is no longer pink; drain. Stir in the pumpkin, tomato sauce, brown sugar, mustard, chili powder and salt. Bring to a boil. Reduce heat; simmer, uncovered, for 10 minutes.

2. Meanwhile, cut American cheese slices with a pumpkin-shaped cookie cutter. Cut mozzarella cheese into shapes (triangles, half-circles, etc.) to make pumpkin faces. Spoon meat mixture onto buns and top each with a pumpkin.

1 CUP: 250 cal., 8g fat (3g sat. fat), 28mg chol., 607mg sod., 30g carb. (9g sugars, 3g fiber), 15g pro.

HALLOWEEN PUNCH

My bright orange sipper fits right in with silly October fun. To serve it in a festive way, I sometimes set the punch bowl inside a large hollowed-out-pumpkin.

—Sue Thomas, Casa Grande, AZ

Prep: 10 min. + chilling • **Makes:** 24 servings

- 1 can (46 oz.) pineapple juice, divided
- 1 pkg. (3 oz.) orange gelatin
- 1 carton (64 oz.) orange juice
- 1 liter ginger ale, chilled
- 1 qt. orange sherbet

In a saucepan, bring 1 cup pineapple juice to a boil. Stir in gelatin until dissolved. Cool; transfer to a large pitcher or container. Add orange juice and remaining pineapple juice. Chill. Just before serving, pour into a punch bowl; add ginger ale and mix well. Top with scoops of sherbet.

1 CUP: 132 cal., 1g fat (0 sat. fat), 1mg chol., 23mg sod., 31g carb. (28g sugars, 0 fiber), 1g pro.

READER REVIEW

"Very light and refreshing, and it tastes really good too. Looks pretty at any fall event."

COOKINDIVA, TASTEOFHOME.COM

BAT CUPCAKES

Even my adult children love these Halloween cupcakes! We serve them every year at our pumpkin-carving party. You can also make them with the fudge stripes on their wings facing up for variety.
—*Joyce Moynihan, Lakeville, MN*

Prep: 25 min. • **Bake:** 20 min. + cooling
Makes: 2 dozen

- 1 pkg. chocolate cake mix (regular size)
- 1 can (16 oz.) chocolate frosting
- 24 fudge striped cookies
- 24 milk chocolate kisses
  White decorating icing

1. Prepare and bake cake mix according to the package directions for cupcakes. Cool cupcakes completely.
2. Spread frosting over cupcakes. For bat wings, cut cookies in half; insert two cookie halves into each cupcake.
3. Gently press chocolate kisses into frosting for heads. Add eyes with decorating icing.
1 CUPCAKE: 284 cal., 14g fat (5g sat. fat), 27mg chol., 249mg sod., 37g carb. (25g sugars, 1g fiber), 3g pro.

PAMELA SHANK
Parkersburg, WV

HALLOWEEN PARTY CUTOUT COOKIES

I've been making these Halloween cookies for about 40 years—first for my children and now for my grandchildren and all their friends. I make about 20 trays a year to give away to all of our trick-or-treaters.
—*Pamela Shank, Parkersburg, WV*

Prep: 1 hour + chilling
Bake: 10 min./batch + cooling
Makes: 2 dozen

- ½ cup butter, softened
- ¾ cup sugar
- 1 large egg, room temperature
- 1 tsp. vanilla extract
- 1½ cups all-purpose flour
- 1 tsp. baking powder
- ½ tsp. salt

FROSTING
- 3¾ cups confectioners' sugar
- ¼ cup shortening
- 4 to 6 Tbsp. water

  Yellow, orange, green and black paste food coloring, optional

1. In a large bowl, beat butter and sugar until light and blended. Beat in egg and vanilla. In another bowl, whisk flour, baking powder and salt; gradually beat into creamed mixture. Shape dough into 2 portions. Shape each into a disk; wrap and refrigerate 1 hour or until firm enough to roll.
2. Preheat oven to 350°. On a lightly floured surface, roll each portion of dough to ¼-in. thickness. Cut with floured 2½ in. Halloween-shaped cookie cutters. Place 2 in. apart on ungreased baking sheets. Bake 8-10 minutes or until edges are light brown. Remove from pans to wire racks to cool completely.
3. In a large bowl, beat confectioners' sugar, shortening and enough water to reach spreading consistency. Tint frosting and decorate as desired. Let stand until set.
1 COOKIE: 182 cal., 6g fat (3g sat. fat), 18mg chol., 103mg sod., 31g carb. (25g sugars, 0 fiber), 1g pro.

THANKSGIVING

AUNT MARGARET'S SWEET POTATO CASSEROLE

My great-aunt made an incredible sweet potato casserole for our holiday dinners. I've lightened it up a bit, but we love it just the same.
—*Beth Britton, Fairlawn, OH*

Prep: 50 min. • **Bake:** 50 min.
Makes: 12 servings

> 3 **lbs. sweet potatoes (about 3 large), peeled and cubed**
> **TOPPING**
> ¾ **cup all-purpose flour**
> ¾ **cup packed brown sugar**
> ¾ **cup old-fashioned oats**
> ⅛ **tsp. salt**
> ⅓ **cup cold butter, cubed**
> **FILLING**
> ½ **cup sugar**
> ½ **cup 2% milk**
> 2 **large eggs, lightly beaten**
> ¼ **cup butter**
> 1 **tsp. vanilla extract**
> 2 **cups miniature marshmallows**

1. Preheat oven to 350°. Place sweet potatoes in a 6-qt. stockpot; add water to cover. Bring to a boil. Reduce heat; cook, uncovered, until tender, 10-12 minutes. Meanwhile, make topping by combining flour, brown sugar, oats and salt; cut in butter until crumbly.
2. Drain sweet potatoes; return to pan. Beat until mashed. Add sugar, milk, eggs, butter and vanilla; mash. Transfer to a broiler-safe 13x9-in. baking dish. Sprinkle topping over potato mixture.
3. Bake, uncovered, until topping is golden brown, 40-45 minutes; let stand 10 minutes. Sprinkle with marshmallows. If desired, broil 4-5 in. from heat until marshmallows are puffed and golden, 30-45 seconds.
½ CUP: 373 cal., 11g fat (6g sat. fat), 56mg chol., 134mg sod., 66g carb. (39g sugars, 4g fiber), 5g pro.

> **TEST KITCHEN TIP**
> If you add the marshmallows when the casserole comes right out of the oven, they will start to melt together and form a silky marshmallow layer.

MARINATED THANKSGIVING TURKEY

My family enjoys this turkey because it cooks up tender, tasty and golden brown. Build up flavor by marinating the meat, then grill it for a truly unique holiday bird.
—*Ken Churches, Kailua-Kona, HI*

Prep: 10 min. + marinating
Grill: 2½ hours + standing
Makes: 12 servings

> 2 **cups water**
> 1½ **cups chicken broth**
> 1 **cup reduced-sodium soy sauce**
> ⅔ **cup lemon juice**
> 2 **garlic cloves, minced**
> 1½ **tsp. ground ginger**
> 1 **tsp. pepper**
> 2 **turkey-size oven roasting bags**
> 1 **turkey (12 to 14 lbs.)**

1. Combine the first 7 ingredients; set aside and refrigerate 1 cup for basting. Place 1 oven roasting bag inside the other. Place the turkey inside the inner bag; pour in the remaining marinade. Seal bags, pressing out as much air as possible; turn to coat turkey. Place in a shallow roasting pan. Refrigerate overnight, turning several times.

2. Remove turkey; drain and discard marinade.
3. Prepare grill for indirect medium heat. Tuck wings under turkey and arrange breast side down on grill rack. Grill, covered, for 1 hour.
4. If using a charcoal grill, add 10 briquettes to coals; turn the turkey. Baste with reserved marinade. Cook, covered, 1½-2 hours, adding 10 briquettes to maintain heat and brushing with marinade every 30 minutes until a thermometer inserted in thigh reads 170°. Remove turkey from grill; tent with foil. Let stand 20 minutes before carving.
CONVENTIONAL ROASTING METHOD: Follow steps for marinating turkey overnight. Preheat oven to 325°. Place turkey on a rack in a large roaster. Bake, uncovered, 3-3½ hours or until a thermometer inserted in a thigh reads 170°. Baste frequently with reserved marinade. When turkey begins to brown, cover lightly with a tent of aluminum foil. Remove turkey from oven; tent with foil. Let stand 20 minutes before carving. If desired, skim fat and thicken pan drippings for gravy; serve with turkey.
9 OZ. COOKED TURKEY: 407 cal., 12g fat (4g sat. fat), 171mg chol., 383mg sod., 5g carb. (0 sugars, 1g fiber), 67g pro.

GREEN BEAN & CAULIFLOWER CASSEROLE

I like to make a savory homemade cream sauce for the timeless green bean casserole. This time I added another vegetable for a delicious twist that sets my casserole apart from the rest! You can always omit the vermouth by substituting another half cup of chicken broth.
—Ann Sheehy, Lawrence, MA

Prep: 45 min. • **Bake:** 30 min.
Makes: 10 servings

- 1 lb. fresh cauliflowerets, cut into 1-in. pieces
- 1 lb. fresh green beans, trimmed and cut into 2-in. pieces
- 4 tsp. olive oil, divided
- 1 cup panko bread crumbs
- 1 cup french-fried onions, crumbled
- 2 Tbsp. butter
- 8 oz. thinly sliced fresh mushrooms
- 1 shallot, finely chopped
- 2 garlic cloves, minced
- ¼ cup all-purpose flour
- ½ cup dry vermouth or reduced-sodium chicken broth
- 1½ cups reduced-sodium chicken broth
- 1 tsp. salt
- 1 tsp. dried thyme
- ½ tsp. pepper
- ¼ tsp. ground nutmeg
- ½ cup cubed fully cooked ham
- ½ cup sour cream
- 1 cup plain Greek yogurt

1. Preheat oven to 375°. In a Dutch oven, bring 12 cups water to a boil. Add cauliflower and beans; cook, uncovered, just until the beans turn bright green, 1-2 minutes. Drain and immediately drop vegetables into ice water. Drain and pat dry.

2. In a large skillet, heat 1 tsp. oil over medium-high heat. Add bread crumbs; cook and stir until lightly browned, 2-3 minutes. Stir in french-fried onions; set aside.

3. In the same skillet, heat butter and remaining oil over medium heat. Add mushrooms and shallot; cook and stir until tender, 8-10 minutes. Add garlic; cook 1 minute longer. Stir in flour until blended. Gradually whisk in vermouth; cook, stirring until most of the liquid is gone. Whisk in broth and seasonings. Stirring constantly, bring to a boil; cook and stir until thickened, 6-8 minutes. Remove from heat; stir in ham, sour cream, yogurt and reserved vegetables. Transfer to a greased 13x9-in. baking dish.

4. Bake, uncovered, until casserole is bubbly, 30-40 minutes. Sprinkle with bread crumb mixture before serving.

1 CUP: 217 cal., 13g fat (6g sat. fat), 19mg chol., 539mg sod., 19g carb. (5g sugars, 3g fiber), 7g pro.

5i QUICK CRANBERRY GELATIN SALAD

Since this tangy salad keeps well, I make it a day ahead for my menus. It's also a smart choice to take to a Thanksgiving dinner or perhaps to a holiday potluck—even people who aren't fond of cranberries think it's yummy. I got the recipe from a friend at church who likes to cook and bake as much as I do.
—Betty Claycomb, Alverton, PA

Prep: 10 min. + chilling • **Makes:** 10 servings

- 1 pkg. (6 oz.) cherry gelatin
- 1½ cups boiling water
- 1 can (20 oz.) crushed pineapple, undrained
- 1 can (14 oz.) whole-berry cranberry sauce
- 1½ cups seedless red grapes, halved
- ¼ cup chopped pecans

In a large bowl, dissolve gelatin in water. Stir in pineapple and cranberry sauce. Refrigerate for 30 minutes. Stir in grapes and pecans. Pour into a 2-qt. serving bowl. Refrigerate until firm.

½ CUP: 146 cal., 2g fat (0 sat. fat), 0 chol., 62mg sod., 32g carb. (0 sugars, 0 fiber), 1g pro.
DIABETIC EXCHANGES: 2 fruit, ½ fat.

CARAMEL PECAN PIE

This is hands down the best pecan pie—it's so good, it's scary! I'm making it for Thanksgiving because there will be others around to share it with me. Here's the trick: Toss the bag of caramels to your kid or spouse and promise they can eat whatever is left after they unwrap your 36 caramels.
—Dorothy Reinhold, Malibu, CA

Prep: 25 min. • **Bake:** 35 min. + cooling
Makes: 8 servings

- 36 caramels
- ¼ cup water
- ¼ cup butter, cubed
- 3 large eggs, room temperature
- ¾ cup sugar
- 1 tsp. vanilla extract
- ⅛ tsp. salt
- 1⅓ cups chopped pecans, toasted
- 1 frozen deep-dish pie crust (9 in.)
  Pecan halves, optional

1. Preheat oven to 350°. In a small heavy saucepan, combine the caramels, water and butter. Cook and stir over low heat until caramels are melted. Remove from the heat and set aside.

2. In a small bowl, beat the eggs, sugar, vanilla and salt until smooth. Gradually add caramel mixture. Stir in chopped pecans. Pour into crust. If desired, arrange pecan halves over the filling.

3. Bake until set, 35-40 minutes. Cool on a wire rack. Refrigerate leftovers.

1 PIECE: 541 cal., 29g fat (7g sat. fat), 88mg chol., 301mg sod., 68g carb. (49g sugars, 2g fiber), 7g pro.

HANUKKAH

CHICKEN MATZO BALL SOUP

The keys to this amazing chicken matzo ball soup are slow-cooking it and using boxed matzo ball mix. Some people swear by seltzer, but I find it's not necessary—the mix makes perfect, fluffy matzo balls every time due to its baking powder. Add chicken fat (schmaltz) for extra-authentic flavor. I think that these lovely matzo balls taste as if they came straight from Grandma's kitchen.
—*Shannon Sarna, South Orange, NJ*

Prep: 30 min. + chilling • **Cook:** 1½ hours
Makes: 26 servings (6½ qt.)

- 1 broiler/fryer chicken (3 to 4 lbs.)
- 1 lb. chicken wings
- 6 qt. water
- 3 large carrots, chopped
- 2 medium parsnips, peeled and chopped
- 1 medium turnip, peeled and chopped
- 1 large onion, chopped
- 1 bunch fresh dill sprigs
- 1 bunch fresh parsley sprigs
- 1½ tsp. whole peppercorns
- 3 tsp. salt

MATZO BALLS
- 1 pkg. (5 oz.) matzo ball mix
- 4 large eggs
- ¼ cup safflower oil
- ¼ cup rendered chicken fat
- 2 Tbsp. snipped fresh dill
- 2 Tbsp. minced fresh parsley
- 10 cups water

1. Place chicken and wings in a stockpot; add water, vegetables, herbs and seasonings. Slowly bring to a boil. Reduce heat; simmer, covered, 1-2 hours.
2. Remove chicken and wings and cool. Strain broth through a cheesecloth-lined colander; reserve vegetables. Skim fat. Remove meat from bones and cut into bite-sized pieces; discard bones. Return broth, vegetables and meat to pot. If using immediately, skim fat. Or cool broth, then refrigerate 8 hours or overnight; remove fat from surface before using. (Broth may be refrigerated up to 3 days or frozen 4-6 months.)
3. Meanwhile, in a large bowl, beat matzo ball mix, eggs, oil, chicken fat, dill and parsley until combined. Cover and refrigerate for at least 30 minutes.
4. In another stockpot, bring water to a boil. Drop rounded tablespoonfuls of matzo ball dough into boiling water. Reduce heat; cover and simmer until a toothpick inserted into a matzo ball comes out clean (do not lift cover while simmering), 20-25 minutes.
5. Carefully remove matzo balls from water with a slotted spoon; place 1 matzo ball in each soup bowl. Add soup.
1 CUP: 167 cal., 10g fat (2g sat. fat), 60mg chol., 523mg sod., 8g carb. (1g sugars, 1g fiber), 11g pro.

CRANBERRY SHORT RIBS

We live in the Yukon bush, so I often pick wild cranberries for this incredibly tender, comforting entree.
—*Cathy Wylie, Dawson City, YT*

Prep: 20 min. • **Bake:** 1½ hours
Makes: 2 servings

- 1½ lbs. bone-in beef short ribs
- ½ tsp. salt, divided
- ¼ tsp. pepper
- 1 Tbsp. all-purpose flour
- 1 Tbsp. brown sugar
- ⅛ tsp. ground mustard
  Dash ground cloves
- ¾ cup water
- 2 tsp. cider vinegar
- ½ cup fresh or frozen cranberries
- 1½ to 2 tsp. grated lemon zest
- ½ tsp. browning sauce, optional

1. Preheat oven to 350°. Place ribs in a greased 8-in. square baking dish; sprinkle with ¼ tsp. salt and pepper. Bake, covered, until tender, 1¼-1½ hours.
2. In a small saucepan, combine flour, brown sugar, mustard, cloves and remaining salt; gradually whisk in water and vinegar until smooth. Stir in cranberries, lemon zest and, if desired, browning sauce; bring to a boil. Cook and stir until thickened, about 2 minutes.
3. Drain ribs. Pour cranberry mixture over ribs. Bake, uncovered, 15 minutes longer.
1 SERVING: 314 cal., 16g fat (7g sat. fat), 82mg chol., 645mg sod., 13g carb. (8g sugars, 1g fiber), 28g pro.

POTATO LATKES

These potato and onion pancakes are tasty at any meal. For the ultimate crispiness, squeeze out all the liquid from the grated veggies before you fry them up.
—Taste of Home *Test Kitchen*

Prep: 20 min. • **Cook:** 20 min.
Makes: 2 dozen

- 2 lbs. russet potatoes, peeled
- 1 medium onion
- ½ cup chopped green onions
- 1 large egg, lightly beaten
- 1 tsp. salt
- ¼ tsp. pepper
  Oil for frying
  Optional toppings: Applesauce, sour cream, lox, chives, pearl onions and lemon wedges

1. Coarsely grate potatoes and onion; drain any liquid. Place in a bowl; add green onions, egg, salt and pepper.
2. In a cast-iron or electric skillet, heat ⅛ in. of oil to 375°. Drop the batter by heaping tablespoonfuls into hot oil. Flatten to form patties. Fry until golden brown; turn and cook the other side. Drain on paper towels. If desired, serve with toppings.
2 PANCAKES: 115 cal., 7g fat (1g sat. fat), 16mg chol., 205mg sod., 11g carb. (1g sugars, 1g fiber), 2g pro.

SUFGANIYOT

Sufganiyot are believed to have come from Spain, adapted from a similar treat, sopaipillas. Others say the sopaipilla was borrowed from Jewish cuisine. Either way, as a tradition, doughnuts are an easy one to adopt.
—David Feder, Buffalo Grove, IL

Prep: 35 min. + rising • **Cook:** 10 min.
Makes: 1½ dozen

- ½ cup whole wheat flour
- 1 pkg. (¼ oz.) active dry yeast
- ¼ tsp. ground cloves
- 1½ to 2 cups all-purpose flour
- ½ cup water
- ¼ cup honey
- 2 tsp. canola or peanut oil
- 1 large egg
- ½ tsp. vanilla extract
  Oil for deep-fat frying
- ¾ cup seedless raspberry preserves
  Confectioners' sugar

1. In a large bowl, mix the whole wheat flour, yeast, cloves and 1¼ cups all-purpose flour. In a small saucepan, heat the water, honey and oil to 120°-130°. Add to dry ingredients; beat on medium speed for 2 minutes. Add egg and vanilla; beat 2 minutes longer. Stir in enough remaining flour to form a soft dough (dough will be sticky).
2. Turn onto a floured surface; knead until smooth and elastic, 6-8 minutes. Place in a greased bowl, turning once to grease the top. Cover and let rise in a warm place until doubled, about 1 hour.
3. Punch down dough. Turn onto a lightly floured surface; roll dough to ¼-in. thickness. Cut with a floured 2-in. biscuit cutter.
4. In an electric skillet or deep fryer, heat oil to 375°. Fry doughnuts, a few at a time, until golden brown, about 45 seconds on each side. Drain on paper towels.
5. Cut a small hole in the tip of a pastry bag or in a corner of a food-safe plastic bag; insert a small tip. Fill bag with preserves.
6. With a small knife, pierce a hole into the side of each doughnut; fill with preserves. Dust with confectioners' sugar. Serve warm.
1 FILLED DOUGHNUT: 133 cal., 4g fat (0 sat. fat), 12mg chol., 5mg sod., 23g carb. (12g sugars, 1g fiber), 2g pro.

CHRISTMAS DINNER

3. Mix marmalade and reserved orange juice mixture; spread over ducklings. Bake, uncovered, until a thermometer inserted in thigh reads 180°, 30-40 minutes. Discard oranges, rosemary and cranberries from cavities. Let ducklings stand 10 minutes before carving.

8 OZ. COOKED DUCK: 373 cal., 21g fat (7g sat. fat), 61mg chol., 517mg sod., 31g carb. (27g sugars, 1g fiber), 16g pro.

MERRY BERRY SALAD

Every fall and winter we go through a cranberry craze, and we love developing recipes that celebrate the season with a subtle twist. Dried cranberries drizzled with a fresh cranberry vinaigrette infuse this salad with the holiday spirit everyone looks forward to.
—Taste of Home *Test Kitchen*

Takes: 20 min. • **Makes:** 10 servings

- 1 pkg. (10 oz.) mixed salad greens
- 1 medium red apple, diced
- 1 medium green apple, diced
- 1 cup shredded Parmesan cheese
- ½ cup dried cranberries
- ½ cup slivered almonds, toasted

DRESSING
- 1 cup fresh cranberries
- ½ cup sugar
- ½ cup cider vinegar
- ¼ cup thawed apple juice concentrate
- 1 tsp. salt
- 1 tsp. ground mustard
- 1 tsp. grated onion
- 1 cup canola oil

Combine the first 6 ingredients. To make dressing, pulse the next 7 ingredients in a blender, covered, until well mixed. While processing, gradually add oil in a steady stream. Drizzle desired amount of dressing over salad; toss to coat. Refrigerate any leftover dressing.

1 SERVING: 367 cal., 28g fat (3g sat. fat), 6mg chol., 398mg sod., 28g carb. (22g sugars, 3g fiber), 5g pro.

CRANBERRY-ORANGE ROAST DUCKLINGS

I came up with this recipe a few years ago. The first time I served it, not a speck of food was left on the platter—and I knew I had a winning recipe.
—Gloria Warczak, Cedarburg, WI

Prep: 20 min. • **Bake:** 3 hours + standing
Makes: 10 servings

- 2 domestic ducklings (4 to 5 lbs. each)
- 2 medium navel oranges, quartered
- 2 sprigs fresh rosemary
- 1½ cups fresh or frozen cranberries, divided
- 4 cups orange juice
- 1 cup chicken broth
- ¼ cup soy sauce
- 2 tsp. sugar
- 2 garlic cloves, minced
- 1 tsp. grated fresh gingerroot
- ⅔ cup orange marmalade

1. Preheat oven to 350°. Pierce duckling skin all over with a fork. Place 4 orange quarters, 1 sprig of rosemary and ¼ cup cranberries in each duckling cavity; tie drumsticks together. Place ducklings on a rack in a roasting pan, breast side up.

2. In a bowl, mix orange juice, broth, soy sauce, sugar, garlic and ginger. Refrigerate ½ cup for glaze. Pour 1 cup over ducklings; sprinkle with remaining cranberries. Cover and bake 1 hour. Uncover and bake 1½ hours longer, basting frequently with remaining orange juice mixture. (Drain fat from pan as it accumulates.)

PESTO STAR BREAD

I was excited to work with the *Taste of Home* Test Kitchen to make a savory version of my Christmas Star Twisted Bread. It's perfect for the holidays (but it's a showstopper any time of the year).
—Darlene Brenden, Salem, OR

- -

Prep: 45 min. + rising
Bake: 20 min. + cooling
Makes: 16 servings

- 1 pkg. (¼ oz.) active dry yeast
- ¼ cup warm water (110° to 115°)
- ¾ cup warm 2% milk (110° to 115°)
- 1 large egg, room temperature
- ¼ cup butter, softened
- 2 Tbsp. sugar
- 1 tsp. salt
- 3¼ to 3¾ cups all-purpose flour
- ½ cup prepared basil pesto
- 6 Tbsp. grated Parmesan cheese, divided
- ¼ cup sun-dried tomato pesto
- 2 Tbsp. butter, melted
  Optional: Additional grated Parmesan cheese, basil pesto, torn fresh basil and marinara sauce

1. In a small bowl, dissolve yeast in warm water. In a large bowl, combine milk, egg, butter, sugar, salt, yeast mixture and 2 cups flour; beat on medium speed until smooth. Stir in enough remaining flour to form a soft dough (dough will be sticky). Turn dough onto a floured surface; knead until smooth and elastic, 6-8 minutes. Place in a greased bowl, turning once to grease the top. Cover and let rise in a warm place until doubled, about 1 hour.

2. Punch down dough. Turn onto a lightly floured surface; divide into 4 portions. Roll each into a 12-in. circle. Place 1 circle on a greased 14-in. pizza pan. Spread with half the basil pesto to within ½ in. of edges; sprinkle with 2 Tbsp. Parmesan. Place second circle of dough on top; spread with sun-dried tomato pesto and sprinkle with 2 Tbsp. Parmesan. Top with third circle of dough, remaining basil pesto and remaining 2 Tbsp. Parmesan; top with final portion of dough.

3. Place a 2½-in. round cutter on top of the dough in center of circle (do not press down) With a sharp knife, make 16 evenly spaced cuts from round cutter to edge of dough, forming a starburst. Remove cutter; grasp 2 adjacent strips and rotate twice outward. Pinch the ends together. Repeat with the remaining strips.

4. Cover with a kitchen towel; let rise in a warm place until almost doubled, about 30 minutes. Preheat oven to 375°. Bake until golden brown, 18-22 minutes. Remove from oven; brush with melted butter, avoiding areas where pesto is visible. Cool completely on a wire rack. If desired, sprinkle with additional cheese and basil before serving; serve with pesto or marinara.

1 PIECE: 192 cal., 9g fat (4g sat. fat), 26mg chol., 355mg sod., 23g carb. (3g sugars, 1g fiber), 5g pro.

HOLIDAY EGGNOG PIE

When I created this pie, I was trying to use up a few things I had on hand—and everyone loved it! With pumpkin pie spice and eggnog, this creamy, dreamy pie has fantastic holiday flavor.
—Shirley Darger, Colorado City, AZ

- -

Prep: 15 min. + freezing
Makes: 8 servings

- 4 oz. cream cheese, softened
- 1 Tbsp. butter, softened
- ½ cup confectioners' sugar
- ¼ cup eggnog
- 2 Tbsp. sour cream
- 1 tsp. pumpkin pie spice
- 1½ cups whipped topping
- 1 graham cracker crust (9 in.)
- ⅛ tsp. ground nutmeg

1. In a small bowl, beat the cream cheese, butter and confectioners' sugar until smooth. Beat in the eggnog, sour cream and pie spice. Fold in whipped topping; spread into crust. Sprinkle with nutmeg.

2. Cover and freeze for 4 hours or until firm. Remove from the freezer at least 15 minutes before slicing.

1 PIECE: 253 cal., 15g fat (8g sat. fat), 27mg chol., 179mg sod., 26g carb. (19g sugars, 0 fiber), 2g pro.

CHRISTMAS PARTY PINWHEELS

These festive appetizers look so special and pretty that folks can't resist them! Refreshing ranch dressing and crisp colorful vegetables make the pinwheels a pleasure to serve to holiday guests.
—Janis Plourde, Smooth Rock Falls, ON

- -

Prep: 15 min. + chilling
Makes: about 6½ dozen

- 2 pkg. (8 oz. each) cream cheese, softened
- 1 pkg. (0.4 oz.) ranch salad dressing mix
- ½ cup minced sweet red pepper
- ½ cup minced celery
- ¼ cup sliced green onions
- ¼ cup sliced pimiento-stuffed olives
- 4 flour tortillas (10 in.)

In a bowl, beat cream cheese and dressing mix until smooth. Add red pepper, celery, onions and olives; mix well. Spread about ¾ cup on each tortilla. Roll up tightly; wrap. Refrigerate for at least 2 hours. Unwrap; using a serrated knife, cut into ½-in. slices.

1 PINWHEEL: 34 cal., 2g fat (1g sat. fat), 6mg chol., 84mg sod., 2g carb. (0 sugars, 0 fiber), 1g pro.

CHRISTMAS TREATS

ANN BUSH
Colorado City, CO

SANTA CLAUS SUGAR COOKIES

I've used this recipe for almost 40 years, and I love it because it's a little different from most. My mom always made Santa cookies, and we'd put them into little clear bags tied with ribbon to hang on the tree.
—*Ann Bush, Colorado City, CO*

- -

Prep: 45 min. + chilling
Bake: 10 min./batch + cooling
Makes: about 4 dozen

- 1 cup unsalted butter
- 1½ cups sugar
- 2 large eggs, room temperature
- 1 tsp. vanilla extract
- 3½ cups all-purpose flour
- 1 tsp. baking soda
- 1 tsp. cream of tartar
- ½ tsp. ground nutmeg
- ¼ tsp. salt

FROSTING
- ¾ cup unsalted butter, softened
- 6 Tbsp. 2% milk
- 2¼ tsp. vanilla extract
- ¼ tsp. salt
- 6¾ cups confectioners' sugar
  Optional: Red colored sugar, miniature semisweet chocolate chips and Red Hots

1. In a large bowl, cream butter and sugar until light and fluffy, 5-7 minutes. Beat in the eggs and vanilla. In another bowl, whisk flour, baking soda, cream of tartar, nutmeg and salt; gradually beat into creamed mixture.
2. Divide dough in half. Shape each into a disk; wrap and refrigerate 1 hour or until firm enough to roll.

3. Preheat oven to 375°. On a lightly floured surface, roll each portion of dough to ¼-in. thickness. Cut with a floured 3-in. Santa-shaped cookie cutter. Place 2 in. apart on greased baking sheets.
4. Bake 8-10 minutes or until light brown. Remove from the pans to wire racks to cool completely.
5. For frosting, in a large bowl, beat butter until creamy. Beat in milk, vanilla and salt. Gradually beat in confectioners' sugar until smooth. Pipe onto the cookies and decorate as desired.
1 COOKIE: 186 cal., 7g fat (4g sat. fat), 27mg chol., 56mg sod., 30g carb. (22g sugars, 0 fiber), 1g pro.

HOLIDAY DIVINITY

I've been whipping up this Christmasy treat—with its jolly red and green candied cherries and scrumptious chopped nuts—since 1955. It's so light it melts in your mouth.
—*Helen White, Kerrville, TX*

Prep: 25 min. • **Cook:** 15 min.
Makes: 1¼ lbs.

- 2 cups sugar
- ½ cup water
- ⅓ cup light corn syrup
- 2 large egg whites
- 1 tsp. vanilla extract
- ⅛ tsp. salt
- 1 cup chopped walnuts, toasted
- ¼ cup diced candied cherries
- ¼ cup diced candied pineapple

1. In a heavy saucepan, combine the sugar, water and corn syrup; cook and stir until sugar is dissolved and mixture comes to a boil. Cook over medium heat, without stirring, until a candy thermometer reads 250° (hard-ball stage). Remove from the heat.
2. Meanwhile, in a stand mixer, beat the egg whites until stiff peaks form. With mixer running on high speed, carefully pour hot syrup in a slow, steady stream into the mixing bowl. Add vanilla and salt. Beat on high speed just until candy loses its gloss and holds its shape, about 10 minutes. Stir in nuts and fruit.
3. Drop by teaspoonfuls onto waxed paper. Store in airtight containers.
1 SERVING: 289 cal., 7g fat (0 sat. fat), 0 chol., 59mg sod., 56g carb. (49g sugars, 1g fiber), 4g pro.

FESTIVE HOLIDAY FRUITCAKE BARK

Every year I make brandy-soaked dried fruit for fruitcake, but I always make too much. When I tried turning the extras into candy, the result was a sweet and colorful bark for grown-ups.
—*Susan Bickta, Kutztown, PA*

Prep: 25 min. + standing • **Makes:** 2 lbs.

- ⅔ cup chopped mixed candied fruit
- 2 Tbsp. brandy
- ½ cup walnut pieces, toasted, divided
- 20 oz. white candy coating, coarsely chopped
- ⅔ cup miniature marshmallows
- 10 shortbread cookies, coarsely chopped

1. In a small bowl, combine the candied fruit and brandy. Refrigerate, covered, 2 hours, stirring occasionally.
2. Line a 15x10x1-in. baking pan with waxed paper. Reserve 2 Tbsp. candied fruit and 2 Tbsp. walnuts for topping. In a microwave-safe bowl, melt candy coating; stir until smooth. Stir in marshmallows, cookie pieces, and remaining fruit and walnuts.
3. Spread into prepared pan (pan will not be full). Sprinkle with reserved fruit and walnuts; press into candy coating. Let stand until set. Break or cut bark into pieces. Store in an airtight container.
1 OZ.: 148 cal., 7g fat (5g sat. fat), 2mg chol., 22mg sod., 20g carb. (17g sugars, 1g fiber), 1g pro.

EGGNOG COOKIES

This cookie's flavor fits right into the holiday spirit. Pick your favorite cookie cutter shapes to make them even more festive.
—*Myra Innes, Auburn, KS*

- -

Prep: 25 min. + chilling • **Bake:** 10 min./batch
Makes: about 7 dozen

1   cup butter, softened
2   cups sugar
1   cup eggnog
1   tsp. baking soda
½   tsp. ground nutmeg
5½ cups all-purpose flour
1   large egg white, lightly beaten
    Colored sugar
    Vanilla frosting, optional

1. Cream butter and sugar. Beat in eggnog, baking soda and nutmeg. Gradually add flour and mix well. Cover and chill 1 hour.

2. On a lightly floured surface, roll out half of the dough to ⅛-in. thickness. Using floured 3½-in. cookie cutters, cut into desired shapes; place on ungreased baking sheets. Repeat with remaining dough. Brush with egg white; sprinkle with colored sugar.

3. Bake at 350° until the edges are lightly browned, 6-8 minutes. Cool on wire racks. If desired, decorate with frosting.

1 COOKIE: 71 cal., 2g fat (1g sat. fat), 8mg chol., 35mg sod., 11g carb. (5g sugars, 0 fiber), 1g pro.

HOLLY WREATHS

Cream cheese helps to keep these wreaths tender for a long time while adding delicious flavor. Candied green cherries and spicy Red Hots make them merry and bright!
—*Dee Lein, Longmont, CO*

Prep: 20 min. • **Bake:** 10 min./batch + cooling
Makes: about 3 dozen

- 1 cup butter, softened
- 3 oz. cream cheese, softened
- ½ cup sugar
- 1 tsp. vanilla extract
- 2 cups all-purpose flour
  Green candied cherries, thinly sliced
  Red Hots
  Decorating icing

1. Preheat oven to 375°. Cream butter and cream cheese. Add sugar; beat until light and fluffy, 5-7 minutes. Stir in vanilla. Gradually beat in flour.
2. Using a cookie press fitted with a star piping tip, shape dough into 2½-in. wreaths 1 in. apart on ungreased baking sheets. Bake until set (do not brown), 8-10 minutes. Cool on wire racks.
3. Decorate with green cherry pieces for leaves and Red Hots for berries. Use red decorating icing to form bows and to adhere candy to wreaths.
1 COOKIE: 90 cal., 6g fat (4g sat. fat), 16mg chol., 48mg sod., 8g carb. (3g sugars, 0 fiber), 1g pro.

READER REVIEW
"My mom made these cookies with my great-grandma, and I've made these with my mom since I can remember. Christmas wouldn't be the same without them."
NEWTER5, TASTEOFHOME.COM

ALPHABETICAL INDEX

SUBSTITUTIONS & EQUIVALENTS

EQUIVALENT MEASURES

3 teaspoons	= 1 tablespoon	**16 tablespoons**	= 1 cup
4 tablespoons	= ¼ cup	**2 cups**	= 1 pint
5⅓ tablespoons	= ⅓ cup	**4 cups**	= 1 quart
8 tablespoons	= ½ cup	**4 quarts**	= 1 gallon

FOOD EQUIVALENTS

Macaroni	1 cup (3½ ounces) uncooked	= 2½ cups cooked
Noodles, Medium	3 cups (4 ounces) uncooked	= 4 cups cooked
Popcorn	⅓-½ cup unpopped	= 8 cups popped
Rice, Long Grain	1 cup uncooked	= 3 cups cooked
Rice, Quick-Cooking	1 cup uncooked	= 2 cups cooked
Spaghetti	8 ounces uncooked	= 4 cups cooked

Bread	1 slice	= ¾ cup soft crumbs, ¼ cup fine dry crumbs
Graham Crackers	7 squares	= ½ cup finely crushed
Buttery Round Crackers	12 crackers	= ½ cup finely crushed
Saltine Crackers	14 crackers	= ½ cup finely crushed

Bananas	1 medium	= ⅓ cup mashed
Lemons	1 medium	= 3 tablespoons juice, 2 teaspoons grated zest
Limes	1 medium	= 2 tablespoons juice, 1½ teaspoons grated zest
Oranges	1 medium	= ¼-⅓ cup juice, 4 teaspoons grated zest

Cabbage	1 head = 5 cups shredded	**Green Pepper**	1 large = 1 cup chopped
Carrots	1 pound = 3 cups shredded	**Mushrooms**	½ pound = 3 cups sliced
Celery	1 rib = ½ cup chopped	**Onions**	1 medium = ½ cup chopped
Corn	1 ear fresh = ⅔ cup kernels	**Potatoes**	3 medium = 2 cups cubed

Almonds	1 pound = 3 cups chopped	**Pecan Halves**	1 pound = 4½ cups chopped
Ground Nuts	3¾ ounces = 1 cup	**Walnuts**	1 pound = 3¾ cups chopped

EASY SUBSTITUTIONS

WHEN YOU NEED...		USE...
Baking Powder	1 teaspoon	½ teaspoon cream of tartar + ¼ teaspoon baking soda
Buttermilk	1 cup	1 tablespoon lemon juice or vinegar + enough milk to measure 1 cup (let stand 5 minutes before using)
Cornstarch	1 tablespoon	2 tablespoons all-purpose flour
Honey	1 cup	1¼ cups sugar + ¼ cup water
Half-and-Half Cream	1 cup	1 tablespoon melted butter + enough whole milk to measure 1 cup
Onion	1 small, chopped (⅓ cup)	1 teaspoon onion powder or 1 tablespoon dried minced onion
Tomato Juice	1 cup	½ cup tomato sauce + ½ cup water
Tomato Sauce	2 cups	¾ cup tomato paste + 1 cup water
Unsweetened Chocolate	1 square (1 ounce)	3 tablespoons baking cocoa + 1 tablespoon shortening or oil
Whole Milk	1 cup	½ cup evaporated milk + ½ cup water

GET COOKING WITH A WELL-STOCKED KITCHEN

In a perfect world, you plan weekly or even monthly menus and have all the ingredients on hand to make each night's dinner. The reality, however, is that you may not get to think about dinner until you walk through the door.

With a reasonably stocked pantry, refrigerator and freezer, you'll still be able to serve a satisfying meal in short order. Consider these tips:

QUICK-COOKING MEATS—such as boneless chicken breasts, chicken thighs, pork tenderloin, pork chops, ground meats, Italian sausage, sirloin and flank steaks, fish fillets and shrimp—should be stocked in the freezer. Wrap individual pieces and portions, so you can remove only the amount you need. For the quickest defrosting, wrap meats for freezing in small, thin packages.

FROZEN VEGETABLES are a real time-saver. Simply pour out the amount needed—no additional preparation is required.

PASTAS, RICE, RICE MIXES AND COUSCOUS are great staples to have in the pantry—and they generally have a long shelf life. Remember that thinner pastas, such as angel hair, cook faster than thicker pastas, and fresh (refrigerated) pasta cooks faster than dried.

DAIRY PRODUCTS like milk, sour cream, cheeses (shredded, cubed or crumbled), eggs, yogurt, butter and margarine are perishable, so check the use-by date on packages and replace as needed.

CONDIMENTS like ketchup, mustard, mayonnaise, salad dressings, salsa, taco sauce, soy sauce, stir-fry sauce, hot sauce, lemon juice and lime juice add flavor to many dishes. Personalize the list to suit your family's tastes.

FRESH FRUIT AND VEGETABLES can make a satisfying pre-dinner snack. Oranges and apples are not as perishable as bananas. Ready-to-use salad greens are perfect for an instant salad.

DRIED HERBS, SPICES, VINEGARS and seasoning mixes add lots of flavor and keep for months.

PASTA SAUCES, OLIVES, BEANS, broths, canned tomatoes, canned vegetables and canned or dried soups are ideal to have on hand for a quick meal—and many of these items are common recipe ingredients.

GET YOUR FAMILY INTO THE HABIT of posting a grocery list. When an item is used up or is almost gone, just add it to the list for your next shopping trip. This way you're less likely to run completely out of an item, and you'll also save time when writing your grocery list.

MAKE THE MOST OF YOUR TIME EVERY NIGHT

With recipes in hand and the kitchen stocked, you're well on the way to a relaxing family meal. Here are some pointers to help get dinner on the table fast:

PREHEAT THE OVEN OR GRILL before starting on the recipe.

PULL OUT THE REQUIRED INGREDIENTS, mixing tools and cooking tools before beginning any prep work.

USE CONVENIENCE ITEMS whenever possible. Think pre-chopped garlic, onion and peppers, shredded or cubed cheese, seasoning mixes and jarred sauces.

MULTITASK! While the meat is simmering for a main dish, toss a salad together, cook a side dish or start on dessert.

ENCOURAGE HELPERS. Have younger children set the table. Older ones can help with ingredient preparation or can even assemble the recipes themselves.

TAKE CARE OF TWO MEALS IN ONE NIGHT by planning main-dish leftovers or making a double batch of favorite sides.

TRICKS TO TAME HUNGER WHEN IT STRIKES

Are the kids begging for a pre-supper snack? Calm their rumbling tummies with nutritious, not-too-filling noshes.

START WITH A SMALL TOSSED SALAD. Try a ready-to-serve salad mix, and add their favorite salad dressing and a little protein, like cubed cheese or julienned slices of deli meat.

CUT UP AN APPLE and smear a little peanut butter on each slice, or offer other fruits such as seedless grapes, cantaloupe, oranges or bananas. For variety, give kids vanilla yogurt or reduced-fat ranch dressing as a dipper, or combine a little reduced-fat sour cream with a sprinkling of brown sugar. Too busy to cut up the fruit? A fruit snack cup will also do the trick.

DURING THE COLD MONTHS, a small mug of soup with a few oyster crackers on top can really hit the spot.

RAW VEGGIES such as carrots, cucumbers, mushrooms, broccoli and cauliflower are tasty treats, especially when served with a little hummus for dipping. Many of these vegetables can be purchased already cut.

OFFER A SMALL SERVING of cheese and crackers. Look for sliced cheese, and cut the slices into smaller squares to fit the crackers. Choose a cracker that's made from whole wheat, such as an all-natural seven-grain cracker.